Enhancing Resilience in Survivors of Family Violence

Kim M. Anderson, PhD, LCSW, is an associate professor in the School of Social Work at the University of Missouri, where she teaches clinical practice and evaluation courses at the graduate level. Dr. Anderson's scholarship bridges gaps between theory and practice by offering conceptual frameworks that capture the interplay of trauma and resilience for survivors of family violence and mental health practitioners. Specific populations of women that she studies (although not mutually exclusive) include survivors of childhood incest, adult children of battered women, and individuals formerly in a domestic violence relationship. Her research interests include assessment of risk and resiliency in trauma populations and implementation of strengths-based mental health practice. Throughout the past 20 years, she has embraced the roles of practitioner, researcher, educator, and advocate to help survivors of family violence and the practitioners who serve them.

Character cannot be developed in ease and quiet. Only through experience of trial and suffering can the soul be strengthened, ambition inspired and success achieved.

—Helen Keller

Contents

Foreword

This book is a welcome and bracing addition to the mental health literature in general and the literature on female sexual abuse, and oppression and violence against women, in particular. I was privileged to be Dr. Anderson's dissertation advisor as she began her exploration of this subject. She has derived some of her samples for this book from the 26 incest survivors in that study. This book is also informed by her subsequent research on, teaching about, and practice in the field of family violence. This more recent research includes 12 women who witnessed the sexual, physical, and emotional abuse of their mothers and 20 women who had been in relationships characterized by domestic violence. This violence is a serious and abiding social problem. Consider that 1 in 3 women is molested before the age of 18 and that incest is the most common form of violence. About 43% of children who are sexually abused are abused by family members. But Dr. Anderson's lifelong interest in the self-renewal that may come from trying to defy and rebound from abuse, seasoned with her continuing study and practice, has given her insights and an approach that show remarkable conceptual ripening and practical leavening and point the way to a hopeful and strengths-based approach to helping women who suffer these indignities and insults.

The appreciations that guide this work include: feminist standpoint theory, grounded theory (developing theory from the direct experience of individuals and building a conceptual and methodological superstructure from that), resilience research, constructivist self-development theory, ideas about trauma and posttraumatic growth and development, and the strengths perspective. This is a broad conceptual canvas to work, but Dr. Anderson's brush strokes are sure and true. The core of her work is represented by the idea of resistance. Furthermore, their (the subjects') acts of resistance served as a catalyst to their resilience and became an enduring strength that was drawn upon throughout their lives" (chapter 3). They resisted, often in remarkable fashion and as best they

could, the powerlessness, isolation, and enforced silence that characterized their lives as targets of male violence. It was out of this resistance
and struggle that they were able to build capacities, competencies, skills,
points of view, and values that would come to stand them in good stead
the rest of their lives. Out of brutality came eventual resistance; out of
resistance came psychological, spiritual, moral, and emotional growth.
At no time, however, does Dr. Anderson diminish the horror and suffering that these women faced or witnessed. When listening to their stories,
she always encourages these women to add to their frightening narratives the plotlines and occasions of strength, courage, and pure grit.

The joy of this book (and there is joy in the outcomes we are privileged to witness) lies in the stories that Dr. Anderson elicits from these
gutsy women about their tribulations, but, most importantly, about their
triumphs. The many ways in which they surmounted adversity and confronted their challenges, not to mention their abusers, is astonishing.
Heroic is not too strong a word to use in describing these women and, in
the words of an ancient proverb, "Heroism is endurance for one moment
more." Clearly these women have endured, but, more than that, they
have surpassed most expectations, probably including their own, about
how far into personal renewal they could venture. The stories they tell
are "documents of identity" (Robert Hutchens' phrase), recounting the
reformation of the self. To help these survivors "speak the unspeakable"
(chapter 6), Dr. Anderson employed many devices. One of the most profound and telling was her use of digital storytelling. In a six-week group
format, 8 to 10 of these women gather together and are encouraged not
just to tell their stories but to make montages that include photos, videos,
voiceovers, music, and movement. These are edited into a 2- to 5-minute
"show." At the end of the workshop, these are shared with the group on a
large screen. While they may include a sense of the hideous trauma they
faced, the stories are primarily a vehicle for celebrating the resistance,
recovery, and growth in formerly defeated and "damaged" women.
There are also valuable instructions here for employing digital storytelling using Photo Story 3 (Windows XP and Vista) in practice or teaching.

Another beneficial and constructive part of this book is the inclusion
of chapters on survivor-to-survivor advice and survivor-to-professional
advice. In the former, advice such as "hold onto hope, life does get better" or "find meaning and purpose in suffering" would mean a lot coming from someone who has been through a literal hell. Or, in the case of
counsel to professionals, "support client strengths, resourcefulness, and
competence" and "convey an outlook of hope and possibility" may seem

obvious, but, as Dr. Anderson makes plain, negative and hope-deprived attitudes are far too common in this field of practice. This material, found in chapters 8 and 9, is gold, both for survivors and helpers. As one of the participants said, "If you don't know your stuff, if you're in over your head, for God's sake, please, go read some more, go do the research, go talk to someone who has experience with this. Don't play it by ear" (a 45-year-old survivor of childhood exposure to domestic violence).

In chapter 10, Dr. Anderson confronts some of the realities that face professionals and volunteers who work in this area, from burnout to vicarious trauma to compassion fatigue. She has helpful and prudent advice for those who need to deal with these realities. Her idea of compassion satisfaction is a positive remedy for some of the common sequelae of work with the ordeals, suffering, and trauma that these women have had to contend with. She recounts a very helpful dialogue between a supervisor and a worker who seems on the edge of vicarious trauma that ultimately articulates the dimensions of the problem and the shape of the solutions.

This book will help to change the paradigm that has gripped the mental health professions for so long and will be a positive boost for those who know there must be a better and more affirmative way to do this important work.

Dennis Saleebey, DSW
Professor Emeritus
School of Social Welfare
University of Kansas
Lawrence, Kansas

Preface

My interest in resiliency began 20 years ago in my first postgraduate position at a mental health center. I worked in a rural community and became the area "expert" on working with child sexual abuse cases; simply, because my caseload primarily consisted of such cases. During graduate school, interestingly, I did not intend to work in the area of sexual trauma; yet, upon the initial days at my job I was handed 10 cases, all children who had been sexually abused. I felt under prepared and so proceeded to read up on everything related to child sexual abuse trauma and recovery. It was the late 1980s and the seriousness of childhood victimization had been recognized; thus, much of the professional literature centered on ameliorating the consequences of such trauma. The treatment concentrated on acknowledging one's sexual abuse experiences and on identifying their connection to existing dysfunctional patterns of living. What became to be more and more emphasized was how their victimization was the centerpiece to their identities rather than being viewed as something that happened to them. Consequently, addressing individuals' deficits, problems, and pathology were central to intervening with survivors and thus lessening the aftereffects of childhood sexual abuse.

Although it was essential to validate the pain that individuals experience as a result of childhood sexual abuse, I was seeing in my clients the other side of their victimization: the positive ways in which they coped, survived, and resisted. Basically, the children and adults that I worked with who had been sexually abused did not fit with descriptions of being deficit-ridden. Instead, I saw strength, courage, and determination. This awareness led to a lifelong desire to address strengths and resiliency in survivors of family violence (e.g., child abuse and domestic violence) and to challenge existing helping paradigms that put problems before possibilities. I pursued my doctorate at the School of Social Welfare at the University of Kansas, pioneers in the strengths perspective in social work practice. I was fortunate to have Dennis Saleebey as my PhD chair who encouraged me to challenge both practice and research paradigms in the area of trauma and recovery. I disputed traditional concepts of resilience that focused solely on capturing competence through standardized measures of functioning. I questioned the purpose of resiliency research in regard to differentiating people into classifications of either success or failure. Instead, I engaged in research that drew from the wisdom and experience of participants; thus, survivors—the people most significantly affected by family violence—assisted me to shape practice theory and methodology in the area of trauma and recovery. In doing so, I have learned that resiliency is not a scarce commodity in which some have it and some do not. Instead, there are many roads to surviving, persevering, and thriving if we are prepared to listen and learn from individuals' experiences with suffering and healing.

This book addresses the suffering that ensues from being abused by a family member and the strengths it takes to prevail over experiences of torture, humiliation, and betrayal. There are strong commonalities in those survivors I have crossed paths with in my practice and research. I have learned that the human spirit prevails and ultimately wants to heal. Additionally, I have learned that individuals have unrecognized or underappreciated enduring strengths that can be used for their healing. Clients often ask me how I can be so positive. I find this an interesting question, as I cannot imagine the alternative in working with them. I see growth and change daily and with that healing that exceeds expectations. I refuse to see them in the restricted and negative ways they or others view them. The healing journey is arduous; yet, mental health practitioners who convey hope, possibility, empathy, acceptance, and compassion help to ease the burden.

The hope is that this book will assist practitioners in developing their practice with survivors of family violence in a manner that supports and enhances their resilience.

I explore and highlight the many facets of surviving, prevailing, and ultimately triumphing over family violence. Empirical findings, conceptual insights, assessments, and interventions are presented as a way for practitioners to gather information that is unique to the abilities of each client and further delineate the available repertoire of strengths one might possess. Such information may then be used to develop an intervention plan that builds on clients' abilities to manage traumatic experiences. Additionally, it embodies a philosophy of hope, underscores the resourcefulness of clients, and illuminates the many ways people prevail during and in the aftermath of family violence. Ultimately, this book challenges the premise that survivors who have suffered family violence will remain wounded or become less than the persons they might otherwise have been.

Acknowledgments

This book would not exist without my good fortune in crossing paths with survivors on their healing journeys. I am in awe of your courage, compassion, and determination. Thank you for sharing your personal accounts regarding your trials and tribulations on the road to recovery. You are truly inspirational for others who may be suffering without a sense of purpose, direction, or meaning. I hope I have done justice to your experiences.

I have had the honor of teaching social work students for several years. This book emerges from your requests to write about my work and translate it into practice principles for the classroom and beyond. Thank you to the students in my solution-focused practice course who helped me discover the answers for my writing block and thus finish this book.

I would like to thank my editor at Springer Publishing, Jennifer Perillo, whose interest, support, and assistance is greatly appreciated.

My husband and best friend, Kelly Anderson, has consistently encouraged, supported, and validated my true self. Thank you for your input in writing this book; I am forever grateful for our rich and enjoyable discussions on spirituality.

Enhancing Resilience in Survivors of Family Violence

1

Dynamics and Consequences of Oppression and Violence

In response to a disproportional emphasis on pathology in mental health practice (Ai & Park, 2005; Barnard, 1994; Goldstein, 1990; Ickovics & Park, 1998; Saleebey, 2009), this book provides empirical findings and conceptual insights from the author's research for those who are interested in facilitating resilience in female survivors of family violence. Helping professionals may use this book to better understand how protective processes develop and contribute to hardiness in the case of survivors of family violence (i.e., childhood incest and domestic violence). Helping professionals cannot change the abusive experiences encountered by their clients; they can only hope to influence reactions to the abuse. Since individuals often internalize shame and blame about their victimization experiences, providing a view of themselves as resourceful individuals gives credit to their ability to prevail despite seemingly insurmountable odds (Miller, 1996). Therefore, they may view themselves differently, particularly their strengths, by recognizing their active response to adversity in the past. This new awareness can help them to confront present struggles by channeling their survival strategies.

Sharing one's story of adversity, whether in a research or clinical setting, can be an opportunity to contextualize the experience and to make choices about nesting the narrative as an event in the life course as a subplot in a complex biography with parameters, limits, and lessons (Anderson & Hiersteiner, 2007). Through the author's research, participants are given a forum for voicing their experiences, which is essential to break down the barrier of silence that often occurs around family violence. The author's inquiry explores survivors' perspectives on the personal qualities and social conditions that enhanced their ability to survive traumatic experiences and to persevere. The interaction between personal and environmental strengths demonstrates how resourceful these females are as they negotiate the challenges of their oppression. The roots of their resilience are forged in their resistance to abusive behavior and domination by the male perpetrators.

A subtopic of inquiry involves exploring participants' perspectives on how social workers and other mental health service providers can support and mobilize survivors' resilient capacities throughout the therapeutic process. Consequently, participants identify recommendations for mental health practice to honor and support women's resourcefulness when providing supportive and therapeutic services.

LIMITATIONS OF TRAUMA-FOCUSED TREATMENT

Questioning individuals in detail about their recovery stories can pose a challenge to mental health practitioners who operate from a trauma-focused treatment paradigm that may obscure resilience by focusing on posttrauma stress, which tempers the significance of individual survival strengths over the life course (Anderson, 2006; Gasker, 1999; Naples, 2003).

Naples (2003) suggests that the trauma paradigm/recovery discourse that has developed in the professional field over the last 20 years may be a disempowering healing strategy for some survivors of family violence because it focuses on symptoms and diagnosis. As a result, individuals' interpretations of their survival and the strengths that led to that survival are overshadowed. In other words, we know more about survivors' posttraumatic stress disorder (PTSD) symptoms than we do their acts of strength and courage (Bhuvaneswar & Shafer, 2004).

Adapting the word *trauma* to include survivors of family violence was helpful in shifting helping paradigms from "blaming the victim," thus minimizing their experiences, to fully exploring the short- and long-term consequences of trauma (Burstow, 2003). Trauma theory was significant in taking the blame off victims of traumatic events. It validated psychological injury, drew parallels to other types of trauma, explained what people were experiencing, and led to treatment interventions such as cognitive-behavioral therapy to lessen symptoms (Gilfus, 1999). Although the seriousness of individuals' victimization is recognized, the unintended consequence includes reinforcing the role and status of being a victim. Instead of victimization being viewed as something that has happened to someone, it is seen as the centerpiece to one's identity. Although the language may change from *victim* to *survivor*, the underlying assumptions continue to remain the same: that one will inevitably endure long-term mental health hazards. Although it is essential to validate the pain that individuals experienced as a result of victimization, it makes the other side of their victimization—the positive ways in which they coped, survived, and resisted—invisible.

PTSD has come to be used as a conceptual model for describing and understanding the psychological symptoms and struggles of survivors in addition to guiding treatment interventions, including cognitive-behavioral therapy (Herman, 1997; Saakvitne, Gamble, Pearlman, & Lev, 2000). Although it is helpful in understanding trauma and its aftermath, PTSD is rooted in a medical model that categorizes symptoms for the purpose of discrete diagnosis (Armstrong, 1994). The medical model often leads to objectifying individuals as diagnoses or "cases." The risk of looking at the medical model as a basis for trauma frameworks is the classification of "normal" reactions to abnormal circumstances as symptoms (e.g., dissociation) rather than signs of creative survival (Graybeal, 2001).

This way of viewing individuals and their responses to trauma leaves many facets of their experiences unnoticed (e.g., survival strengths) or distorted (e.g., coping skills are viewed as pathological). Therefore, survivors may not interpret their strengths because their stories are centered, with the encouragement of professionals, on the damage resulting from the devastating effects of family violence. In other words, the pathology model of trauma leads practitioners to interpret the pain and hurt expressed by survivors as evidence of psychopathology (Anderson, Cowger, & Snively, 2009).

Because many helping professionals understand institutional and social problems at a discrete micro level and, consequently, locate the source of problems exclusively within the individual, clients' traumatic reactions are often perceived as some disorder or deficit that then creates negative expectations about their potential to address the stressors in their lives (Deitz, 2000). If a professional's practice orientation is restricted to the containment of problems, it is difficult to perceive clients as being resourceful. The problems (e.g., depression) overshadow the survivor's strengths (e.g., determination) and, therefore, become the central focus in treatment. Consequently, among helping professionals and clients there is a general lack of understanding about problematic behavior and the fact that it is originally produced within an oppressive context, often as a coping strategy or method of survival (Wade, 1997). Therefore, it is important to cultivate ways to assist clients with the expression of suffering and to connect such expressions to an analysis of systemic oppression (Wineman, 2003).

Traumatic experiences incapacitate one's normal mechanisms for coping and self-protection; therefore, one often resorts to extraordinary measures in order to survive physically and psychologically (Bussey & Wise, 2007). Essentially, wherever you find violence, you find people trying to defend and protect themselves. At the moment when abuse takes place, therefore, individuals are figuring out how to survive and thrive. In the moment of trauma, the victim's psychological task is to maintain some semblance of normalcy, coherence, integrity, meaning, control, value, and equilibrium (Briere & Scott, 2006; Wade, 1997). This must be done in the face of an overpowering assault that threatens to annihilate the victim psychologically and, in some cases, physically. The effects of oppression may never disappear completely. However, focusing on strategies of resistance can promote individual resilience and recovery and lessen and/or alleviate personal suffering. So a helping framework that not only encompasses the damage inflicted upon survivors but also includes their resourcefulness is necessary; such an archetype nourishes and honors the potential in each individual who is coping or has coped with family violence.

In trauma recovery, resilience and impairment are not necessarily opposites, but, instead, are different aspects of the overall experience of coping and adjustment (Bussey & Wise, 2007; O'Leary, 1998). Standing alongside the entire range of debilitating effects of trauma, most survivors display a stunning capacity for survival and perseverance. The following example of childhood resistance is from the author's (Anderson, 2006) research with incest survivors. Jennifer[1] (age 35) was sexually abused between the ages of four and six by three people, with her father as the primary perpetrator. The abuse decreased once she started school because Jennifer put tremendous energy into avoiding being alone with her father throughout her childhood, thus cutting off his access to her:

> I always made sure that if my father was around that I was with my mother. I always arranged so I would never be alone with my father. There was one

---

[1] All names used in this volume are pseudonyms.

point in time where I was supposed to ride the bus home, and my father worked out of the house, and rather than ride the bus home and get home early, I would sit in my mother's car, where she worked at this clothing store, and I would sit in the car for three hours and wait for her to get off work, rather than ride the bus home, because I didn't want to be alone with my father.

Jennifer graduated from college and was employed full time for ten years. She had a positive work history and received the employee of the year award at her job. Eventually, though, Jennifer's depression became overwhelming and her suicidal thoughts consumed her. She was hospitalized for inpatient psychiatric treatment and has not been able to work since that time. Jennifer has experienced obstacles (e.g., judgmental helping professionals) in her recovery. Yet, she has continued to persevere in addressing her traumatic experiences:

I've learned that I can't let the incest break me, even though at times it seems like it has and I think what has really helped me in this is that I've felt like the perpetrators would be winning if I gave up. And I don't want to give them that satisfaction.

The incest cannot "break" Jennifer if she does not let the aftereffects dominate her life. Consequently, she is determined to work toward self-restoration. The perpetrators cannot "win" if Jennifer does not give up her battle to heal from her traumatic childhood. This participant's resilience emerges from her resistance to her perpetrators' domination when she was a child and continues onward as an adult as she is active in confronting the aftereffects.

This book offers new insights and conceptual frameworks for survivors and practitioners that allow for varied individual experiences of trauma, trauma recovery, and resilience. The author's research with females who have experienced family violence has found that survivors interact with stressors over time and are able to access resources within themselves and their environments that often go beyond initial coping efforts. Examples of populations studied (although not mutually exclusive) include female survivors of childhood incest, adult daughters of battered women, and women formerly in a domestic violence relationship. Although these added exemplars are drawn from the author's research in the area of family violence, they may be transferred to other experiences of oppression as well.

TYPES OF FAMILY VIOLENCE EXPLORED IN THIS VOLUME

The author's research is guided by a feminist theoretical perspective that sets out to gather women's stories to understand their oppression, recognize their strengths, and allow space for them to voice their experiences. Feminism is a standpoint theory that asserts the purpose of research must be to advance the causes of the participants (Davis, 1986). The author's research standpoint reinforces the notion that survivors have strengths and that the process of telling their stories gives voice to their resourcefulness and is a form of consciousness-raising for themselves and others (i.e., researchers, practitioners). Consequently, participants' quotes from the author's research are used throughout this book. Pseudonyms are used to protect their confidentiality.

For this book, the social problem of family violence is viewed within a context that addresses power relations. This framework, therefore, allows for understanding female participants' experiences within an oppressive family context that was dominated by their male perpetrators. Although there are certainly male victims of violence, the author's research is only dealing with female victims within a familial context (e.g., female incest survivors rather than children who are abused by nonfamily members). Certain forms of family violence, such as elder abuse or same-sex partner violence, are beyond the scope of this volume.

Childhood Incest

Although both males and females are sexually abused, girls comprise most victims of childhood incest while their perpetrators are often male family members (Blake-White & Kline, 1985; Valentine & Feinauer, 1993). O'Hyde (1984) defines child sexual abuse as contact or noncontact interactions between a child and someone else, when the child is being used for the sexual stimulation of that person or persons.

For the purpose of the author's research, incest is defined as both nongenital (i.e., exhibitionism, sexual kissing, masturbating in front of the child) and genital contact (i.e., manual or oral genital contact, digital penetration, attempted or competed anal or vaginal intercourse) between a female child (birth to age 18) and a male, who is perceived by the child as a family member. This may include a father, stepfather, a surrogate parent (e.g., mother's boyfriend), a brother (half-, adopted, or stepbrother), grandfather, or any other male adult (e.g., fictive kin, such as a godparent).

Being sexually assaulted in a close and trusting relationship such as one with a father, stepfather, brother, or grandfather may cause harmful long-term consequences because of the betrayal by a trusted family member and the lack of escape for the child, not to mention the physical harm (Beitchman, Zucker, Hood, DaCosta, & Akman, 1992). The child victim of incest is denied the essential ingredients for developing healthy relationships, such as trust, intimacy, security, and personal boundary setting (Dinsmore, 1991). The victim is readily accessible, and there are many opportunities for incestuous abuse that the child is powerless to fend off.

Childhood incest takes place in a familial climate of pervasive fear and terror where ordinary caretaking relationships are disrupted. As children, incest survivors learn that the most powerful male adults in their family environments are unsafe to them and that the other adults responsible for their care cannot or do not offer protection (Herman, 1997). Browne and Finkelhor (1986) identify the incest dynamics of traumatic sexualization (i.e., coerced sexual relations), betrayal, stigmatization, and powerlessness as being core experiences for psychological injury.

Sexual violence against girls is probably the issue most commonly associated with childhood trauma, and for good reason: nearly one-in-three women are molested before the age of 18 (Anderson, Martin, Mullen, Romans, & Herbison, 1993). Incest has been noted as the most common form of child sexual abuse. Studies conclude that 30% to 40% of sexually abused children are abused by family members (Kilpatrick, Saunders, & Smith, 2003; Snyder, 2000). Incest in the United States remains an under-reported crime, which contributes to the discrepancies in statistics. Pressure from family members and threats from the perpetrator all too often result in extreme reluctance to report abuse and subsequently obtain help (Matsakis, 1991). Jane's (age 37) story from the author's research illustrates the coerciveness of perpetrators of child abuse. Jane's brother-in-law abused her between the ages of 6 and 12. She was the youngest of eight siblings, and there were 20 years between herself and the oldest sibling. Her perpetrator was the husband of her second oldest sister. Her mother was often in frail health due to diabetes and died when Jane was 15. Her perpetrator would tell her that if she told anyone it would kill her mother. The following excerpt highlights the extent of her perpetrator's domination:

> I can remember the beatings—wanting to go hide and it was always a fall at the playground or something, which I made [up]. You look back as an

adult and you think, "How did they not notice the hand marks on my neck? How did that look like a swing?"...And I remember one time trying to tell my mom I didn't want to go. I didn't want to leave her and I didn't want to go. And she thinks he's bein' nice, and I'm being irresponsible and ungrateful for not going, and she forces me to go. And he took me into this little hallway, he took me back in the corner and pulled me up by my neck [and said], "Don't you ever tell her you don't wanna go again. Do what I say or else."

Jane's perpetrator also used verbal threats to coerce her into submission:

The threats were always based on that my mother would die if I told. As I got older, where that was not as easily bought by me, it changed to the threatening nature that "If [your] Mom finds out about you, it'll kill her because she won't be able to stand the fact that she has such a whore of a daughter." Because it was, "You started this. This was your idea. You propagated this."

During adulthood, Jane confronted her perpetrator, but he denied sexually abusing her. She also disclosed to her father and siblings about the sexual abuse. Her father was accepting and supportive of her, but his health was failing and died shortly after she told him about the abuse. Unfortunately, the majority of her siblings minimized or failed to acknowledge her disclosure. Jane decided to take control of her life and although it was difficult, she began separating from her siblings so she would not have to endure their negative reactions. After ten years, she and her siblings have begun to make amends and she does not find it essential anymore to have their validation regarding the sexual abuse because she believes and trusts in herself. The following illustrates her siblings' reactions when she initially disclosed the sexual abuse to them:

I'm talking with my family, brothers and sisters and letting 'em know this [sexual abuse] is what happened. I'm getting responses from like my one sister I lived with, "This is too much. I can't deal with this. You're doing this for [their father's] money." Just myriads of reasons not one, "You can't do that to my sister," which is what I was looking for...So, at that point, I just basically divorced the family.

As a result of experiencing childhood incest, individuals may exhibit significant impairment in their functioning if the trauma remains unaddressed in treatment or in their natural environment (Everett & Gallop, 2001). Child incest can have a range of effects on its survivors, such as a violation of their personal boundaries, trust in the world, and sense of meaning. If the child does not receive help and the opportunity to work through the experiences in a supportive network of social relationships, the effect and memories of the experience can lay dormant until adulthood, prompting a search for professional help, guidance, and understanding (Harvey, Mishler, Koenen, & Harney, 2001). The majority of research on adult survivors of incest consists primarily of quantitative studies that identify the characteristics of the survivors, compare survivors with nonabused persons on different areas of functioning, or that determine if a history of sexual abuse is more common within certain clinical populations (Cole & Putnam, 1992).

Research has also suggested that childhood incest is strongly associated with the adult disorders Borderline Personality Disorder (BPD) (Bryer, Bernadette, Nelson, Miller, & Krol, 1987; Lobel, 1992; Wheeler & Walton, 1987), Dissociative Identity Disorder (DID) (Anderson, Yasenik, & Ross, 1993; Blake-White & Kline, 1985; Coons, 1986; Chu & Dill, 1990), and Posttraumatic Stress Disorder (PTSD) (McNew & Abel, 1995; Patten, Gatz, Jones, & Thomas, 1989). Studies show that adult survivors of incest are found to be more maladjusted because of the long-term consequences of their abuse, with a particularly greater degree of personality disturbance, when compared to nonabused persons (Parker & Parker, 1991; Wheeler & Walton, 1987). The results of these studies demonstrate the obstacles to achieving successful intrapsychic and interpersonal functioning in adulthood.

Childhood Exposure to Domestic Violence

Another vast amount of traumatic experiences includes the 3.3 to 10 million children exposed to interparental conflict or domestic violence each year in the United States (Fantuzzo, Boruch, Beriama, Atkins, & Marcus, 1997). In the past 20 years, research has highlighted the stressors related to domestic violence in the lives of children (Peled & Edleson, 1999; Graham-Bermann & Edleson, 2001). Studies show that many children who have been exposed to acts of violence between their parents or parental figures are found to be more maladjusted when compared to individuals from non-violent families. Findings suggest that there is a link between domestic violence exposure and the development of symptomatology for children, including behavioral problems (particularly physical aggression and noncompliance), anxiety, depression, concentration difficulties, low self-esteem, somatic complaints, and revictimization

(Cummings, Peplar, & Moore, 1999; Jaffe, Wolfe, & Wilson, 1990; Kolbo, Blakely, Engelman, 1996; McGee, 1997; Mitchell & Finkelhor, 2001). In addition, witnessing parental violence is found to be a significant predictor of PTSD (Kilpatrick, Litt, & Williams, 1997). The results of these studies demonstrate that children are highly affected by exposure to violence involving people who are close to them.

Living with a father who is abusive to your mother creates an oppressive home environment characterized by fear and powerlessness. The following excerpts from the author's research (Anderson & Danis, 2006) highlight quotes for two adult daughters of battered women regarding how their fathers persisted in pursuing opportunities to assault their intimate partners, whose efforts to protect themselves and their children were often subverted, perpetuating a feeling of captivity for the child:

> Dad used his size, his voice, and his strength to hurt her over and over and over again. I first remember seeing it and knowing that he was hurting her when I was four years old...The abuse toward Mom continued every moment that he was in the house with us until he was no longer in the home. It didn't stop, and he was abusive not only to her but to all of us as well...I never felt, well, quite frankly, I didn't think anybody could help us. I really thought that we were all going to die and that there was nothing that we could do about it. I really thought we were totally trapped. (Donna, age 45)

> The most vivid memory that I have would be when my father decided that he was going to kill us and he took his truck and he drove it to the top of our driveway, which was a quarter mile along, and he raced it down the driveway and he hit the house. He smashed into the house and he backed up and he smashed into the house again. (Moberly, age 32)

Intimate Partner Violence

Violence against females all too often does not end with childhood. According to the National Violence Against Women (NVAW) survey, every year an estimated 5.3 million Intimate Partner Violence (IPV) victimizations occur among women aged 18 and older (Tjaden & Thoennes, 2000). Domestic violence often continues for several years, leads to severe physical, emotional, and sexual assaults, and is associated with disruptive and devastating consequences. Survivors of battering learn on a daily basis that their intimate partners are a danger to them (Herman, 1997; Lempert 1996). Women's experiences with domestic violence may produce longlasting effects, including PTSD, loss of identity, disruption of core beliefs and values, depression, decreased self-esteem, eating disorders, and substance abuse (Bogat, Levendosky, Theran, von Eye, & Davidson, 2003; Jones, Hughes, & Unterstaller, 2001; Lewis, Griffing, Chu, Jospitre, Sage, Madry, & Primm, 2006; Lynch & Graham-Bermann, 2000; Orava, McLeod, & Sharpe, 1996). Domestic violence research shows that survivors suffer aftereffects that may leave them lacking in several areas of psychosocial functioning.

The following quote from a survivor of domestic violence from the author's research is an example of typical methods used by batterers to control their intimate partners:

> I was married when I was 20 years old, and after a week, there was a violent episode. He didn't hit me, but he tore up things in the household, and it was all due to, he didn't like what I was cooking for supper. But by the end of the following week, which was two weeks into the marriage, I took my first hit from him. Looking back, every time that I experienced physical contact from him, the first thing that he would always say is "if you hadn't of made me," whatever the situation was, he would say that "I wouldn't have had to hit you." After two months into the marriage, he put a loaded gun to my head. I'd never felt that kind of scaredness before. (Betsy, age 50, married 12 years)

DYNAMICS AND CONSEQUENCES OF OPPRESSION AND VIOLENCE

Trauma is a psychological dimension of oppression. Oppression, the systemic abuse of power, renders people subjectively powerless as is the case with individuals subjected to family violence (Wade, 1997). The essence of victimization is that you are acted upon against your will. In turn, powerlessness—the experience of being without options—is the hallmark of traumatic experience (Herman, 1997; Wineman, 2003). In most cases the lasting, major damage caused by abuse is emotional and psychological. Common responses to trauma include substance abuse, self-injury, depression, suicide, violence against others, shame, chronic fear, eating disorders, anxiety, dysfunctional relationships, psychotic episodes, and physical illness (Briere & Runtz, 1993; Burgess & Holmstrom, 1974; Gilfus, 1999; Herman, 1997; Janoff-Bulman, 1992; Koss & Harvey, 1991; McCann & Pearlman, 1990.

Family violence involves a deep sense of helplessness and isolation, both of which are central to experiences of psychological trauma. Psychological trauma is often a response to an unexpected event that an individual has experienced forcefully and intimately (Everstine & Everstine, 1993). "Traumatic events overwhelm the ordinary systems of care that give people a sense of control, connection, and meaning" (Herman, 1997, p. 32). Traumatic responses vary for each individual. Reactions to stress and trauma are best understood as adaptive efforts to abnormal conditions (Allen, 1995). Herman (1997) addresses the "dose-response" curve that indicates that the more one is exposed to trauma, the more severe the symptoms will be, and consequently, the more difficulty one will have recovering from it. "People subjected to prolonged, repeated trauma develop an insidious progressive form of posttraumatic stress disorder that invades and erodes the personality" (Herman 1997, p. 78). Personality changes occur including the inability to relate and thwarted identity development (Herman, 1997).

Neurobiological Responses to Trauma

Living in a constant state of agitation without a way to take action alters brain functioning to a point of heightened sensitivity to alarming stimuli. Terror and fear alters chemical functioning because when the *locus ceruleus* (neurons in the brain stem) is activated it sends adrenaline (i.e., norepinephrine) into many areas of the brain, consequently increasing arousal and preparing one for action. Individuals become excessively sensitive to stressors that trigger an alarm response even when the threat is no longer present. Stressors or triggers can create adrenaline surges that set off hyperreactive aroused states that stimulate a survival response that is generalized to nonthreatening stimuli (Bolen, 1993). "Long after the danger is past, traumatized people relive the event as though it were continually recurring in the present" (Herman, 1997, p. 34). Consequently, chronic trauma conditions people to be hypervigilant, anxious, and agitated.

Trauma may become encoded as an abnormal memory in the form of vivid sensations and images. The amygdala in the brain stores emotional memories intact but without cerebral integration (i.e., cognition and evaluation) for that emotion. So, emotions may remain in memory but they are disconnected from the original experiences that provoked them (Bremner & Marmar, 1998). Memory deficits, dissociation, and amnesia are characteristic responses to trauma. Dissociation is self-protective because it excludes painful experiences from normal awareness through altering one's consciousness (Allen, 1995; Chu & Dill, 1990). "Dissociation falls on a continuum ranging from full awareness through suppression to repression and, finally to dissociative identity disorder. It has been characterized as the lack of normal integration of thoughts, feelings, and experiences into the stream of consciousness and memory resulting in disturbances of identity" (Anderson & Alexander, 1996, p. 240). Dissociative "disorder" may be viewed as the creation of a manageable way of maintaining memories of one's experiences of abuse.

Psychological Responses to Trauma

Trauma invades and breaks down the psychological structures of the self (Herman, 1997; Janoff-Bulman, 1992; Koss & Harvey, 1991; McCann & Pearlman, 1990). When traumatic events occur during childhood they are more likely to be a part of one's permanent sense of identity, serving as the basis for perceiving, thinking, and reacting to life circumstances (Tedeschi & Calhoun, 1995). Trauma requires accommodation or a modification of cognitive schemas as individuals adjust to interacting with their traumatic situations. Unfortunately, assumptions that guide schema development, such as one's beliefs about personal invulnerability, a meaningful world, and a positive self-image, are disrupted by traumatic experiences as well. In fact, chronic trauma may cause the victim to lose her sense of self because her experiences with continuity, cohesiveness, unity, integrity, wholeness, and identity have been shattered (Allen, 1995).

Upon leaving an abusive relationship, battered women report feeling traumatized and lacking a sense of identity. Practically every aspect of life has been altered in the aftermath of domestic violence. This struggle takes tremendous strength as one's energy shifts from survival mode to starting life anew (Senter & Caldwell, 2002). Leaving an abusive partner involves transitioning from being controlled to being in control, while coping with the costs of a domestic life filled with fear, terror, and devastation. The following quotes from the author's research with battered women recovering from abusive relationships illustrate their transformations as they progressed in beliefs about self (from vulnerability to strength), victimization (from questioning their suffering to finding meaning in their struggles), and life purpose (from doubting their existence to valuing their lives):

> I tell you it was the worst experience in my life, but it was also the best experience in my life... It made me a stronger person, and I feel like that

what I have gone through, I can pass along to others, and I feel like I have this intuition when I'm around people that are in those situations, and I try to make it evident but not obvious, that I'm there for them if they need anything. (Denise, age 42)

There were many nights I prayed. I prayed either to get me out of the situation or to give me the knowledge to get me out of the situation. Maybe the good Lord knew that I needed to go through this to get to where I'm at now. I really believe that everything happens in your life for a purpose. I think I had to go through what I went through... and I know mine wasn't as bad... because a lot of women have it a lot worse than I did. (Karen, age 52)

I'm strong. I'm capable of doing whatever I want to do, as long as I set my mind to it. I just want to live my life to the fullest. I'm happy. I'm content. Because you know he [the batterer] had me believe, "you can't do nothing without me." Oh, yes I can. I'm here. I look good. I feel good. Gotta icebox full of food, my house is clean, got a good job, I can open up my curtains any time I want to, or then I can close them any time I want to. (Vera, age 46)

Trauma can disrupt individuals' views of themselves, relationships with others, and their core assumptions as well. Yet, according to Constructivist Self-Development Theory (CSDT), facing these disruptions may also promote expanded perspectives, the development of additional personal and social resources, and new ways of coping (Calhoun & Tedeschi, 1998; McCann & Pearlman, 1990; Saakvitne, Tennen, & Affleck, 1998). CSDT posits that inevitable changes occur for the individual in regard to identity, relationships, and worldview as one attempts to construe meaning in response to a traumatic event. Hence, individuals' identities are shaped by the sense they make of their own life stories (Docherty & McColl, 2003). Therefore, when a highly stressful event seriously invalidates or challenges an individual's assumptive world, growth may be triggered. However, the presence of growth does not necessarily alleviate grief, emotional distress, or suffering. Although researchers agree that this process is highly individualized, many propose that it cannot occur in isolation, but is the product of social learning and support as much as it is one's own deliberate effort at meaning-making (Aldwin & Levenson, 2004). Evidence varies as to whether or how posttraumatic growth is related to severity of trauma, as the perceived impact of it appears more significant to growth than its exact nature (Helgeson, Reynolds, & Tomich, 2006).

SUMMARY: RECOVERY, RESILIENCE, AND RESISTANCE IN THE MIDST OF OPPRESSION

The pain and discomfort individuals experience from family violence should not be minimized. Yet, it does not have to be the centerpiece to one's identity. Mental health professionals often focus on pathology when attempting to explain individual behaviors in response to violence and abuse (Ai & Park, 2005; Ickovics & Park, 1998), but this focus does not take into account how individuals actively engage in resisting their oppression and its consequences. "Persons continue to resist, prudently, creatively, and with astonishing determination, even in the face of the most extreme forms of violence" (Wade, 1997, p. 31). Survivors of family violence are heroic, and treatment that focuses on their resiliency would reinforce this conceptualization. These resilient capacities are often submerged beneath pain and discomfort, and are difficult to access if those engaged in the helping relationship are not equipped to view these protective strategies as strengths (Anderson, 2001).

Engaging clients in a conversation regarding the details and implications of their resistance may assist them in experiencing themselves as stronger, more insightful, and more capable of responding to the difficulties in their current lives (Wade, 1997). Individuals typically are resistant to their oppression and use a variety of mental and behavioral strategies to prevent, withstand, stop, or oppose their subjugation and its consequences. Sometimes these behaviors promote health and well-being beyond the initial survival from the oppression. Other times, the behaviors become maladaptive. Exploring oppression and its consequences assist in understanding why and how personal strategies of resistance develop. Individuals' acts of resistance may thus serve as the catalyst for survival perseverance, and the subsequent development of strategies that promote resilience and recovery. As individuals come to understand the injurious actions perpetrated on them, they may, for example, resolve to be different from their oppressors and, therefore, choose to end a cycle of harming self and others rather than perpetuating it.

Survivors of family violence often underestimate their potential because their victimization has negatively affected their perceptions of self-worth. Since survivors often internalize shame about their abuse experiences, providing a view of themselves as being resilient gives credit to their abilities and determination to persevere and prevail. In the following quote from a helping professional who is an incest survivor, she emphasizes how difficult it is to cultivate one's resourcefulness and tenacity when trauma has become the center of a person's being.

> I think my experience in treating a lot of survivors is the thought that any strengths once developed are not valuable somehow because they generated up out of the sexual abuse experience...There's a tendency to define everything good as somehow less than or not worthy because it came up as a result of the abuse instead of seeing it as tenacity or resourcefulness. They see it as some kind of response to a horrible event in their life and therefore it has no value. (Sara, age 44)

Clearly, the research shows that survivors of family violence suffer adverse consequences that may leave them lacking in several areas of psychosocial functioning. Yet, symptom inventories tell us little about survivors' experiences of violence and about what they can teach us. Having individuals share their stories of trauma recovery validates their wisdom and experiences and, at the same time, helps to develop a deeper understanding regarding the many dimensions of healing from family violence. In the author's research, consequently, survivors—the people most significantly affected—help to shape practice theory and methodology in the area of trauma and recovery.

2

The Power of Recovery: Resilience, Posttraumatic Growth, and Strengths

Resiliency research, posttraumatic growth literature, and strengths-based social work practice contribute to a helping framework that optimizes human potential while counterbalancing a more traditional vulnerability/deficit model in mental health practice. Integrating these cutting edge trends into work with survivors of family violence provides a more comprehensive view of trauma recovery. Therapeutic paradigms that operate with a focus on pathology are less likely to tap into clients' resilience because "...we can only see and know that which our paradigms allow us to see and know" (Barnard, 1994, p. 137). Although each of these trends has different origins (e.g., psychopathology, existential psychology, social work), they share common assumptions regarding the positive aspects of the human condition, including growth from adversity (Saleebey, 2009; Tedeschi, Park, & Calhoun, 1998; Wolin & Wolin, 1993). They recognize that people strive towards growth even under the most ominous conditions. In addition, they identify that people's ability to live well in the present depends upon recognizing and uncovering their strengths. Furthermore, they understand that people are doing the best that they can with the resources available to them. This chapter discusses these mental health trends more fully as each credits individuals' abilities to triumph in the face of adversity, thus creating important and new implications for working with survivors of trauma.

RESILIENCY RESEARCH

Recognition that not all children exposed to adverse conditions develop adult pathologies led to the emergence of resiliency research (Fraser, 1997; Glicken, 2006; Masten, 2001; Wolin & Wolin, 1993). Much of resiliency research focuses on uncovering those attributes that help at-risk children resist stress. Protective factors in children, their families, and external support systems are identified (Garmezy, 1987; Werner & Smith, 1992). These protective factors evolve from the adaptive changes that occur when children successfully cope with stress. If one does not experience impaired functioning then an individual is perceived as competent or "thriving" despite encountering adversity. Experiences and conditions are categorized as risk factors because their presence deprives youth of important developmental experiences, relationships, and opportunities, making them vulnerable to participation in antisocial activities or ill health (Safyer, Griffin, Colan, Alexander-Brydie, & Rome, 1998). Some of these adverse conditions studied include poverty (Werner & Smith, 1992), parental mental illness (Beardslee & Podorefsky, 1988), inner-city living (Luthar, 1993), and child abuse and neglect (Farber & Egeland, 1987).

Over the years, resiliency literature has emerged from studies in developmental psychopathology that focused on the "adverse" conditions placing children at risk for developing adult pathologies (Byrd, 1994) and the ways in which youth avoid problems despite exposure to adverse conditions. To this end, risk and protective factors have been identified within individual, family, and community domains (O'Leary, 1998; Patterson, 2002; Walsh, 2003). Much of resiliency research focuses on uncovering those attributes that help at-risk individuals withstand stress (Fraser, 1997; Garmezy, 1987; Masten, 2001; Rutter, 1987; Werner & Smith, 1992). These factors include attributes in individuals, their families, and in external support systems that serve as protective mechanisms and appear to foster resilience (Howard, Dryden, & Johnson, 1999; Mandleco & Perry, 2000). Benard's (1996) listing of protective factors is frequently cited including: social competence, problem-solving skills, autonomy, sense of purpose and future, caring and supportive environment, high positive expectations, and opportunities for meaningful involvement. The Search Institute's developmental assets framework contains a similar list of internal and external assets (Leffert, Benson, Scales, Sharma, Drake, & Blyth, 1998).

The resiliency literature has progressed to recognizing complex interaction of individual attributes, family milieu, and social context as indicators that play into the capacity to overcome adversity and remain resilient under stressful life events (Glicken, 2006). The studies progressed from defining attributes of resiliency to exploring processes over time that protect one from risk. Instead of viewing resiliency as the avoidance of stress factors, researchers recognized that resiliency was a process whereby risk was successfully engaged (Egeland, Carlson, & Sroufe, 1993). The protective factors evolved from the adaptive changes that occurred when children successfully coped with stress (Rutter, 1987). Successfully engaging in risk fostered outcomes of adaptation and competence (Cohler, 1987). The resiliency studies refocused after discovering that identifying these attributes was not sufficient in explaining why a person overcomes adversity. Instead, it was a process that unfolded over time, in which the child learned to positively adapt to stress and adversity. Therefore, it was not a matter of being "resistant" to stress but engaging in it, and this process fostered outcomes that were characterized by adaptation and competence. These children were finding ways to manage the stress and anxiety of a troubled family life.

A literature review on resilience is presented to provide conceptual sensitivity and serve as a background for the author's research. Resilient capacities are presented through addressing the bio-psycho-social-spiritual dimensions of the phenomena, recognizing these dimensions are not mutually exclusive, nor do they operate void of an environmental context. The literature review highlights the many ways in which individuals perceive, seek to make sense of, and respond to adverse life situations.

BIO-PSYCHO-SOCIAL-SPIRITUAL PROTECTIVE FACTORS

Initial studies on resilience focused on children's risk for developing adult pathologies because of their exposure to adverse conditions, such as parental mental illness. These studies discovered that there were children who were unusually competent and creative although they had endured highly stressful environments (Rutter, 1987). Research findings suggested that factors such as being highly intelligent, having a sociable temperament, and being exceptionally creative (e.g., artistically) may be biologically based and significant contributors to the hardiness of these "super kids" (Luthar & Zigler, 1991; Rutter, 1987; Smith & Prior, 1995).

These early studies tended to view these children as unique, biologically, constitutionally, or temperamentally regarding their ability to thrive. As research on resilience evolved, studies began to focus on other components in children and their environments in an attempt to further address the question of how individuals can engage with stressful factors and remain competent. In more recent studies on resilience (Fraser, 1997; Masten, 2001; Valentine & Feinauer, 1993), a biological-based dimension has not been found as significant as other attributes and processes of individuals and their environments.

The psychological dimensions of resiliency include cognitive, behavioral, and emotional strategies used to survive adverse experiences and to persevere in life. Although intelligence is a significant contributor to one's mental capabilities, many elements of cognitive functioning are learned through interacting with environmental stressors. For example, cognitive appraisal of those parts of a sexually abusing family environment that are controllable and those that are not is dependent upon efforts employed to affect the abuse situations. These attempts to affect the abuse experience may have started out as accidental, such as being sick, but recognizing that this prevented one from being sexually abused, the child may have figured out that this and other ways to influence the abuse situation, either directly or indirectly existed (Ceresne, 1995). They may not have always been successful in stopping the abuse, but they were active in trying to escape or resist it (Morrow & Smith, 1995).

Lazarus and Folkman (1984) argue that how one cognitively appraises a stressful event and how one copes with it are more significant than the actual event itself in determining a person's adjustment. Appraisal of a stressful event occurs before cognitive and behavioral strategies are employed. Primary appraisal involves assessing what is at stake. The event may be appraised as benign, irrelevant, or stressful. Secondary appraisal involves making decisions about what may be done about the situation. Appraisal of the event, therefore, guides selection of cognitive and behavioral strategies that are either oriented toward or away from the stressor (Roth & Cohen, 1986). According to Lazarus and Folkman (1984) coping can either be emotion-focused or problem-focused depending on how the situation is appraised. If an event is appraised as uncontrollable then emotion-focused coping is used to regulate one's response to the problem. This includes cognitive strategies that serve to alter one's feelings about a situation. On the other hand, if the situation is appraised as having potential for control, then problem-focused coping is used and action is directed toward managing or changing the problem. Stressful events are cognitively appraised and reappraised throughout one's life (Lazarus & Folkman, 1984).

Research on coping is often presented as a dichotomy in that one is either emotion-focused or problem-focused. Emotion-focused coping is believed to be a passive means of adapting to a problem, while problem-focused coping is thought to be more active and, consequently, a healthier way to confront the stressors of a situation.

Banyard and Graham-Bermann (1993) discuss the limitations of viewing coping as being either emotion-focused or problem-focused in relationship to gender. In coping research, females are often found to use emotion-focused strategies and consequently are portrayed as passive victims of their environments. Males, on the other hand, use problem-focused strategies; and, as a result, are believed to be more active and effective in their coping. Women's coping is viewed as more maladaptive than men's is because assessments of their overall functioning focus on psychological adjustment in which they are more likely to internalize what is happening to them rather than to take action in confronting the problem (Gutierrez, 1994). The central organizing trait of women's development is an inner sense of connection to others (Miller, 1976). Research needs to understand women's coping strategies within a larger social context in which women's choices are made for the good of others rather than personal survival. Theorizing that effective coping is exhibited by problem-focused methods sets predetermined boundaries of how we think positive adaptation should be exhibited. Without a contextual understanding, the scope of inquiry is limited because researchers, then, don't hear or see other ways that individuals may be coping as "healthy" (Massey, Cameron, Ouellette, & Fine, 1998).

For example, Morrow and Smith (1995) contend that the overwhelming predominance of emotion-focused coping in sexually abused victims is due to the powerlessness of females in our society and the lack of dependable resources for intervention available to the victims. "What appears at first glance to be a profusion of dysfunctional symptoms becomes, upon closer examination, rational and reasonable coping strategies given the extremity of the stressors to which these women, as children, were subjected" (Morrow & Smith, 1995, p. 32). Society's denial of and secrecy surrounding sexual abuse further exacerbates a choice to use emotion-focused coping. Incestuous families are usually unresponsive and nonsupportive of the child victim. Consequently, children end up blaming themselves for their victimization. When coping strategies are abstracted from the context of their lives, adult survivors' experiences are reduced to individual deficiencies rather than obstacles to resources, such as lack of social support.

The child who has experienced family violence is under a threat in the most intimate environment, which places her on constant guard because she does not know when the abuse will occur again. To establish feelings of safety, it is essential for the child to figure out cognitive, behavioral, and emotional avenues of protection, escape, and resistance (Henry, 1999). Resiliency studies indicate that fantasizing helps one to escape through developing imaginary friends, families, havens, or futures that would allow them to psychologically distance themselves from the trauma (Byrd, 1994). Many resilient individuals are involved in extracurricular activities that assist them in escaping their trauma by connecting with caring adults and providing a safe haven that allows opportunities for resilience to grow and develop (Tiet, Bird, & Davies, 1998). Emotional strategies often involve protecting oneself from the overwhelming feelings caused by the trauma and by letting out their emotions by talking to themselves, toys, or pets. Another emotional strategy is to find protection by channeling their emotional pain through painting, writing, drawing, playing music, and developing a sense of humor (Wolin & Wolin, 1993).

The social dimension involves relationships between individuals, their families, and external support systems. The significance of having one supportive adult in one's life is illustrated in resiliency research due to the many functions that these relationships provide: being a role model for appropriate behavior, offering affirmation, providing safety, and reinforcing the idea that the individual deserves to be loved (Garmezy, 1987; Laws, 1995; Rubin, 1996). These adults may be family members, friends' parents, teachers, clergy, coaches, or other community members. Other relationships, including the caring of pets or time spent outdoors in a natural setting, also provide sources for nurturance. Another important area in social relations is individuals' caretaker roles within their families-of-origin. They are caring and nurturing in their relationships, but remain distant in a manner in which they are not consumed by family problems and chaos. Taking care of certain family members and responsibilities allows for opportunities to give and receive nurturance, establish autonomy, develop self-reliance, and achieve a sense of accomplishment (Werner & Smith, 1992).

The spiritual dimension addressed in resiliency literature involves both religious and nonreligious expressions of spirituality and meaning that serve various functions for those enduring adversity. Resilience research indicates that spiritual beliefs, activities, and supports are important in giving a sense of purpose to individuals' lives and their traumatic experiences in a manner that frees them from guilt and shame (Valentine & Feinauer, 1993). Spirituality during childhood is mainly expressed within religious institutions. Attending a religious institution on a regular basis provides structure in their lives, connects them with a consistent source of support, allows respite from their trauma, and provides comfort in the belief that there is a Higher Power on which they can depend (Ceresne, 1995). The act of prayer affords opportunities to express what is happening and to ask for help in getting them through their troubles. Their spiritual beliefs help them feel that they can prevail regardless of what the future has in store (Henry, 1999). In thinking about their childhood adversity, some resilient individuals indicate that it is part of a life plan guided by a Higher Power and see themselves as becoming stronger from their experiences.

THE EBB AND FLOW OF RESILIENCE ACROSS THE LIFE SPAN

The majority of research on children's resilience is conducted through assessing children's competence at one point in time, and then making conclusions about their adaptation and competence in life (Laws, 1995). The data from these risk and protective studies are important in identifying protective mechanisms in children, their families, and external support systems. However, the impact of risk and protective factors may change at various times throughout a child's life. Therefore, conducting longitudinal studies is important for gaining a better understanding of the processes that support or limit the development of resilience over time (Garmezy & Masten, 1986; Luthar & Zigler, 1991). Longitudinal studies show that individuals demonstrate their "power of recovery" repeatedly as different stressors arise throughout their lives (Laws, 1995).

There are times in their lives when resilient individuals are able to persevere better than others because of life experiences and developmental demands that vary throughout their lives. Some critical events or turning points include leaving the family environment (moving out), marriage or being involved in a serious relationship, having children, going to college, getting a job, chance events (e.g., seeing a television program on domestic violence and realizing that is what one has experienced), and maturing (Garmezy, 1987; Laws, 1995; Rubin, 1996). The following section discusses

Werner and Smith's (1992) longitudinal studies of individuals who endured childhood poverty, but grew up to be caring and competent adults.

Werner and Smith (1992) studied a birth cohort who were born into poverty on the Hawaiian island of Kauai in 1955, and followed their development across the life span. The birth cohort included 505 individuals. The purpose of the Kauai longitudinal studies was to monitor a variety of risk factors and protective mechanisms over the life span of these individuals. The high risk cohort (210 individuals) endured a greater number of stress factors than the others, putting them at low odds for successful development. These children experienced poverty, perinatal stress, and parental discord or psychopathology. Two out of three children in the high-risk group developed serious behavior problems such as juvenile delinquency, mental disorders, or teenage pregnancy. The remaining one-third (30 males and 42 females) of the high-risk group developed into confident, caring, and competent individuals by the age of 18. Of the two-thirds in the high-risk group who were having difficulty functioning at the age of 18, half of them had turned their lives around by the age of 31. Overall outcomes for the high-risk group show that by the age of 31 there was an enormous capacity for recovery. The following section discusses how individuals in the resilient group maintained their competence throughout their lives, and how others in the high-risk group corrected their lives after struggling during childhood.

The resilient group (72 individuals) showed adaptive capacities throughout their development from birth to 31 years of age in contrast to their counterparts in the high-risk group. Looking at their development helps us understand that confidence, competence, and a caring attitude can flourish, even against strong odds. As we look at them in different development stages, the rise of their resilient capacities are evident. As infants, they were good-natured, easy to deal with, and elicited positive attention from family members. They had fewer sleeping and eating problems that caused stress for their parents. Their positive temperament elicited appropriate care and attention from their environment even in conditions of poverty. During their first year, they rarely experienced extended separation from their primary caretaker.

As toddlers, the children in the resilient group continued to attract attention through their positive social orientation. They were cheerful, agreeable, friendly, responsive, and relaxed. They were also self-confident and more advanced in their verbal ability than their high-risk counterparts. By the age of 10, the resilient group had better reading and reasoning skills than others in the high-risk group. They continued to be friendly and got along well with their peers. These children were not unusually gifted; however, they were able to make good use of the skills they possessed. The girls were often caretakers of younger siblings, which allowed them to develop a sense of responsibility and competence. Resilient boys often thrived at home due to the presence of their fathers.

At the age of 18, the resilient group had developed a positive self-concept and had an achievement-oriented attitude toward life. They demonstrated a greater degree of maturity, responsibility, and nurturing behavior. They expressed an internal locus of control, believing that their actions and decisions could determine outcomes in their lives. The resilient group exhibited insight into what was necessary for them to achieve, such as having structure in their lives. They were able to comfort themselves, but were also caring toward others.

Protective factors in their families and external support systems of the resilient group helped to nourish and maintain resilient adaptive capacities. They often sought and received support from many informal sources, and they had a close relationship with at least one caregiver or substitute parent. Their own families were consistent in enforcing rules and in expressing a positive attitude toward academic achievement. Resilient individuals were often put in caretaker roles that they viewed positively, because it gave them opportunities to manage responsibility and to act autonomously. Sibling caretaking appeared to be a significant antecedent to responsible and nurturing behavior that lead to positive relationships in adulthood.

As children, resilient individuals sought relationships outside the family and were often involved in extracurricular activities although they were lacking in financial resources. They sought refuge in activities through church youth organizations, 4-H, the YMCA, and the YWCA. These activities gave them distance from what was occurring at home and connected them with adults who gave them emotional support. The help of caring individuals, such as religious mentors or teachers, allowed them to have faith in their abilities and provided meaning to their lives. The Kauai children did not name mental health professionals among those who made a difference in their lives.

Werner and Smith (1992) gathered data through quantitative measures of health, well-being, and life satisfaction to assess attributes of resilience in the participants at the age of 31 years old. In addition, they conducted semi-structured interviews to determine participants' perceptions of significant stressors and supports throughout their lives. The resilient adults considered personal competence and determination as their most effective means of coping with the stressors in their lives. Also, having the support of a family member or partner, having a sense of faith, and being achievement oriented were helpful in managing their adversities during adulthood. The majority of resilient adults were industrious and had career or job success as a primary objective. They had acquired additional education after high school and were employed in managerial or professional positions. Overall, they were satisfied with their lives.

Resilience in one-third of the high-risk group was a constant throughout their lives, supported by individual and environmental protective factors. Of the remaining two-thirds in the high-risk group, half of them had made significant changes in adulthood; so that by the age of 31, they were also assessed as resilient on measures of competency and life satisfaction. This figure demonstrates that the road to recovery takes different forms; and that for some individuals, resilience continues to develop as they leave adverse childhood environments. Their recovery in adulthood provides a perspective on the developmental process of adaptation and demonstrates that resilience can flourish anytime throughout one's life. Once people are able to leave their adverse environments, many are able to be productive by taking on the responsibilities of work, intimate relationships, and parenthood.

POSTTRAUMATIC GROWTH LITERATURE

A complementary but distinct concept in relation to childhood resilience is posttraumatic growth, which may account for Werner and Smith's (1992) findings regarding how some individuals turn their lives around upon leaving an adverse environment. In the aftermath of stressful or traumatic life experiences (i.e., the trauma has ended or the person is no longer in the harmful environment), many people report personal growth in the midst of their struggles to heal (Saakvitne, Tennen, & Affleck, 1998). These positive changes are often referred to as "posttraumatic" growth and highlight the human capacity for transformation in even the most ominous circumstances. "*Transformation* is change, change that involves being strengthened, rather than destroyed, by trauma" (Bussey & Wise, 2007, p. 7). Areas strengthened as a result of posttraumatic growth include: intimacy in one's interpersonal relationships, the ability and desire to help or protect self and others, spirituality, and resilience to future stressors due to a foundation of past coping and survival skills (Helgeson, Reynolds, & Tomich, 2006; Linley & Joseph, 2004; Roche & Wood, 2005). Posttraumatic growth is noted in various disrupting and devastating circumstances including war combat, natural disasters, death of a loved one, and terminal illness (Helgeson et al., 2006; Linley & Joseph, 2004).

Drawing upon conceptual insights from studies conducted with trauma populations (i.e., female survivors of childhood sexual abuse, women who suffered domestic violence, and female sexual assault victims), the markers of posttraumatic growth are briefly described to provide a context in which to better understand how one develops new understandings of life's meaning and purpose after such injurious and debilitating events (Cobb et al., 2006; Frazier, Conlon, & Glaser, 2001; McMillen, Zuravin, & Rideout, 1995). One key to the transformation process includes the ability for the survivor of violence to step back and detach from events and the environment that characterized the trauma experience (Tedeschi, Park, & Calhoun, 1998). Such disengagement allows the opportunity for rumination on one's thoughts, emotions, and beliefs from a safe distance and provides the path for examination of the past. Lev-Wiesel and Amir (2003) note that breaking attachment to a violent perpetrator may be of utmost value to this process. From this new vantage point one can begin the process of deconstructing old schemas and worldviews on the nature of families, relationships, accountability, and other often previously unchallenged ideas about life that were part and parcel of the abuse environment.

As old ways of thinking become invalidated through cognitive restructuring, they are replaced with new ways of understanding the self and one's place in the world. The process involves accepting the limitations of human beings and how one's previous assumptions about life have been broken down by the reality of trauma. This can result in the paradoxical understanding that one is both vulnerable yet powerful as a human actor in an often chaotic and unjust world. Integrating one's reactions to and cognitions about the past with the new schemas that emerge from this rumination process allow for both an acceptance (rather than avoidance) of traumatic events and for an informed outlook on oneself and the future (Cadell, Regehr, & Hemsworth, 2003; Cobb et al., 2006). The growth experienced in this renewal process may then inform survivors' decision making, perception of possibilities, and appreciation for life, self-efficacy and the value of choice. Although these constructs assist in conceptualizing posttraumatic growth theoretically, there is no magic formula as one must go through the cognitive and affective processing of adverse experiences to get to the other side and reap the hard-won benefits of reconstructing a self-narrative of strength, resiliency, and agency.

THE STRENGTHS PERSPECTIVE IN SOCIAL WORK PRACTICE

The strengths perspective emphasizes a helping framework that honors people's abilities and potential for growth and has its roots in the social work profession (De Jong & Miller, 1995). The underlying premise is that a helping paradigm that honors and supports individuals' strengths, capabilities, skills, and talents offers a more productive avenue for helping than focusing on problems, pathology, and disorders (Saleebey, 1992). The strengths perspective is a practice orientation that helps clients to recognize the individual and environmental resources available to help them heal and make positive changes in their lives. Over the past 30 years, the strengths perspective has developed into a model for social work practice found to be effective in working with a variety of populations including the chronic mentally ill, people with disabilities, the elderly, children, and families (Saleebey, 2009).

The application of the strengths perspective includes the practitioner firmly believing in and supporting a client's aspirations, perceptions, and strengths despite the problems that are presented (Saleebey, 1997). "To really practice from a strengths perspective demands a different way of seeing clients, their environment, and their current situation. Rather than focusing on problems, your eye turns to possibility" (Saleebey, 1997, p. 3). This provides a holistic view of clients because it highlights the positives of the person in all life domains (e.g. social, educational, vocational, etc.) along with their struggles. The strengths perspective allows for a collaborative process between the client and practitioner as they mutually share their strengths, life stories, and aspirations (Sullivan & Rapp, 1994). The relationship is of central importance and builds on the resourcefulness of the client. The continued focus on the positive assists clients to get back in touch with their natural resources and bring out additional strengths to assist in achieving their aspirations.

Instead of a problem-centered focus, individual and environmental strengths are emphasized as vital to good social work practice. The focus of the client and practitioner's work revolves around what the client has done to manage their life experiences, what resources have been or are currently available to the client, and the aspirations and dreams the client may hold. The strengths perspective recognizes that clients have coped with their situation in the best way that they know (Weick, Rapp, Sullivan, Kisthardt, 1989; Saleebey, 1992). The client's knowledge and experiences, therefore, are of central importance in guiding the helping process. The identification and rediscovery of a client's individual and environmental resources occurs through the use of a strengths assessment. A strengths assessment often explores the life domains of daily living, education/vocation, health, recreation, and social supports. The individual and environmental strengths available to the client are examined within each of these areas (Kisthardt, 1992).

Clients may not achieve their life's potential because the array of their abilities is not fully expressed (Weick et al., 1989). Operating from a strengths orientation guides social work practitioners to unleash the potential in individuals who have experienced family violence. The struggles and hardships individuals face may obscure their skills, talents, and competencies (Saleebey, 1996, 1997). Therefore, the helping process focuses on uncovering these "lost" strengths and to build on them in order to help each client achieve his or her treatment goals. The strengths perspective focuses on identifying the specific pattern of individual and environmental strengths for each individual (Kisthardt, 1997). Emphasizing the unique skills and competencies for each client individualizes the helping process. The client's strengths are drawn upon to formulate an intervention plan that is specific to his/ her situation. Clients achieve positive treatment outcomes when their individual abilities are validated and mobilized into an action plan (Saleebey, 1997).

SUMMARY

Clients have survived and coped often against immense odds such as in the case of family violence. Yet, mental health practitioners cannot assist individuals to uncover and to tap into these abilities if they are not equipped to see them as strengths. By overlooking strengths and ignoring resilience, traditional vulnerability/deficit models of mental health practice encourages survivors to describe, dissect, and document repeatedly how they were hurt. Initially, naming a person's "damage" (e.g., symptoms, diagnosis) may provide relief; yet, this may restrict opportunities of growth, because the assumption is that to live well one must "undo" the damage (Wolin & Wolin, 1993). This chapter, in contrast, highlights how the contributions of resilience research, posttraumatic growth literature, and strengths-based social work practice may assist practitioners to shift the focus of their helping frameworks from problems and pathology to strengths and resilience. In doing so, the potential of each client, particularly how one has prevailed, may be nurtured and honored.

3 Broadening the Focus of Resilience Research

Resilience research has uncovered an array of individual and environmental factors that contribute to adaptation and competence. Competence is often viewed as the absence of psychopathology (e.g., depression, anxiety) and is conceptualized through its implications for at-risk children and adolescents rather than for adults (Miller, 2003). Yet, a definition of resilience based on competence is restrictive because it categorizes people who are exposed to adversity as either being resilient, if they are doing well, or dysfunctional, if they are having problems (Luthar, Cicchetti, & Becker, 2000). Is the purpose of resiliency research to differentiate people into classifications of either success or failure (Miller, 2003)? If so, we run the risk of inadvertently "blaming the victim" when persons fall short of achieving predetermined criteria of resilience (Ungar, 2003). As highlighted in Werner and Smith's (1992) research, resilience is a process and an individual's growth is likely to have its ups and downs in the face of adversity (Massey, Cameron, Ouellette, & Fine, 1998). Surviving traumatic experiences, such as family violence, often leaves psychological sequelae that impede positive adaptation (Briere & Runtz, 1993). Therefore, survivors who seek mental health treatment would not be considered resilient, according to the traditional definition, because their adaptive capacities are diminished by the damage or expressed as dysfunctional behaviors; consequently, on measures of psychological distress (e.g., Brief Symptoms Inventory [BSI]) they would not appear competent.

Resilience research—along with the posttraumatic growth literature and the strengths perspective—is particularly limited with its narrow focus on individual conditions and its exclusion of oppressive social circumstances (Massey et al., 1998). Individual and environmental protective factors are explored by researchers, but they remain underdeveloped concepts, particularly in their relationship to adversity (Cowger, Anderson, & Snively, 2006; Masten, 2001). To truly understand resilience the context of adverse conditions—from which resilience emanates—needs further explication in resilience research and trauma theory. Consequently, previous research and theory building are insufficient in specifying hypotheses for testing resilience. There are tools that address aspects of resilience such as coping, social adjustment, and self-esteem. Yet, there is minimal if any detail given to how resilience is forged within a particular context of oppression. Consequently, a resiliency theory that integrates risk and protective factors into a coherent whole is lacking. The term *adverse* is used to describe difficult or even traumatic family environments; yet, the context for these conditions are stripped or minimized (Cowger et al., 2006). Therefore, the supposed commonalities across different studies in regard to biological, psychological, social, and spiritual protective factors are presented as if all adverse environmental conditions (e.g., poverty, parental mental illness, family violence) are similar in risk factors. Figure 3.1 presents a traditional conceptual structure of resilience.

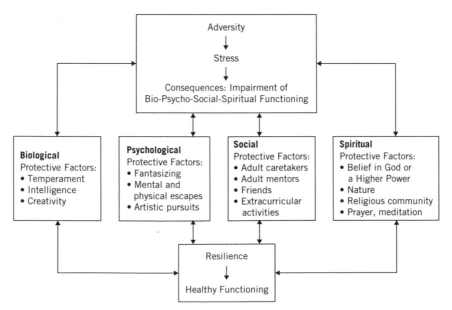

Figure 3.1 Adversity, Protective Factors, and Resilience

USING QUALITATIVE RESEARCH METHODOLOGY TO CONTEXTUALIZE RESILIENCE

The contextual problems that plague resilience research can be addressed through the use of qualitative approaches (Ungar, 2003). Qualitative methods allow for inquiry that attends to how respondents make meaning of their lives (i.e., the contexts, transitions, challenges, stressors, obstacles, and networks of support) without limiting them to the meanings that researchers decide in advance as useful, relevant, or even healthy (Denzin & Lincoln, 1998). In the case of studying resilience, qualitative research addresses the contextual nuances of the solutions at-risk populations find to cope with high-risk environments (Massey et al., 1998). For example, using a naturalistic approach to grounded theory building (as in the author's research) provides an opportunity to develop concepts of resilience that go beyond restrictive traditional definitions (i.e., competence). The grounded theory approach uses a systematic set of procedures to develop an inductively derived grounded theory about a phenomenon (Glaser, 2001). The adequacy of the theory is judged on its ability to not only fit the phenomenon under study, but to provide understanding of it and to be general enough to encompasses a range of situations without being so abstract as to lose its relevance to any one situation (Glaser, 2001).

If little is known about a topic and few adequate theories exist to explain or predict a group's behavior, the grounded theory method is especially useful. The method of theory generation includes the discovery of a basic psychosocial process or a core variable that explicates what's going on in the data. A core variable is distinguished by reoccurring frequently in the data, linking a range of data together, and explaining much of the variation in the data (Oktay, 2004). This variable becomes the basis for the generation of the theory. Researchers also hope that the resulting theory's implications will have useful application (Glaser, 2001). Because of its practical implications, grounded theory research can be classified as applied research and is used widely in social work, in other professions (e.g., nursing, education), and in the social sciences (e.g., sociology). Therefore, the theory needs to provide some application so that practitioners can develop hypotheses regarding how to act in a particular case (Charmaz, 2006).

Data analysis is conducted using a constant comparative method; a qualitative procedure that identifies and extracts significant statements or "meaningful units" from in-depth interview transcripts to be conceptualized and reconstructed in new ways (Denzin & Lincoln, 1998;

Glaser, 2001). A constant comparative method "is time consuming and demanding because it involves intensive fieldwork, simultaneous collection of data and analysis of data, sampling on the basis of emerging theory, and the generation and integration of abstract concepts" (Wells, 1995, p. 35). The aim of this data analysis method is the generation of theoretical constructs that, along with substantive codes and categories and their properties, form a theory that encompasses as much behavioral variation as possible (Denzin & Lincoln, 1998; Glaser, 2001). While coding and analyzing the data, the researcher looks for patterns.

Comparative analysis forces the researcher to expand or "tease out" the emerging category/construct by searching for its cause, structure, temporality, dimensions, consequences, and its relationship to other categories (Oktay, 2004). For instance, the author's research initially involved searching for units of data (e.g., risk and protective factors) that could stand on their own and were associated with the overall purpose for each study. Through coding, data was then grouped into final categories that represented key psychosocial issues and patterns (e.g., protective processes) related to resilience, which were analyzed by comparing them with one another, so that relevant themes (e.g., resistance to oppression) addressing the research questions could emerge. Finally, a resiliency conceptual model was generated around the core category (e.g., oppression) that describes the central phenomenon relating to participants' experiences.

A significant component of the author's research focuses on how strategies of resistance to oppression develop across the life span and promote the development of resilience (i.e., one's ability to survive trauma and persevere in life) for survivors of family violence. Developing grounded theory from the perspectives of individuals experiencing the social problem directly helps to serve the population for which it is carried out. The intent of the following research is to carefully explore the dynamics and consequences of individuals' exposure to family violence and abuse, particularly regarding how one's survival abilities develop amongst chaos and pain.

The author's research process includes an interconnected relationship between her and the participants. The intent is to capture the complexity of women's suffering and their resilience. It allows participants to tell their stories in their own voices, work together to have a common understanding of what is being created, and affirm their knowledge and wisdom. Additionally, the research process provided an opportunity for participants to receive affirmation of their resilient capacities. Another benefit includes thinking about their strengths in new and different ways:

> This is a gift to me in many ways.... It really gave me the opportunity to think about myself in a very, very positive way. So, that was really nice. (Holly, age 58)

Participants felt positive regarding their involvement in the studies and viewed it as a way to give back to others.

> I thought I had something to give back and that I really wanted to help women know that they can survive.... I want to make a difference. (Patricia, age 50)

RESILIENCE IN ADULT SURVIVORS OF INCEST

In the author's study of female incest survivors ($N = 26$), participants' strategies of resistance began as spontaneous protective reactions to their childhood victimization and, consequently, helped these women defend themselves against the destructive aftereffects of their troubled childhoods. Furthermore, their acts of resistance served as a catalyst to their resilience and became an enduring strength that was drawn upon throughout their lives (Anderson, 2006). The core category of "childhood oppression" provided a contextual thick description of the risk factors (i.e., abuse and violence) that participants had experienced and helped to explain how protective processes had developed. A resilience theory was generated around this category to describe and explain the nature and workings of the psychosocial relations within the conceptual model. Participants were not idle or silent in regard to their abuse. They used a variety of strategies to prevent, withstand, stop, or oppose their childhood victimization and its consequences.

Figure 3.2 reveals how these protective strategies were organized around three ontological themes: Resistance (a) of powerlessness (e.g., "I purposely did not do everything the abuser demanded of me."); (b) to silence (e.g., "I told a family member about the abuse."); and, (c) of isolation (e.g., "I sought out activities such as sports, art, music, or drama."). This study is the first to investigate strategies of resistance to childhood oppression as leading to resilience. Consequently, the findings of this

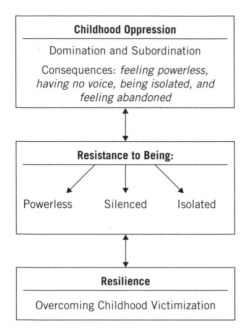

Figure 3.2 Conceptual Model of Adult Incest Survivors' Resistance to Childhood

study provide a set of conceptually meaningful categories for theory development regarding resilience and adult incest survivors, thus, adding to existing protective factors identified by prior resiliency research and trauma theory.

Case Example of Resistance to Being Powerless

Kelly, age 58, was brutally raped between the ages of 12 and 15 by her stepfather. Her attempts at stopping the incest were futile, but she was tenacious in her battle to defy her perpetrator. A driving force was to not let her perpetrator "win" that continued throughout her life. The following quotation tells of Kelly's initial attempt to stand up to her perpetrator and reveals the consequences of doing this:

> My parents had divorced. My mother was shopping around and she met this man, who worked at the same [place] she did, and they were to get married. I was a very needy child. I wanted a daddy like everybody else. [I] missed my own father, and my mother was put in the hospital for an intestinal ailment. I had been at the hospital visiting her. He [perpetrator] came to the hospital and offered to take me home. He took me home to an empty house, and he was talking about how he missed his little girl, and I had offered to make him coffee.... suddenly, things started feeling strange to me. He started pawing me, and I didn't know what to do. I was confused and agitated. And

I didn't say, "No." I just kept scooting away, and he kept scooting forward. Finally, he pinned me against the end of the divan. I scooted down, trying to get away and ended up on the floor, and he raped me. There was no one in the house to help, and yelling didn't help. It seemed to make him enjoy it more. He slapped me around a little. And sent me up to the bathroom to clean up. And came to the bathroom while I was cleaning up and cried and told me if I told anybody that they would blame me. That I had tempted him, and that it was my fault. I told him he would never do that to me again. He said, "Oh, yes, I will. Anytime I want."

Although he had threatened her to not tell, Kelly attempted to disclose the rape to her mother in an effort to stop it. When her mother ignored her attempt at disclosure, Kelly figured that she was in it alone and would have to protect herself. The following excerpt presents her attempt to disclose and the extreme measures she took to stop her perpetrator:

I went to the hospital to see my mother a couple of days later, and I tried to tell my mother what had happened, and she told me she didn't want to hear anymore and that I was jealous of her happiness and I would have to get over that my father wasn't there anymore, and she didn't want to hear anything more about it. So, I didn't tell her....So, anyway, intermittently for the next three years [he raped me]—I got so angry at him. He bought wine by the gallon, and I poured some of the wine out and put bleach in it, hoping to poison him. It made him sick, but it did not poison him.

Unfortunately, Kelly ended up getting pregnant when she was 13 years old by her perpetrator after being repeatedly raped. She sought out the services of Planned Parenthood for her pregnancy. Although she could not stop her perpetrator, she did not get pregnant from him ever again. The following is an excerpt discussing the protective strategies she took to prevent further pregnancies:

Well, they [Planned Parenthood] told me that when I woke up I wouldn't be pregnant anymore. And they had me come a week later. They fitted me with a diaphragm. I still have the scars because I put the diaphragm in every day. I wore it every day and every night, and when I went for my premarital exam at the doctor's, he did a pelvic on me. He said, "My God, woman, what happened to you!" because I did have scars. He wasn't kind when he raped me, but I never got pregnant again. I couldn't stop him, but I could stop having a baby, and I didn't want a baby.

Kelly's doggedness to survive during childhood enabled her to persevere in adulthood and was a part of her healing. She declared, "I clung to the mantra I would not let that evil bastard [perpetrator] win." When she encountered obstacles to her healing, she drew on her will to "live well," which offered the best revenge because then her perpetrator and what he had done to her could no longer dominate her life.

Case Example of Resistance to Being Silenced

Rosie's (age 56) perpetrator was her maternal grandfather, who sexually abused her for eight years. Rosie did not have a name for what her grandfather was doing to her, but knew she did not want it to continue. Rosie did not disclose to her parents because she perceived it would not make a difference in stopping the abuse. At the age of 10, she wrote a letter to her grandfather in an effort to stop his abuse. Her mother intercepted the letter and went into a "rage" over it. Rosie stated that her mother's intense and unsupportive reaction was as traumatic as her sexual abuse. Rosie never brought it up again to her mother. However, she did not continue her silence in adulthood and told her father and sister. Her father was shocked and her sister validated her experiences because their grandfather had tried to molest her as well. The following is an excerpt of Rosie's description of her mother's reaction when her mother found the letter:

> When I was 10 years old...my mother found a letter that I had written to him about [the incest]. I was becoming increasingly uncomfortable and frightened, and she found the letter and went into hysterics, and when I got home from school that afternoon, she took me into her bedroom, closed the door, turned off all the lights, sat me down in a chair and she sat on the bed, and she ranted and raved and screamed and blamed me for everything. And just asked God's forgiveness for me and what will we do and how could this happen. It was a major trauma. That was even more traumatic than the abuse itself.... That session lasted for hours. It was dark, and she still wouldn't turn on the light, and she was still screaming. I don't know what time it was, maybe 9 o'clock at night, before she let me out of that room. And after that, I was just numb.

Case Example of Resistance to Being Isolated

Becci, age 34, and the youngest in the family, was sexually abused from the ages of 3 to 8 by her half-brother, 10 years her senior and the second oldest of her two brothers. The incest stopped when her brother moved out of the house. She reported having mixed feelings about her brother and the abuse. For example, when she was in preschool and it started she thought it was her brother showing love to her. She was finally receiving attention, she thought, in a family environment that neglected her emotional needs. Her father was often away from the home due to his job. Her mother was physically but not emotionally present because of alcohol abuse. Her brother's demeanor was unpredictable. He could be kind and caring and then instantly become violent. Becci recalled feeling fearful and agitated because of his anger and his forcefulness toward her.

> He [her brother] was very angry, very violent. Would just grab me out of different parts of the house and make me go down to like the bathroom or the closet or whatever, where he would make me like perform oral sex on him and sticking fingers, objects, I'm pretty sure even his penis up inside me even when I was little.... I can remember the pressure of him being on top of me or whatever and not being able to breathe and how my body felt and staring out the window.... The things that I would think about when he was doing that and stuff like that. Just to get me through that time until it was over.

Becci remembers having a connection to God at a very young age that helped her to cope with the incest.

> I remember being in my bedroom and having that [sexual abuse] happen and—and staring out the window and just having a real clear feeling that there was a God. I didn't know how to say that. I probably didn't even know how to define God. But, knowing that there was something out there that was like bigger than all of this. I mean, I've always had that.

Becci stated it was always easy to leave her body and let her imagination "go wild." This kind of "dissociation" allowed her to live in an "altered" reality. Although her Native American heritage was not discussed within her family, she identified with it, particularly having relationships to her ancestors.

> Now as I delve a little bit into like the Native American spirituality, beliefs and stuff like that, I call it journeying now. It's so easy for me to meditate and to journey and to like connect with maybe ancestors or just different spirit guides that I probably felt even as a child.... I just always had a real connection to like the whole Native American concept of living or spirituality—my grandmother was Cherokee Indian. I don't know if that just like got in my blood or what, because, even as a little kid, I mean, she would always tease me about taking off my shoes no matter what. I mean, the first

thing I would do when I was anywhere was take off my shoes and just get close to the earth and go barefoot. Just maybe that's where that kind of spiritual concept came from or somethin'.

Becci has always felt connected to her pets because they provided safety and gave her nurturance.

I always had a dog or hamster or somethin' like that. I wanted to have a whole lot. I just have a real love for animals. I have a cat now, and I've had a lot of different animals along the way.... I just really understand 'em. I understand their wisdom and simplicity and all that. I feel more like one of them sometimes than a human being.

Becci was often angry as an adolescent and fortunately found sports to channel her physical energy and her emotions, particularly her anxiety.

I think being active in sports just saved my life, really. Because I think I would have quit school or just I don't know what. Just really pursued drugs and alcohol if I hadn't been so active in particularly volleyball. Because I did well and we had a good team. And it was really important.... It felt like a life saver because it was—it helped dissolve some of that energy, so I could like sleep at night. Everyday we'd have two-hour practices or whatever, and it helped me sleep. It helped me not have panic attacks. It helped me kind of stay calm. It helped me fit in. It helped me have some peers and some people that were complimentary of me. I was just a real physical person that needed that kind of outlet. I really experienced the world a lot through my physicalness.

For Becci school was a safe haven and provided connections with caring adults who supported and believed in her.

The relationships I had from teachers I think were very important. I mean whether it was my coaches or music teacher that even when I was getting suspended from school kept believing in me and kind of saw through all that to the good person I was.... I think I put a lot of energy into bonding with them on whatever they were in to. I wanted them to like me, so I tried to do real well at sports or music or English or whatever it was. And go talk to 'em after school. I was just always searching for that parent just everywhere. Probably still am.

Another important connection for Becci was her relationship with her maternal grandparents. She visited them almost every weekend throughout her childhood. They provided structure, safety, and unconditional love in her life.

> I can remember so many times walkin' into my grandparents' house. They were the ones that set the rituals. That offered sobriety and attention....I never got that from my parents. My grandfather was just always affectionate and hugged me. My dad wasn't into that and everything. They were very, very important. Probably the one stabilizing family connection that I had....We spent a lot of time together. I just knew that I was always loved....I just felt safe being there.

RESILIENCE IN ADULT DAUGHTERS OF BATTERED WOMEN

Additional lines of inquiry include other individuals victimized by family violence, such as adult daughters (N = 12) of battered women (Anderson & Danis, 2006). This exploratory study also used a naturalistic inquiry approach to grounded theory building to explore participants' views of reality and enable the researchers to generate resiliency theory in a population where little is known. As shown in Figure 3.3, the authors

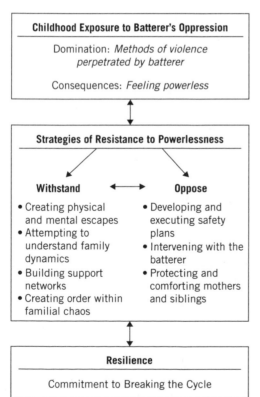

Figure 3.3 Conceptual Model of Children's Resistance to Batterer's Oppression

discovered that during participants' childhood, they used a variety of different protective strategies (N = 75 strategies) to "withstand" (n = 48 strategies) and "oppose" (n = 27 strategies) a sense of powerlessness due to the batterer's oppression of their mothers and of themselves.

Strategies of "withstanding" the violent environment were used in relationship to protecting themselves so they could endure the abuse (e.g., "I stayed away from home as much as possible"). Strategies of "opposing" the abuse were used in relationship to preventing or stopping the violence (e.g., "I argued with the batterer to divert the violence"). Although these acts of resistance began as spontaneous reactions to their mothers' and consequently their own subjugation, they were reshaped into adaptive strategies that were used throughout their lives to break the cycle of violence. This study's findings may serve to make domestic violence prevention programs aimed at children more meaningful and effective.

Case Examples of Withstanding Powerlessness

Adult daughters identified safe places within their childhood homes where they could leave behind what was happening to them by hiding out in closets, under blankets, and in bathrooms, particularly shower stalls. They also escaped into creative activities, such as music, dance, and acting, which not only allowed them to escape, but also allowed them an emotional channel for their family stressors. Cognitive strategies to distance themselves from the violence included reading books, watching television, creating fantasy families, and dissociating. The following quotes demonstrate participants' creative outlets for escaping their unsafe environment:

> I just remember when I was on stage when I was young and growing up like that was definitely my outlet for dealing with everything I was going through and I think that is a lot of how I got through. Because I would get up there and it was like I could, I guess in a way it is almost disassociating, but I could just go into a different space and get to this point to where I could watch myself be on stage in a way and just not have to deal with everything that was going on in my family and that kind of freed me from that and gave me a place to relax and not have to worry. (Melissa, age 27)

> I don't know if it was a gift, but I was a very intelligent child, and my grandmother really fostered that in me, taught me how to read and write well before I started school. And I loved to read. And I read books well beyond my age, well before I started school and first grade. And so that is how I

would try to escape was to read. And then also, as another way, I don't know how this all came about, but I can remember dissociating. I didn't know what it was, but I dissociated a lot where I would just be kind of watching but not actually being a part of. I never understood that until just recent years, about what I did, but I just knew that I couldn't interfere, when I was very small, I couldn't interfere. All I could do was just get out of the way. But if we were out somewhere, in a tavern, there really wasn't any way to get away. I mean I was there with them. There was nowhere to go. If we were in a car going somewhere, I guess that's when I learned to dissociate was by being in such close proximity to what they were doing. (Maggie, age 45)

A second strategy involved attempting to understand what was going on in the family. Adult daughters revealed that they had difficulty making sense of what was happening to their mothers. Yet, as shown in the following quotes, even at a young age some participants realized that their mothers were not at fault and that their fathers were in control:

> By the time I was nine, I knew for some reason that it wasn't Mom's fault. I didn't really know why, but I was no longer angry at her, because she was a victim too. She was hurting as bad as we were hurting. So by nine I didn't want Mom to know how hard it was. I didn't want Mom to know that I wanted to be doing other things. (Donna, age 45)

> I knew very early on, I don't know that I didn't know that it wasn't normal, but I knew that it was a choice, if that makes any sense. I mean that I knew that he [her father] had the control. I knew that he was making it happen or not happen. I knew that. And I recognized very early on that she would cower and do things to make things not happen, let's say, or to try to make things good. You could see that. It was an underlying nervousness. If he didn't see that, it seemed like there always had to be that constant upheaval. There always had to be something going on. I call it now "drama." There always had to be some drama, and I just couldn't stand it. I couldn't stand it. And, like I said, I guess it did become normal, but I refused, even then, to let anybody violate me in any way, including him. And that was scary sometimes, but if there ever was a physical confrontation between he and I, I always stood my ground with him. (Trish, age 37)

A third strategy involved building support networks. Adult daughters worked at developing support systems within and outside their families. Connections with grandparents, cousins, aunts, and uncles provided a sense of belonging and a basis for receiving unconditional love; even though no family members offered intervention regarding the batterer's violence. External connections included teachers, coaches, peers, books, television or fantasy families, and God or a Higher Power.

> I was my grandfather's granddaughter I was right there and he was my best friend when I was growing up and then there was grandma and she didn't go around anybody but she was there, so we were blessed also in having them there so I think that they helped, you know it just takes one person to make a difference in your life and maybe grandpa was the one. (Moberly, age 32)

> I really think about the ultimate relationship that has helped me in my life, is my relationship with God. I do not want to sound religious or anything, but God was my companion through all those times. I had nobody to go and talk about this to. So who do I turn to? I turn to this invisible being, my higher help. And what that has done for me is every time I turn to God, it's made me realize that I do not represent just a temporary, material existence of a conscious animal trying to move through her life with as much pleasure and as little pain as possible. We are so much more than that. So my relationship with God made me realize that there's a higher purpose for me being here, so that gives me strength. (Suria, age 35)

The final strategy included attempting to create order within chaotic familial situations. Creating order often included fixing and putting together the physical damages to their homes and its belongings after their fathers' had created destruction and turmoil. For many, these childhood experiences lead participants to live life in an orderly way in adulthood. They regularly strived for lives without chaos, confusion, or an absence of rules.

> You could hear things going on and my mother crying and finally, everything got quiet and we'd [the children] get up and we'd go clean everything up. And, I don't know how I got any sleep at all during all those years. But we'd get up and we'd just put things back together again, of course my ingenuity for fixing wasn't all that terrific, but I did learn how to use my school glue to glue things together and put all the magazines back in the magazine rack, and put all the pots and pans back where they went and hang things up and tidy things up as best you could so that it looked liked everything was okay by the next morning when everybody got up. We were very quiet. We just, scattered like little elves in the night and we'd fix everything all nice again and maybe 4, 5, or 6 o'clock in the morning we'd go to sleep and then we'd have to get up and go to school. I can remember it was just urgent that it had to be cleaned up perfectly and everything just the way it was supposed to be or something awful was going to happen and that was something that I couldn't protect my sisters from and I mean they

had to help. I couldn't do it all by myself and so we just scurried around like crazy. (Susan, age 34)

Case Examples of Opposing Powerlessness

The first strategy consisted of adult daughters developing and executing safety plans, often at a young age. Safety planning also involved the summoning for help, either from relatives, neighbors, and in some cases the police.

> I had already been at 4 years old planning my escape, if you can believe that. We lived across the street from an elementary school, and even though I wasn't in kindergarten yet, I loved it when we'd actually go over to the playground and play on the equipment. So of course we had been all over the school yard, and I remember thinking that there was this little, it was like a cave to me. But I now know it was of course a fire escape from the cafeteria in the basement to get up and out, but it had a concrete cover over the top of it, so it had a roof, and when the wind would blow, it would swirl leaves down in there, so there was always a nice big soft bed of leaves in there and it was warm when the wind was cold and chilly. I remember thinking, if Mommy wasn't going to stand up to him and make him quit hitting all of us, then I wanted to live somewhere else, and I remember planning that I could live down there where it was warm, and that the little grocery store that was just a half a block further down the road had food that I wanted. It was candy and things like that, that was down low. I knew that I had to eat and I knew that I could take some of that stuff and put it in my pockets and walk out without paying for it. I didn't have the foggiest idea what shoplifting was, but I was planning survival, and I was only four years old. (Donna, age 45)

A second strategy involved intervening with the batterer. This may have included trying to stop the batterer, mediating between the batterer and their mothers, or running interference so the batterer could not get to their mothers or access weapons. The following excerpts illustrate the courage and determination of participants as they intervened with their fathers in hope of preventing further violence toward their mothers:

> They had come home from a tavern one night with me and I had gone in the house. I remember them fighting so much and I was so afraid so I locked the door to keep my dad from coming in the house. Well of course my mother unlocked it, and then I tried to call my Grandma for help, and then my dad became more violent. And that stands out very much because I can still see the whole picture. (Maggie, age 45)

As soon as it would happen I'd call the police and I'd also just stop the fight-ing. I'd get in between my parents because, luckily my dad would never hit me, he never was violent towards me and if I got in between them it could cover my mom's body up. Then he couldn't get to her and he wouldn't hurt me to get to her so then he would stop. (Diane, age 27)

Because I was the eldest in the family, I stepped in and was trying to be brave and reprimanded my father for what he did, knowing very well that I might get hit. I was growing older, in my teens. I guess I had a sense of hate. We have a right to have a nonviolent life. That kind of realiza-tion started stepping into my head and I said, "I want to talk to him." So I did. Of course it was to no avail. I mean he didn't change or anything, but he did listen, and he didn't hit me at that time. Right timing maybe. I actually taught my mother some religion, and I also made her aware that she is being abused and this is not right. Because she is so immune to it already that she might think it's okay. It's just part of her life, she might have accepted it. (Suria, age 35)

A third strategy involved protecting and comforting their mothers and siblings. In regard to their mothers, strategies often involved trying to help them leave their abusive partners. This may have involved talking to them about the necessity of leaving or helping them to actually escape the situation. The following quote shows the courageous efforts of the participant to help her mother escape from the batterer's violence:

So, I took her and we ran away, and then we slowly tried to meet up with my brother in a friend's house, which is close by, without him [her father] ever knowing about it. That was the way I helped my mom, and that was the first time I ran away with mom, and it happened again a second time a few years later. The reason I'm saying it happened again, there came a time when mother decided to forgive, and so we went back and lived with him again. And for a while there he was all right, and then he started again. So, we left him again, and we've never looked back since. (Suria, age 35)

Adult daughters' caretaking roles also included protective actions directed toward their siblings. Caretaking responsibilities including comforting their siblings, explaining to them what was going on in the family, and protecting them from the violence and its consequences.

I fuss about not being rescued by these people that were living next door to us because I was basically raising myself plus my brothers and sisters, but as I've gotten older, I've discovered one of the good things they [her parents] did was they left me alone. They didn't parent me. If they had parented me as they did my brothers and sisters, I probably would have had more issues. I was raised by books, and I taught myself the things I needed to know, and I'm very self-reliant. I don't have a victim mentality. (Mary Poppins, age 51)

There was a time when my sisters were young I tried my best to keep them safe and that meant hiding. In the closet. In my sisters' room, they had a big closet that they shared and it wasn't exactly a walk in closet but it was a bigger closet than any of the others and we could have a nest in there. We had a bunch of clothes and blankets and sheets. But you couldn't take the sheets off the beds or anything because it had to look like you were in bed, in case he came in or looked in, but I don't even really know where we got all that stuff but we had a bunch of stuff in the closet and he never came in there. I can remember standing in the closet and holding the door knob to keep him from opening the door, which of course I would have never been able to if he had tried. (Susan, age 34)

Adult daughters opposed the batterer's violence and oppression and sought to actively stop the abuse by directly challenging their fathers or by summoning for help. Somehow these girls instinctively knew that the beatings aimed at their mothers was wrong and was not supposed to happen. They felt a personal responsibility to keep their mothers and siblings safe.

RESILIENCE IN FEMALE SURVIVORS OF DOMESTIC VIOLENCE

The strategies that battered women actively employ to withstand or oppose the violence has been documented (Campbell, Rose, Kub, & Nedd, 1998; Cavanagh, 2003; Geiger, 2002; Hollander, 2002). Research findings indicate that women typically are resistant to violence and use a variety of mental and behavioral strategies to prevent, withstand, stop, or oppose their subjugation and its consequences (Gillum, Sullivan, & Bybee, 2006; Kocot & Goodman, 2003). In fact, in the face of escalating violence women often demonstrate increasing activity in protecting themselves and their children. Various ways of coping include placating the abuser, accessing support networks, seeking legal action, and creating safety plans (Goodman, Dutton, Weinfurt & Cook, 2003; Horton & Johnson, 1993). Much has been written in regard to women's resistance strategies to intimate partner violence and their use of a variety of mental and behavioral tactics to prevent, withstand, stop, or oppose their subjugation and its consequences. Yet, in regard to women's agency and adaptation after they have left an abusive relationship, the professional literature is far more silent.

An important component to recovery includes the many internal and external resources that trauma survivors are able to create and call upon in diverse situations. Although research has begun to recognize recovery outcomes, there is little known regarding how one goes about achieving them. For instance, adaptation has been related to managing post-traumatic symptoms and other life demands (e.g., housing, food, clothing, and medical needs) without indicating what protective processes helps individuals to do this effectively. Consequently, this lack of information on how women regain a sense of order, coherence, and continuity after experiencing domestic violence provided the author's rationale for doing further research in this area.

Research was conducted, therefore, to study the recovery process from domestic violence survivors' perspectives in regard to what factors (e.g., formal and informal support networks) helped or hindered their recovery process. Through the use of the grounded theory method, recovery for these women ($N = 20$) was found to include a process of altering one's assumptive world, as illustrated in Figure 3.4.

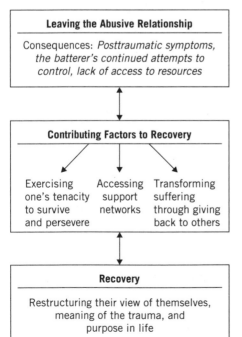

Figure 3.4 Conceptual Model of Women's Recovery from Domestic Violence

Participants' resolve to better their lives involved restructuring their beliefs about self (from vulnerability to strength), victimization (from questioning their suffering to finding meaning in their struggles), and life purpose (from doubting their existence to valuing their lives). Three important strategies were discovered to exist within this complex recovery process:

1. Developing a sense of personal efficacy derived from their tenacity to survive and persevere (e.g., "I did not let the domestic violence 'break' me.")
2. Accessing and eliciting positive responses from informal and formal support networks (e.g., "I reached out for help from family and friends.")
3. Transforming their suffering into giving back to others (e.g., "I turned my struggles into wanting to make a difference for others.")

As a result of their struggles, these women discussed how they were more able to appreciate their strengths, to be compassionate toward others, and to develop a sense of purpose or calling. For the women in this study, their lives did get better as a result of the many internal and external resources they were able to access and develop. Implications for helping professionals and survivors include providing a conceptual framework for better understanding the process of recovery for women who have been out of a violent relationship for several years.

Case Examples of Factors Contributing to Recovery

Personal Tenacity

Throughout and upon leaving the relationship, battered women worked at challenging their inner dialogues of shame and blame. Even though these women were traumatized, they did not give up on themselves or their survival. Participants related numerous examples of their tenacity, courage, and resourcefulness:

> Some people think of tenacity in a bad way, but I think of it as—I never could give up, even when I wanted to. I just couldn't give up. There's something in me that says "I'm going to make it." I never would quit. I remember feeling like I lived in this dark black tunnel, when I would close my eyes that's what I would see. Far off in the distance, I could see a speck of light. As long as I could see that speck of light, I could keep going. I remember feeling one day that I could actually start climbing towards that light. Just that belief that I could make it to that light, and climb out of whatever it was I lived in. (Pearl, age 50)

I don't know if this makes sense, but I just refused to be a victim. And I didn't ever want to be seen as a victim, I didn't want people to feel sorry for me...even when I would get depressed or frustrated or angry or scared, I knew life would go on and that I had...a choice, I had to keep trying and I had goals for myself and things that I wanted to do and so I had to make some changes. (Jane, age 22)

Throughout their recovery, battered women drew upon these survival strengths to face the challenges of reshaping their lives. The next excerpts illustrate how these women often channeled their tenacity into achieving their dreams and aspirations:

The dreams will help you keep your strength, dreams can happen, so just don't give up. If you had a childhood dream, now is your chance to make it happen. I mean, if you dreamed of being an airline pilot, or being a doctor, a nurse, or if your dream is to manage your own business, go for that dream, don't give up on it. It can happen. It can happen right now. I own my own business, so it can happen. Fight for what you want in life, don't just stand and take the back road, just get out there in front and fight for what you want. (Angel, age 42)

I've always wanted to be in the military, never happened—one of those things that you just dream about...One day, me and my two sisters were driving and I see this billboard sign, that said Army National Guard, and I looked up and said "I'm joining the military." They're like "What! Are you crazy? You're 30 years old! Are you nuts?" And I'm like, "No. That's what I want to do."...The recruiter, I think I pushed him more than he pushed me, because I was "Okay, I want in, I want in!" (Jill, age 32)

Supportive Networks

Battered women gave regular testimony on the importance of having other people in their lives as their recovery could not have occurred in isolation. These women discussed how they accessed friends, families, employers, co-workers, counselors, clergy, and neighbors for support and direction in their lives. Overall, people were responsive to participants' efforts of reaching out to them; yet, at times not all responses were immediate or helpful. Participants' stressed how supports systems were essential, particularly during the first two years after leaving the batterer, as they often needed affirmation, encouragement, and resources. They discussed how they were more able to take action in 'their lives because they had support systems available to ease their burdens. These women faced stressors including posttrauma symptoms (e.g., depression, anxiety) and the batterers' persistent attempts at controlling them (i.e., stalking, breaking into their homes, and harassing the women's employers, friends, and family). For these participants, leaving an abusive relationship and working toward recovery, took a tremendous amount of personal strength that was bolstered through their social support systems:

> Don't be afraid to reach out because when you do it is so much relief and I think that most women will really be surprised at how many people are willing to reach out and help you...it is such a shameful feeling, something that you don't want to talk about, you don't want to be seen as weak or a victim or abused...but once you tell it, it's the first step to empowering yourself. (Jane, age 22)

> It was hard to bounce back and get the strength to believe in myself again, but I was able to have a good support background. I feel sorry for anybody out there who doesn't have a loving family, because that's going to be your main strength. I went from wanting to kill myself every day to, right now, just being able to stand up and say "Hey, I'm me, and I love myself." It was really hard to go from one point to the other without support. (Angel, age 42)

During the time of the violence, participants' families-of-origin did not intervene for such reasons as being unaware, not wanting to interfere, or not knowing how to help. Some family members sanctioned the violence by encouraging the participant to remain in the relationship. As one participant, Betsy (married 12 years to the batterer), reported, "My mother said, 'You probably deserved it, you made your bed, now lie on it.'" Although there was a lack of familial response at the time of the violence, interestingly enough, family members often did get "on board" in providing support once the woman decided to leave the batterer. Even in Betsy's case, her parents provided financial support. Some families went to great lengths to protect their loved ones such as the participant whose parents built their retirement home as a safe haven for her and her daughter:

> My mom and dad were building their retirement home, and my dad sat his granddaughter on his lap and he looked at her and said, "You're going to have a home, and nobody's ever going to hurt you again." And that was the moment that he started asking my daughter and I, "What's it going to take for you guys to feel safe?" My parents spent a lot of extra expense in doing

it. The locks are special locks for safety reasons and we're in the ground with concrete all around us. We're safe. (Daisey, age 31)

An essential strength of participants was their ability during times of stress and crisis to know where to turn for help, including accessing both formal and informal networks. For example, a few women sought help from domestic violence shelters or hotlines, which they reported as extremely helpful. Several turned to counseling services and/or support groups. Additional sources of support included health care providers, co-workers, and clergy:

> I thought I would lose my job. But, I asked everybody [staff] to sit down and I just told them, "Here is what is going on in my home life." You could have heard a pin drop. None of them suspected anything. But from that moment on they became my strongest allies. And they were the ones that actually helped me do all the planning. They were the ones that would ensure, that if the vehicle came anywhere on the grounds of the hospital that I was alerted. They were splendid. (Susie, age 56)

> I had to go see a priest before I would even complete the process of getting a divorce. I needed to know that I was not sinning. I'm Catholic, and so, divorce is huge. And so I went to talk to a priest, and I'm like "My mom stayed, and dad [former batterer] got better," and fortunately I had a great priest, who was very reassuring and said, "Your husband broke your marriage vows the first time he laid his hand on you. You have nothing to worry about. Get out." (Trista, age 33)

An important connection for the majority of participants was their relationship to God or a Higher Power. Several were also invested in faith-based activities, such as prayer, meditation, or being a member of a religious community. Many, but not all, participants described the importance of a spiritual relationship to help view their life purpose in a different light. Instead of thinking one's lot in life was to be abused, they were able to appreciate what they had learned from their struggles, such as increased strength, wisdom, and compassion:

> I just look back and I say whatever experiences I lived, it wasn't in vain. It's going to help somebody one day. Maybe one person I can help them to get out of the situation. (Molly, age 36)

> Even though I don't have much, I know I feel the most loved is when I can make somebody else feel good. So as long as I give back to my community, and I keep myself strong so I can do that for my community, I'm okay. (Daisey, age 31)

Giving Back to Others

Participants understanding of their abuse and their responses to it developed over time. Their desire to act on that knowledge was associated with making sense of what happened to them, including turning their experiences with suffering into giving back to others. For some, it went beyond sharing their story for this study, such as writing a memoir about one's domestic violence experiences, entering into a helping profession, doing volunteer work, or advocating for others. It was their hope that something good could come out of the harm they had experienced: They were resolved to be different from their batterers. Participants were caring and compassionate rather than hateful and abusive. They were determined to have a life that was different from what they had endured in their adult relationship. The strengths they forged in regard to their experiences, such as courage and determination, were thought to be of benefit to others who may be struggling to persevere. They used their struggles of adversity as a means of action to help others.

> If I can save one life, that'll be the goal. If I can help someone understand what is happening to them, and how they can move past it, how they can gain the strength to move past fear. And so therefore, that's what this whole book [her memoir] is all about, is how to move past fear. And it's a positive motivational guide to get you into action, and do it. And I pray to God that it will get in the hands of the right people. (Ava, age 58)

> Just the fact that maybe what I have to say or what happened to me is going to be able to help someone out and maybe save a life. Because I know domestic violence sometimes ends in death, and that is not the way a person's life should end. So if anything I have to say, or anything I have to do is going to help someone, then that's all that matters to me. (Angel, age 42)

SUMMARY: IMPLICATIONS OF RESEARCH AGENDA ON MENTAL HEALTH PRACTICE

By focusing on clients' resourcefulness, mental health practice may then tap into their resilience; thereby, allowing for positive ways to work with individuals that honors their survival skills, strengths, and competencies as opposed to their deficits. The heightened focus on strategies of protection and resistance (as in the author's research) encourages researchers and clinicians to get back in touch with the resourcefulness of survivors of violence and provides a background for studying and applying additional strengths.

4   Applying a Strengths Perspective to Problem-Based Assessments

In today's mental health practice settings, the use of the *Diagnostic and Statistical Manual of Mental Disorders*, Fourth edition (*DSM IV-TR*) and various types of diagnostic assessments are often required. The term assessment refers both to a process and a product in mental health practice. Assessment as a process occurs between the practitioner and the client where information is gathered to provide a concise picture of the client and his or her circumstances. Assessment as a product is an actual statement or formulation (at a given time) regarding the nature of a client's problem (Hepworth, Rooney, Rooney, Strom-Gottfried, & Larsen, 2006). Written assessments may range from comprehensive psychosocial reports to brief analyses of specific issues such as the client's suicidal risk, mental health status, or substance abuse. "Because assessments involve social workers' inferences about the nature and causes of clients' difficulties, they serve as the basis for the rest of social workers' interactions with their clients—the goals they set, the interventions they enact, and the progress they evaluate" (Hepworth et al., 2006, p. 179). Although traditional psychosocial assessments acknowledge the importance of strengths, competencies, and protective factors of clients, there continues to be a heightened focus on assessing psychopathology and risk factors (Jordan & Franklin, 2003).

Practitioners often work in mental health settings and institutions that address problem resolution, which fits better with a medical model of practice (i.e., study, diagnosis, and treatment) than a strengths orientation (Jordan & Franklin, 2003). While diagnosis is associated with a medical model of labeling and is incongruent with a strengths perspective, it is often required to access services. A diagnosis, however, should not be viewed as the central feature of clients' identities or life experiences or the only outcome of an assessment. Although mental health service providers and/or third party insurers may require a diagnosis and a substantiation of related symptoms, a practitioner may still modify or add to these problem-based assessments to reflect a strength-based perspective (Graybeal, 2001).

This chapter provides an in-depth dialogue between the author and a client to demonstrate how a strengths perspective may be used throughout the assessment process. In her work, the author draws upon the following strengths-based assumptions (Saleebey, 2009):

1. The practitioner's role is to inquire, listen, and assist clients in discovering, clarifying, and articulating their strengths.
2. Clients' life stories provide numerous examples of strengths as they use their struggles with overcoming their adversity as a catalyst for growth and change.
3. The practitioner can minimize the power imbalance inherent in the helping relationship by stressing the importance of the client's understandings and wants.
4. The client gives direction to the assessment process.
5. Clients, whether they volunteer for services or are mandated, are always striving toward healing albeit encountering frustration, obstacles, and missteps along the way.

MODIFYING A PROBLEM-CENTERED ASSESSMENT PROCESS TO REFLECT A STRENGTHS PERSPECTIVE

Traditional psychosocial assessments often begin with collecting information on the nature of the presenting problem including its history, duration, frequency, magnitude, antecedents, and consequences (Jordan & Franklin, 2003; Poulin, 2000). This involves an unraveling of the problem(s) to uncover information on how one's functioning is affected in different life domains (i.e., family, social supports, education, employment, health/mental health, spirituality, and so on). The synthesis of such data is shaped into a working definition of the problem.

Assessments, therefore, help practitioners to understand a client's history and background along with describing symptoms that support a particular diagnosis (i.e., a categorization of the client's situation based on specifically defined criteria). Prior to goal setting (often the final section of an assessment), personal (e.g., motivation) and environmental (e.g., resources) strengths are listed. After assessment information is gathered, goals and objectives are then designed around ways to reduce or manage the problem(s).

Modifying the assessment process through starting with client goals—rather than the problem situation—provides a course of action that identifies the client's future wants, desires, and aspirations rather than concentrating on past problems, impediments, and mistakes. In the author's experience, clients are not initially comfortable with looking into their future out of the fear of having hope. And, yet, if they cannot imagine a future in which problems are less or resolved, then it is difficult to determine what needs to change in the present to make their future a reality. O'Hanlon (1999), a solution-focused therapist, fittingly asks clients, "If you don't have a dream, how you gonna make a dream come true?" (p. 93).

Survivors of family violence often have tunnel vision in which they maximize negative thinking and diminish positive thinking, where the belief to have hope is dangerous rather than comforting. Thus, in much of the author's work with survivors, she provides them with "considerations" in that if they are going to consider the negative then they also must consider the positive in predicting their future. This helps one to go beyond dichotomous thinking in that you must believe that hope is either dangerous or it is comforting but cannot be both. In response to clients who state that having hope is dangerous, the author may respond, "Well, that is one way of looking at it. However, I also want you to consider that having hope is comforting. And if you are going to predict the future where there is no hope and thus no change then you also must predict a future where there is hope and you can achieve change."

Interestingly, mental health practitioners often also have tunnel vision in predicting a future for their clients perhaps influenced by all of the problems they have uncovered and dissected while doing traditional psychosocial assessments. Consequently, they too may predict a negative future. Or, if they do predict a more positive future it is conditional and includes qualifiers such as the client's attitude, motivation, work ethic, and history. For instance, when a client asks a practitioner, "Do you think

I can change?" A response may include any one of the following worker predictions:

> "I don't know. It's up to you. It depends upon how much you want to change."

> "You have several risk factors that set up you for relapse. It depends upon how motivated you are to change."

> "With your history (i.e., substance abuse, cutting, and so on) you will have to work really hard to make a change."

> "It took a long time for these problems to develop and it will take a long time to change them."

The following example reflects a strengths-based dialogue between the author and a client in regard to the question, "Do you think I can be fixed?" Compare and contrast this with the aforementioned worker predictions.

Client: Do you think I can be fixed?

Author: Yes. And you and I are going to work together to make that happen.

Client: How can you be so sure?

Author: Because you are already in the process of healing, and you and I will build on this to make the changes you want to have happen.

Client: I've been in counseling before and it didn't work, obviously, because I'm having to do it again. I don't see how this will be any different.

Author: Well, that is one way to look at it. I would also like you to consider that it may be different. So, if you are going to predict your future regarding whether or not our work together will be helpful than you have to consider both perspectives: "This isn't going to work" and "This is going to work."

Client: I don't see how it is going to change. It just seems like it will be so much work.

Author: It could take a lot of work but again you have to also consider that it might not.

Client: How can you be so sure that I can change?

Author: Because I see on a daily basis people achieve their goals even though they never expected they would.

Client: But I'm different. I'm sure I'm much worse.

Author: Yes, everybody's situation is different, but it doesn't mean that it is worse or better, it is just different. So, tell me, what changes do you want to make as a result of us working together?

How to Start the Assessment Process with Client Goals and Strengths

Helping clients see and access their future becomes more amenable when the assessment process starts with what they want to achieve rather than after an in-depth exploration of their present and past problems. Questioning techniques from solution-focused therapy (refer to Appendix A for a list of solution-focused questions developed from the work of Corcoran, 1999; De Jong & Miller, 1995; De Jong & Berg, 2002; O'Hanlon, 1999; Walter & Pellar, 1992) may assist in co-constructing goals during the beginning of the assessment process and help clients to think forward in their lives.

Solution-Focused Therapy (SFT) concentrates on strengths and resources rather than on problem, deficiencies, or pathology. This approach is concerned with helping clients co-construct their own "solutions" by exploring the future despite the reality that their future has not yet occurred. This method utilizes specific types of questioning techniques (e.g., exceptions or future-oriented questions) aimed at helping clients think about behavior change. These questions help clients move beyond the sense of failure that they may have experienced through repeated attempts to solve the problem (LaFountain, Garner, & Boldosser, 1995). Consequently, client participation is maximized through tapping into client's inherent competence.

A few beginning solution-focused questions that the author uses interchangeably include: "What do you want different in your life as a result of us working together?" "In three months, how will you know if our work together has been helpful?" Or, "how will you know when you no longer need therapy?" By starting the assessment process with goal setting, the worker and client embark on a world of possibilities rather than problems. Personal and environmental strengths may then be explored in regard to achieving these goals. However, simply asking someone to list their strengths is not fruitful as clients often do not view themselves in this manner and thus cannot volunteer their strengths. For the same reason, the worker initiating a list of strengths is not productive as clients may not see themselves in this same light and as a result do not connect to it.

A case example—drawn from an amalgam of clients and does not represent any specific person—is used for the remainder of this chapter to demonstrate how to modify a problem-centered assessment process to reflect a strengths orientation. The client, Jasmine, is a 29-year-old woman who reports her problem as depression. The author finds that beginning the assessment process with client goals and strengths helps to connect the two and provides avenues and opportunities for carrying out the work to be done.

Author: Jasmine, tell me about what you want different in your life as a result of us working together?

Client: I would like to have more balance in my life.

Author: What would that look like to have more balance in your life?

Client: I would not be so depressed and emotional.

Author: What would you be instead?

Client: I would be free of bad thoughts. I would have some kind of structure in my life. I would want to get out of bed in the morning instead of sleeping 'til noon.

Author: Has what you want to change occurred before in your life— being free of bad thoughts, having structure, and getting out of bed before noon?

Client: Yes, partly, but it's been a long time ago.

Author: Even though it was a long time ago, sharing the experience of what you did to make it happen can help us in our work together as we might be able to build on this to achieve something similar. Let's start with getting out of bed before noon. When is the last time you did this?

Client: Well I have to get out of bed before noon on the days I work, so I guess I'm doing that now some.

Author: So you choose to get out of bed and go to work. How do you make that happen?

Client: I have to. I need the money.

Author: So in the morning you tell yourself that you have to get out of bed because you need the money. What else do you tell yourself so you'll make a choice to get out of bed?

Client: I don't know. (Long pause). I guess because I like work.

Author: What type of work do you do that you like going there?

Client: I work at a daycare.

Author: How did you choose to work at a daycare?

Client: Well I've always liked kids.

Author: How long have you worked at a daycare?

Client: For the past six months.

Author: What other jobs have you worked at?

Client: Bartending, waitressing, mainly. At 29 that gets old, so my mom's friend runs a daycare, so I talked to her about a job and she hired me. It doesn't pay as well as my other jobs but I like it better.

Author: So you have gained many skills through your past and present jobs. What are the particular skills you need to work at a daycare?

Client: A part of you has to still be a kid yourself so you can let loose and have fun being with them. And I have no problem letting loose and being a kid. (Laughs).

Author: So how are you able to let loose and have fun?

Client: I don't know. I just like kids.

Author: Do you have bad thoughts when you are letting loose and having fun?

Client: No. (Pause). I'm not sure why.

Author: Does your future include working with kids?

Client: Yes, I would like to stay at the daycare because I'm going to be full-time soon. Like I told you when I called to set up this appointment, I'll then have insurance to cover therapy. Maybe some day I'll go back to college and get my education degree but I don't know if that is even possible.

Author: I'm very interested in how you make yourself go to your job and also let loose and have fun there even though the depression is a part of your life. Tell me, do you have to provide structure for the children at daycare?

Client: Yes, there are certain times they play, nap, eat. I know what you're thinking about having structure for the kids and not for myself—but it is not so easy to do it for myself.

Author: Actually, I wasn't thinking that and I appreciate you sharing your thoughts to check this out with me. Please feel free to check out anytime what I'm thinking to make sure you and I are on track with each other. I was actually thinking you do have structure at work and maybe those skills can be applied when you're not working too. Plus, I am impressed that you are able to instill and maintain structure with preschoolers!

Client: It's not that bad. If they are in a routine then they get used to it and expect it.

Author: Well, that certainly makes sense. So tell me, what skills and strengths do you have in working at a daycare that may be used to achieve the changes you want in your in life?

Client: I'm a good worker. I'm dependable. I work hard. I care about kids.

Author: Yes, those are important skills to have at work and also in life—to work hard, be dependable, and care about others. What else about you will help you achieve your goals?

Client: Well I've been through more than most people and I'm still alive.

Author: What has helped you to do this?

Client: I don't give up. I keep trying.

Author: How did you get your drive and will to keep going despite facing more than most people have?

Client: I don't know. (Pause). I guess I was born that way. I guess I'm a survivor.

Author: Is there anyone that has helped you along the way of surviving?

Client: My mom. She's like my best friend. Although we weren't always that way, I gave her a hard time when I was younger. Running away, drinking. But we're good now.

Author: Does she know you are in counseling?

Client: Yes, she got me to go back into counseling.

Author: How did you get yourself to listen to your mom?

Client: She cares about me and doesn't like to see me so sad.

Author: Is there anyone else that is there for you?

Client: God. I wouldn't have made it without him.

Author: What makes you open to God?

Client: I don't know. I guess I wouldn't be alive without him.

Author: So, God is a support system for you and has helped to keep you alive?

Client: Yes, and my mom. Also, my dogs.

Author: How did you get yourself to have dogs?

Client: I've always had a connection to animals. They understand me.

Author: So, your mom, God, and your dogs are there for you. Who do you know that has achieved a goal similar to yours?

Client: I don't know. You mean about the depression?

Author: Sure. Who do you know who has the type of balance in their lives that you desire?

Client: My boss. But I don't know if she has ever been depressed but she seems to have it together.

Author: Okay. Well, it might be worth considering her as someone you can check in with to see how she does it—have it together.

Client: I guess. I never thought of that.

Author: Is it okay if I ask you a little more about the depression in your life?

Client: Yes.

How to Talk About "Problems" from a Strengths Perspective

Starting with client goals and strengths during the assessment process builds momentum in regard to client capabilities and aspirations. In doing so, it sets the stage for what the client is able to do despite the problems she is facing. Next in the dialogue between the author and Jasmine, information is gathered regarding the typical content areas of a problem-based assessment starting with the problem situation and proceeds in no particular order with: mental health history, substance abuse history, history of abuse, family situation and history, employment, and education history. The dialogue ends with the author discussing Jasmine's diagnosis with her. Although the typical content areas are addressed, the assessment process is not guided by the author and instead occurs when the client offers them during the dialogue.

Drawing from narrative therapy (to be discussed more fully in Chapter 6), the author refers to the client's depression as "the depression" as a way of externalizing the problem to help the client see that depression is a part of her but not all of who she is. Jasmine may then choose whether or not depression continues to be a part of her life, and thus her life story, or if it is a subplot to be retired (Anderson & Hiersteiner, 2007). Additionally, questioning techniques from solution-focused therapy are used to identify exceptions of when the problem (i.e., depression) is not a problem (Walter & Peller, 1992).

Author: You said that the depression impacts your life including being more emotional, and having problems with getting out of bed and starting your day. How else does the depression affect your life?

Client: I don't sleep well. I'm tired all the time. (Pause). I don't have a problem falling asleep at night, but then I wake up in the middle of the night, around 1 or 2 a.m. and can't get back to sleep because I have all of these thoughts running through my head. About 4 a.m. I fall back to sleep and then sleep until noon.

Author: Except on the days you work you get up before noon. How often do you work?

Client: Two to three days a week.

Author: Does your sleeping patterns differ on the nights before you have to go to work?

Client: I don't know. (Pause). I sleep better at night on the days I work. I guess because I'm worn out after working with kids all day.

Author: What is your level of energy at work?

Client: I'm not sure what you mean.

Author: How is your level of energy different on the days you work compared to the days you don't?

Client: I don't know. I guess I have to be energetic when I'm with the kids, but I'm still depressed. I just act like I'm not.

Author: So the kids or the people you work with would not know you are depressed?

Client: No. Because when I'm at work I'm laughing and playing games with the kids. I don't want to be in a bad mood.

Author: So your caring and fun spirit comes forth. How else does the depression affect your life?

Client: I've lost weight. I don't have much of an appetite.

Author: Has anyone else noticed you've lost weight? Like your mom?

Client: Yes. She tries to get me to eat more.

Author: When is she successful at getting you to eat more?

Client: She's a great cook and she knows I hate cooking. So she brings over food a few times a week and has it already for me to warm up.

Author: What are your favorites that you warm up?

Client: Lasagna. Potato soup. It just depends.

Author: How long has it been since the depression came into your life?

Client: About 5 or 6 months.

Author: How has your mom, your belief in God, and your work helped you to hang on during the past 5 or 6 months?

Client: Well, it's not like I want to end my life or anything. I wouldn't want to hurt my mom and it is not something that God can forgive. Plus no one would be there to take care of my dogs because I live alone. I just want it to be different. More balance, not crying so easily, sleeping better, that kind of thing.

Author: Plus, as you said, you are not one to give up. You keep trying.

Client: Yes.

Author: Have you faced the depression before in your life?

Client: No. Not like this.

Author: What's different this time, that the depression has had more of a hold on you in the past 5 or 6 months?

Client: My brother moved back to town. So now I see him more.

Author: What are your thoughts or theories of why you are more depressed as a result of seeing your brother more?

Client: Because he sexually abused me as a kid and now that he's back I think about it more.

Author: You have good insight to figure out that what happened in the past can affect you in the present. Is it okay if I ask you more questions about the sexual abuse?

Client: I don't mind talking about it. I was in counseling before about it when I was 20.

Author: How did you get yourself to go to counseling before?

Client: I was partying a lot, not working.

Author: And you sought counseling because?

Client: My mom said that I had to. She wanted to know what was wrong. I was living in her house and we were fighting all the time. I wasn't working and she told me I had to get help or move out.

Author: So you chose to get help. That's amazing because not everyone would have made that choice. How long were you in counseling?

Client: I saw the therapist for about a year and a half and then she moved away and I didn't go back. Well, until now.

Author: What, if anything, was helpful about it?

Client: Well I told her about the sexual abuse. She also helped me tell my mom and confront my brother.

Author: I'm sure that took tremendous energy and courage. How did you get yourself to do it?

Client: My therapist asked me if I had ever been abused and I just couldn't keep it to my self anymore.

Author: How did they respond?

Client: My mom got very upset and wanted to know why I never told her about it. But she didn't blame me. She just wished she would have known so she could have done something about it.

Author: And your brother?

Client: He admitted he did it but acted like it was no big deal.

Author: How old were you when it happened?

Client: I was 10 and it lasted until I was about 12. I was slipping away, and I told him I was going to tell our dad who has a bad temper. He probably would have beaten the hell out of my brother. I didn't want him hurt, but I just couldn't take in anymore, so I said, I would tell.

Author: That must have taken much courage. How did you manage to cope with this all by yourself?

Client: I read a lot. Prayed to God, which I was angry at God for a long time, because I didn't think he was answering my prayers. But now I know he was there with me, helping me.

Author: What else did you do to try to protect yourself?

Client: I'd try to not be alone with him, which didn't really work because he had to watch me when my mom was working or gone. He started with making me play strip poker, so I would put on lots of layers of clothing, hoping my mom would come home, before I would have to take off all my clothes. But she never did. Then he would make me do stuff to him or he would do stuff to me. I just wanted it over and would pray that it would stop.

Author: That is amazing that you figured out at such a young age ways to protect yourself. You are creative and courageous. Did he try to sexually abuse you again after you told him you would tell your father?

Client: No. It pretty much stopped.

Author: Do you have other brothers and sisters?

Client: Yes. Two younger sisters.

Author: And did he abuse them?

Client: My mom and dad divorced when I was nine. My dad remarried when I was 10 and then had two children with his new wife. So they are a lot younger and they didn't have much contact with my brother and me. But my dad knows because I wrote him a letter when I was in therapy and told him about it. He was very angry at my brother and refused to have contact with him for several years. I guess my dad told his wife and she became very upset because she had had the same thing happen to her, so she took my sisters to therapy but they said that he had never touched them.

Author: Thank you for sharing about what happened to you. I'm sure that took much strength to do since this is the first time we have met. How else was therapy helpful to you?

Client: I don't know. (Pause). I guess having someone to talk to. Someone who didn't judge me.

Author: So it will be important in our work together that you do not feel that I'm judging you. And if you do, then you'll want to ask me about it much like you did earlier when you checked out what I might be thinking. You mentioned that when you were younger, you were partying a lot. Was that something that you or your therapist saw as a problem to be addressed?

Client: I was drinking and smoking pot a lot. I guess I saw it as a problem but I didn't want to admit it.

Author: What did you discover about yourself in regard to why the drinking and smoking pot had become such a big part of your life?

Client: I liked doing it because I felt free of bad thoughts like about what my brother did to me. I also slept with a lot of guys because I didn't care what happened to me.

Author: That's understandable considering what you had been through. What have you done that's been helpful in regard to ending those behaviors?

Client: Well not working in bars any more! (Laughs) I don't party much anymore and if I do it's just to have a beer or two with some friends. I don't sleep around anymore. I don't go out with anyone for too long. Just not into it. I've been there done that.

Author: You have made some big changes in your life in the past few years. How did you get yourself to do that?

Client: I don't know. I just got sick of it.

Author: That's understandable. So you got sick and tired of being sick and tired?

Client: Yeah.

Author: Now that your brother is back, you said that you think more about the abuse. How do you think this is connected to not having balance in your life, feeling more depressed, being more emotional, and having bad thoughts?

Client: I am thinking more about what he did to me.

Author: That makes sense. Seeing your brother is a trigger for you—it triggers memories of the past abuse. Is that what you meant by having bad thoughts?

Client: Yes, I'd like to not have to think about it as much.

Author: Like when you are working and having fun with the kids and have those times when you are not thinking about it.

Client: I guess so. I hadn't made that connection.

Author: I have asked you a lot of questions. Is there anything that I didn't ask you that I should have?

Client: Not that I can think of.

Author: Well after you leave here if you have additional questions or thoughts, feel free to write them down and bring them for the next time we meet. Do you have something you can use or would you like me to provide you with a journal to write in?

Client: I'm sure I can find something.

Author: In everything that we've talked about today, what would you like to consider working on between now and the next time we see each other?

Client: I don't know.

Author: Well, you have said that you want more balance in your life, to be less emotional, to have less bad thoughts, to have more structure and to get out of bed before noon.

Client: Well since I'm already getting out of bed before noon on the days I work, I guess I can try and do it on the other days.

Author: Okay, so you are going to try and get up before noon on the days you do not work. Is there anything that may get in the way of you trying this?

Client: Trying it? No. Doing it? Yes.

Author: Okay, well then we'll see how it goes trying it. Would it make any sense to ask your mom to help you?

Client: Like asking her to call me on the days I'm not working?

Author: Sure, if you think that would help.

Client: Maybe. I can ask her.

Author: How often do you want to meet?

Client: I don't know. How often do people meet with you?

Author: It depends on how much time you need to try out what you want to work on. Some people choose to meet weekly with me when they first start counseling and then every couple of weeks, once a month, and so forth. It's up to you.

Client: Let's see about every other week for now.

Author: Sounds good. Now before we end today I need to talk to you about a diagnosis. When you were in counseling before, were you given or told of a diagnosis?

Client: I don't remember but I think it was PTSD.

Author: Do you remember if you were on any medication at that time, or since?

Client: I was at the time. I can't remember. Maybe Lexapro? I'm not sure. I stopped taking it after I ended therapy and haven't taken anything since.

Author: Okay, well we can find out for sure if you want to sign a release of information for the counseling agency for us to get that information. I can't request or give out any information without a signed release from you. So, even if you told your mom that she could call me, I wouldn't be able to acknowledge that I even know you without a signed release. This is to protect your confidentiality. However, I do break client confidentiality when clients talk about hurting themselves or someone else. Plus, I'm a mandatory child abuse reporter, which means if you share with me that you know of a child that is being abused, I am required to report it. Here is a "consent to treat" form that explains confidentiality more along with other information including record keeping, diagnosis, client rights and responsibilities, and my professional background and responsibilities in providing services. Take this with you to look over and we will touch base on it when we meet again to answer any questions you have before you sign it.

Client: Okay.

Author: I like to talk with the people I work with in regard to the diagnosis that I am recommending for them so they are fully aware and have access to the criteria for the diagnosis. Also, it gives you an opportunity to discuss your concerns or questions about it. All of the diagnoses come from a book entitled the *DSM-IV-TR*; I have a copy in my office and will be glad to let you refer to it and learn more about what it says regarding your diagnosis. When you do secure health insurance, a diagnosis is required for reimbursement. So, you will need to decide if you want to use your insurance as there will be a diagnosis on record with your health insurance or pay out-of-pocket as you are doing now where the diagnosis is noted in your agency file but is not submitted elsewhere without your permission or unless it is court ordered.

Client: Okay. I thought I had to use my insurance.

Author: It's up to you. You can keep paying for it or use your insurance when you get it.

Client: I'll think about it. I'll talk to my mom about it.

Author: Okay. Your diagnosis is likely to change over time as additional information comes forth and if that is the case then you and I will discuss it. At this point I am recommending Adjustment Disorder with mixed anxiety and depressed mood, chronic. An adjustment disorder occurs when there is an identifiable stressor such as your brother coming back to town. And because you have been feeling this way for six months, it is labeled chronic, actually anything over three months, is considered chronic. Additionally, you have talked about symptoms of depression but I'm also thinking anxiety might be part of the problem with not sleeping well and losing weight so for now I would like to include both. I will make a copy of this diagnosis with its criteria for you to take with you and we can talk about it also the next time we meet.

Client: Okay.

Author: So was meeting with me today like what you expected?

Client: I think it was better but then I didn't really know what to expect.

Author: So do you think you still want to meet again?

Client: Yes.

Author: Okay. Well, I'll just walk you out and we'll get an appointment set up with the receptionist.

SUMMARY

By simply adding strengths questions to an assessment battery, mental health practitioners may assume that they are practicing from a strengths perspective (Blundo, 2001). However, the significance of these ideas is lacking in regard to how it might influence their overall practice as they continue to operate from a problem-centered approach. In other words, a list of client/family strengths may appear in the case record but there is no coherent plan that incorporates them into goal development or action steps. A situation is set up, therefore, where workers may report that they address client strengths, but in practice may still operate from a deficit approach (Anderson & Sundet, 2006). To actually practice from a strengths perspective means practitioners believe that the strengths and resources to resolve a difficult situation lie within the client and his or her environment. Discovering these strengths, then, is central to guiding the assessment process (Anderson, Cowger, & Snively, 2009).

5

Assessments that Capture Client Strengths, Resilience, and Acts of Resistance

This chapter provides assessments and psychometric measures, whose primary focus is to capture clients' strengths and resilience, which may be used to accompany or replace existing problem-based assessments. These tools are presented as a way for practitioners to gather information that is unique to the abilities of each client and further delineate the available repertoire of strengths one might possess. Additionally, the resilience literature and the author's research in family violence helps to expand previous discussions of strengths-based assessments and strategies by providing conceptual frameworks for moving the assessment toward uncovering survival strengths. Such information may then be used to develop an intervention plan that builds on clients' abilities to manage traumatic experiences (Chaffin, Wherry, & Dykman, 1997; Jaffe, Sudermann, & Geffner, 2000; Spaccarelli & Kim, 1995). Clients may view themselves differently, particularly their strengths, by recognizing how they actively responded to adversity in the past, and may now channel their survival strategies into confronting present struggles.

STRENGTHS ASSESSMENT

The strengths perspective recognizes that clients cope with their life circumstances in the best way they know (Saleebey, 1992, Weick, Rapp,

Sullivan, & Kisthardt, 1989). "A strengths perspective is much more than reframing problems and deficits; a strengths perspective identifies the real talents, histories, and aspirations unique to each individual that are often unrecognized and unappreciated to them" (Rapp, 1992, p. 57). In using a strengths assessment the client and worker's perspectives are broadened to include what is working rather than solely focusing on what's not working (Graybeal, 2001). This information assists both the client and the practitioner to mobilize or build on past and present strengths to achieve positive life outcomes. A person's ability to live well in the present, then, occurs through the recovery of these "lost" strengths and building upon them.

The strengths assessment (see Appendix B) gathers information on the client's history of functioning (e.g., "What have I used in the past?"), present status (e.g., What's going on today? What's available now?"), and desires for the future (e.g., "What do I want?"), in each of the following life domains: housing/transportation, financial/insurance, vocational/educational, social supports, health/mental health, and leisure/recreational (Rapp & Cosha, 2006). The assessment process identifies and builds on these resources and gives credit to the unique configuration of individual and environmental strengths for each client. As illustrated in chapter 4, filling out a strengths-based form does not necessarily mean you are working from a strengths perspective, particularly if you do not have a sincere belief in the client's potential.

Individual strengths include personal talents, interests, skills, or creative coping tactics. Additionally, what people have learned from their challenges—as well as their accomplishments—provides important assessment information. Environmental strengths include opportunities, social relations, and resources. Opportunities involve the various prospects in the environment that are available to connect and add to the strengths of the individual. Social supports comprise of caring relationships that offer positive feedback, a sense of being cared for, and positive expectations of the individual's accomplishment. Furthermore, resources entail formal or informal services related to promoting well-being such as mental health services or spiritual activities (Saleebey, 2009).

Although social work literature emphasizes philosophy and theory that presents a strengths perspective (Saleebey, 2009), it continues to lack well-developed practice directives and guidelines for incorporating this perspective into the area of trauma and recovery. If the helping process begins to focus on the positive ways one coped with family violence, for instance, this allows a different way to look at the past and provides an additional life domain to uncover strengths. In other words, the survival abilities of individuals are enduring strengths that develop in relationship to their trauma as a means of self-preservation, rather than deriving from the life domain areas currently specified in the strengths assessment. Incorporating survival strengths into the assessment process allows for a broader perspective to identify individuals' coping abilities.

In turning to the resiliency literature, it further develops the strengths model in regard to individuals' skills and resources to rise above adversity. Exploring the pain and trauma that one has experienced can help to unravel how one survived and prevailed, which may become significant strengths to be used in present circumstances. In other words, addressing the strategies survivors' used to protect themselves and gain strength from their struggles may also be applied to their current problem situations (Wolin & Wolin, 1993). The resiliency literature in developmental psychopathology provides an in-depth exploration of protective strategies that emerge from managing an adverse childhood (refer to chapter 2). Additionally, in this chapter the author's research findings inform us that resistance to powerlessness includes acts of courage, determination, and resourcefulness that are often not legitimized by professionals or institutions as the assessment process often neglects to consider the wider social and political context influencing individual adversity. To deal with this gap during the assessment process, the author's research addresses social and political dimensions, particularly the "resistance to oppression" factor to assist professionals who are seeking to practice in empowering ways.

RESILIENCY ASSESSMENT OF CHILDHOOD PROTECTIVE FACTORS

Resiliency research recognizes a complex interaction of individual attributes, family milieu, and social interactions in promoting well-being. People who have survived stressful childhoods are considered resilient because they have enduring strengths that developed as a means to protect themselves from their troubling circumstances (e.g., parental mental illness, poverty, child abuse). Yet, missing from resiliency literature is a practical application of this information. Therefore, the author presents a 24-item assessment form (see Appendix C) developed from resiliency research to capture people's capabilities, aspirations, and skills in facing childhood adversity. (Note: Biological protective factors are not included as these are innate or something one is born with, such as high intelligence, and thus may not be able to influence.)

A central component to enhancing client resiliency becomes the helping professional's ability to identify client strengths and to make them accessible in a useful way (O'Connell-Higgins, 1994). Using the conceptual framework from chapter 3, as presented in Figure 3.1 ("Adversity, Protective Factors, and Resilience"), allows the practitioner and client to better understand the connections between adverse events, their consequences, and bio-psycho-social-spiritual protective factors. Additionally, the "Resiliency Assessment of Childhood Protective Factors" presented in Appendix C translates the conceptual framework into an assessment to be used with an individual as he or she reviews her childhood adversity. Major constructs of the resiliency conceptual framework are highlighted in bold; however, to simplify the assessment form (e.g., if a worker does not want to include a discussion of the conceptual model) one might only include the 24-item list of protective factors for clients.

The purpose of the resiliency assessment is to highlight the many ways one protected oneself during childhood in the face of a troubling family environment. In the author's experience, simply asking clients the open-ended question, "How did you protect yourself despite facing childhood adversity?" does not often yield much response. Typical responses may include: "I didn't do anything." Or, "I tried to be invisible." Thus, clients minimize their protective strategies or blame themselves for not doing enough. Using the resiliency assessment can prompt them to recognize the many ways they defended themselves and provide a different view of themselves as being resourceful, courageous, and determined. In rediscovering these strengths, a dialogue between the client and worker may then evolve into addressing one's present problem and whether or not these childhood survival abilities are still useful, need to be modified, or retired.

For instance, in reviewing a completed resiliency assessment, the worker and client might note protective factors that were used frequently during childhood and discuss how these may or may not be relevant in regard to coping with current circumstances. The same review process can be done with those rarely used in childhood to see if they may be applicable now in adulthood. Or, some childhood protective factors may not necessarily translate to the present situation and have actually become a part of the problem (e.g., using fantasy instead of making an effort to change one's reality) rather than the solution.

The following dialogue between the worker and client highlights how to use a resiliency assessment and suggests a connection between childhood survival strategies and adult healing activities that contribute to one's resilience. The client, Claire, is a 31-year-old women who defines "an obsession with her weight" as her initial counseling issue that she wants to work on. Her theory on the causes of her weight concerns stem from beliefs that she needs to be "perfect." She believes her perfectionism has its roots in her childhood, including parents who she identifies as alcoholics. As a result of her parents drinking throughout Claire's childhood, she believes that her mother was emotionally unavailable and her father verbally abusive to her.

Worker: Hi, Claire. So tell me what changes do you want in your life as a result of us working together?

Client: I have an obsession with my weight. I worry about how much I eat. I worry about calories and how much I burn off. I'm always thinking about it.

Worker: How has the obsession with the weight become a problem for you?

Client: I'm less social. I turn down invitations with friends because I'm afraid it might involve food. And when I am around friends or just people in general I'm afraid that people are judging me. You know, about my weight.

Worker: What are your thoughts or theories of why there is the obsession with weight?

Client: I've been thinking about it and I think it has to do with trying to be perfect. I want people to think I have it together and that I am someone you can look up to. So, I'm afraid that if people really knew me and the problems I have with weight then they would think less of me.

Worker: You have thought a lot about this and made some important connections of what might be causing the obsession. Do you recall when the weight obsession first started to take a hold of your life?

Client: It seems like it's been all my life. I was never a heavy person but I was always afraid I would be because my mom is.

Worker: Okay. So when do you think the perfectionism started to take hold of your life?

Client: I've never felt that I was good enough. As a kid, I never got much attention from my parents. They were alcoholics. They never should have had kids. I don't remember my parents ever attending any of my school activities—and I was in lot of them. My brothers and I basically raised ourselves. We just didn't get much validation from our parents. I don't ever remember them telling us that they loved us or each other for that matter. My dad was mean when he was drunk, which was a lot. He wouldn't use our names if he wanted us to do something. Instead, he'd say, "Hey, dumb shit, get me a beer." He told us that we were stupid and would never graduate from high school. He told me that I was so ugly that no one would want me. So, I married a jerk who treated me badly and had affairs on me and blamed me for it because I was fat. I wasn't fat. I was pregnant—what an idiot. I did have a tough time taking the weight off after the baby, so he used that against me too and said that no one else would want me because I was so fat. Including him, I guess, because he divorced me.

Worker: And how does this lack of affection and validation impact you now—in addition to the unwanted thoughts of needing to be perfect, such as with your weight?

Client: I just want someone to care about me. I've never really had that.

Worker: So, you want someone to care about you. And what difference in your life would that make if you had someone who cared about you?

Client: I wouldn't be so alone.

Worker: That's understandable. If it is okay with you, I would like to know more about how you survived and persevered your difficult childhood to see if any of those protective factors are still present today and whether or not they may be useful in our work together. I would like for you to take an assessment of childhood protective factors. This is an assessment that I developed based on research in the areas of resiliency and is reflective of this conceptual model (hands client the model) that looks at the connection between childhood adversity, protective factors, and resilience. This applies to any childhood adversity and the research indicates that there are similarities in protective factors that promote well-being and healthy functioning for resilient individuals. So, we'll start at the top of this figure with the childhood adversity itself which you have identified as parental neglect and verbal abuse, which was stressful on you and impacted you, for instance, in the social area in regard to interpersonal relationships. The resiliency assessment itself (hands client the assessment) addresses the protective factors in particular, with the exception of the biological area, because you might not be able to influence what you were born with and thus apply it to your current situation. It asks you to think back to your childhood and rate how frequently you used each protective factor. It is 24-items and takes about 5–10 minutes to complete. There is also space at the end of it to include additional factors that were not addressed in the assessment. What are your thoughts and feelings in regard to completing the resiliency assessment?

Client: Well, I don't think I'm very resilient. So I don't know if this applies to me.

Worker: What does being resilient mean to you?

Client: Not an overweight, divorced, single parent living pay check to pay check. You know, someone who doesn't have problems or if they do they can handle them on their own without help.

Worker: Okay. But I would also like you to consider that being resilient is someone who gets knocked down and gets back up, not once, not twice, but time and time again. And even if that means they fall flat on their face, they are still falling in the right direction—forward.

Client: Well, I've been knocked down plenty of times.

Worker: And yet you picked yourself up and you're here today wanting to make changes. So, I would like you to at least consider that you are resilient. This assessment does apply to you as its purpose is to highlight the ways you protected yourself during childhood in the face of your parents' alcoholism and its consequences on you. We then may be able to use this information to see how these strategies can be used or modified to confront your present struggles.

Client: Okay. (Client completes assessment) I guess I'm done.

Worker: What have you learned about yourself in regard to how you survived and persevered despite a childhood lacking in affection and validation?

Client: I escaped.

Worker: How?

Client: Physically—not in fantasy. When I got older I was never home. I'm from a small town. So you could pretty much be involved in anything and everything at school.

Worker: So you kept yourself occupied to avoid being at home. Did being involved in school activities help you in any other way?

Client: Well, school was a place with rules and structure, which I didn't have at home. Most people would think I'm lucky that I didn't have to follow any certain rules about when I ate, went to bed, or how late I stayed out. But as I said it was rough because I basically raised myself.

Worker: So tell me was there anything that you learned from doing the assessment that surprised you about yourself?

Client: Reading. I read a lot. I didn't think of it as an escape though because it was just something I liked to do.

Worker: Do you think it was an escape, something you liked to do, or both?

Client: Both.

Worker: Do you still enjoy reading?

Client: Yes, but I don't get to do it as much as I would like to.

Worker: What protective factors did you use frequently—marked as 4s or 5s.

Client: Well like I said I escaped a lot. Physically. I just wanted to get away. I didn't really fantasize much.

Worker: What other protective factors did you use?

Client: I was involved in volleyball, softball, and chorus.

Worker: Tell me about each.

Client: I was very athletic. I had a lot of energy, so sports helped me get some of that out of me. And I was in the school chorus—actually anybody could be in the chorus.

Worker: How did you rate adult caretakers and mentors?

Client: Well as I said I didn't really have parents that showed me they cared. I did have a volleyball coach that became like a second mom to me in high school, but that was a long time ago and I haven't kept in touch with her.

Worker: You said that you were away from home a lot. Did you have a job or do volunteer work also?

Client: Yes, I was a cook at a drive-in food place like a Sonic all through high school. We lived in the country, so I had to ride my bike to work, which wasn't always safe especially at night. But my parents wouldn't drive me or let me drive. So, sometimes my friends would give me rides.

Worker: How else were your friends there for you?

Client: I'd stay at their houses especially on nights we had games. My parents didn't care where I stayed. My friends' parents were great—no drama—like mine.

Worker: Where there any spiritual protective factors that you rated as frequently?

Client: We didn't belong to a church. My mom and dad didn't believe in it. But I joined the Lutheran youth group because my friends were in it. My parents didn't care one way or another as long as I got myself there. I didn't always think that God loved me. Because I didn't feel my parents did, so I didn't know how God could. Plus I prayed and nothing seemed to get better, so I didn't think at the time that God was much help.

Worker: Anything else?

Client: I liked school. I did well in school even though my dad said that I was too stupid to learn. Unfortunately, I believed him, so I never went on to school. I wanted to be a vet and work with animals.

Worker: Were there any other ways you protected yourself that you wrote down?

Client: I think just trying to be perfect. Not cause any problems or waves at home or at school.

Worker: In reviewing the childhood protective strategies, are there any you still use today that are helpful? Not helpful? Or, any that you would like to start doing again?

Client: Well being perfect isn't working for me anymore. I don't give myself a break and recognize what I've done. Instead, I move on to the next thing.

Worker: Anything else?

Client: Well I still escape but probably not in the best way because I isolate myself.

Worker: Anything that is helpful?

Client: Friends. I do have good friends. I like animals. I have cats. My job. I'm a good worker.

Worker: Anything you would like to start doing that you don't anymore?

Client: Maybe I'll contact my old volleyball coach. I don't know if she would want to hear from me or not.

Worker: Is there a reason she wouldn't want to hear from you? Did things end badly between you and your coach?

Client: Oh, no, not at all. I just didn't keep in touch with her.

Worker: Well, then it sounds worth checking out. Anything else?

Client: I think I do better playing team sports instead of just working out on my own. I'd like to get back into playing volleyball or softball.

Worker: How do you think contacting your former coach or playing team sports again, will help you with your weight concerns and your need to be perfect?

Client: I guess I might just feel better about myself and then not obsess so much.

Worker: Anything else?

Client: Maybe going to college. I don't know.

Worker: How will that help you?

Client: I guess I'd have something else to focus on—instead of my weight. I was pretty good at school.

Worker: Of everything we talked about today, is there anything you want to consider trying before the next time we meet?

Client: I think I'm going to call my old coach.

Worker: Anything that might get in the way of you contacting your old coach?

Client: No, I just need to do it. She's still a coach at my old high school, so I could probably get her phone number.

Worker: So a sign that you are moving in the direction of what you want to change in your life is to contact your old coach?

Client: Yes.

Worker: We'll set up your next appointment then after you have had a chance to do this.

Client: Okay. I'll let you know.

The dialogue between Claire and the worker helped her to explore past survival strengths that may be used to address her present circumstances. Throughout the dialogue, Claire offered several past and present problems for further exploration including: the weight obsession, her perfectionism, a failed marriage and parental alcoholism, neglect, and abuse. Yet, the worker did not follow these avenues, at the time, because unraveling layers of problems would not necessarily lead to what Claire desired, which was for someone to care about her so she would not feel so alone. Instead, the worker pursued Claire's strengths to help her see herself in a different light, including being resilient, as a means of showing her that she can achieve what she wants and already has some of the internal and social resources to do so. However, this did not mean that Claire immediately embraced this resiliency, due to her problems or for the reason that she is not where she would like to be in her life.

If one views Claire from a problem-focused helping paradigm, then the initial solution of calling a former coach may seem simplistic because she has too many problems that need to be addressed, such as, an eating disorder, low self-esteem, and intimacy issues. This belief is guided by the assumption that for Claire to achieve feeling cared about and less lonely, she would need to explore the deep-rooted causes of these experiences, which in her case go back to a "damaged" childhood. In contrast, a strengths-based helping paradigm broadens the lens into Claire's life to include the survival strengths she used to endure and prevail along with the challenges she has faced. By doing so, Claire is allowed to guide the direction she would like to pursue either unraveling her past or making changes in her present life. At this point in time, she chose the latter.

BROADENING RESILIENCY ASSESSMENTS TO INCLUDE THE RESISTANCE-TO-OPPRESSION FACTOR

Protective factors identified in resiliency research provide significant contributions to the assessment process for mental health practitioners and their clients. These resilient capacities are often buried beneath pain and discomfort and are difficult to access if clients and workers are not equipped to view these protective strategies as strengths. Yet, a limitation of the resiliency research includes presenting all adverse environmental conditions as similar; thus, all protective factors are also viewed in this same light. So whether one experienced parental mental illness or parental abuse during childhood, he or she develops similar biological, psychological, social, and spiritual protective factors. There is no differentiation between various childhood adverse circumstances and their risk factors. Therefore, to address this gap in the literature, the author's research differentiates social problems and their risk factors to uncover protective factors (i.e., acts of resistance) unique to each of the following: childhood incest, childhood exposure to domestic violence, and adult intimate partner violence. In doing so, the author's findings are translated into assessment forms (see Appendixes D, E, F) distinctive for each type of family violence.

Developing a knowledge base on resilience that encompasses resistance provides a new direction in mental health practice with survivors of family violence because it not only addresses the trauma but focuses on participants' resourcefulness as well within a context of oppression. Individuals may not interpret their strengths, such as ways of resisting, because their stories are centered, often with the encouragement of professionals, on the damage resulting from the devastating effects of oppression. Yet, "alongside each history of violence and oppression, there runs a parallel history of prudent, creative, and determined resistance" (Wade, 1997, p. 23). Understanding resistance as opposition to oppression is useful in developing an intervention plan that builds on these strategies and assists clients to manage the difficulties in their current lives. From the beginning of treatment then, the mental health practitioner and the client consider all the dimensions of one's life story including both oppression and resistance. Thus, definitions of resiliency should be broadened to include the concept of resistance.

In order to acknowledge, affirm, and extend clients' acts of resistance, practitioners have to be knowledgeable of them. "To resist is to oppose actively, to fight, to refuse to cooperate with or submit" (Kelly, 1988, p. 161). Focused listening enables helping professionals to detect opposition to oppression within clients' terminology including words such as: resist, take back, stand-up to, confront, oppose, challenge, win, defy, fight, battle, protect, defend, rebel, question, contest, object, go up against, disagree, and argue. Unfortunately in helping professions the term "resistance" has negative connotations; psychoanalysis uses the term to refer to psychological defenses against threatening material in the unconscious mined. Resistance also is defined as a refusal to comply with the advice of professionals or the prescribed process of therapy. Historically, in other words, "resistance" has pathology-oriented meanings rather than self-preserving ones. Instead, resistance to oppression may be looked upon as indicative of health and is "health inducing" (Wade, 1997), which is how it is applied throughout this book.

A pathology model of trauma leads practitioners, who lack the ability to understand the full meaning of victimization and its consequences, to interpret the pain and hurt expressed by survivors as evidence of psychopathology. To label as pathology rather than acts of resistance and signs of creative survival obscures and denigrates courageous coping efforts in the face of immense adversity. Therefore, mental health assessment tools that highlight survivors' capacity for agency, resistance, and resilience are necessary (Gilfus, 1999). "Clinicians cannot change the abusive experiences encountered by their clients; they can only hope to influence reactions to the abuse" (McMillen, Zuravin, & Rideout, 1995, pp. 1042–1043). As a result, the task of the helper is to support individuals to find "space" within their narratives to allow the opportunity for a different understanding (Gasker, 1999). For some individuals this may include recognizing resistance strategies that evolved from their struggles to overcome their family violence experiences.

The author's qualitative research addresses the contextual nuances of the solutions at-risk populations find to cope with high-risk environments. As a contextual understanding of oppression evolved, the roots of one's resilience can be seen forged in their resistance to subjugation that consequently promoted their survival and perseverance. Their resistance served as a catalyst to their survival and perseverance that may be drawn upon throughout their lives. Particularly, identifying and building on the positive aspects of the self that had their origins in the resistance of their oppressive experiences. Consequently, protective factors are broadened to include individuals' survival strengths that developed as a means to protect themselves from oppression. Research has confirmed that many mental health practitioners "understand institutional and social problems at a perceived, discrete micro level, focusing their interventions on individuals while failing to confront institutionalized oppression" (Dietz, 2000, p. 371). Mental health practitioners during the assessment process, then, would need to merge an understanding of individual issues with an awareness of power relations that are embedded in the larger social environment.

Assessment of Resistance Strategies to Childhood Incest

Twenty-six adult females were interviewed in order to collect and explore information about the meanings they attributed to their childhood incest experiences. The traumatic sexualization of these women was but one layer of an oppressive and often violent family environment. The participants' victimization involved an extreme misuse of power by adolescent and adult male relatives. Although they did not use the term "oppression" to define their experiences, all participants discussed how, in their intimate worlds, male relatives used their authority to dominate them. The perpetrators (the terms *perpetrator* and *abuser* were often used by participants as they discussed their incest experiences) dominated their victims by violating their bodies and by creating a climate of fear. Participants' lives involved protecting themselves by being vigilant of their abusers' demeanor in order to prevent their trauma from reoccurring. Unfortunately, their attempts were often futile, and their abusers continued to coerce (e.g., threatened to physically harm them) them into sexual submission. When participants did take risks to disclose their incest experiences to family members, the abuse was usually minimized, denied, or ignored. Consequently, familial intervention, if any, to protect them was minimal and unreliable.

During childhood, participants were not idle or silent regarding their victimization. They typically were resistant to their perpetrators' domination and used a variety of mental and behavioral strategies to prevent, withstand, stop, or oppose their subjugation and its consequences. Participants were extremely determined to not let their perpetrators "break" them. They developed a resolve to be unlike their perpetrators, a resolve that served them well in adulthood because they chose to live lives without hatred or malice. Each participant's story was distinctive. However, three ontological themes emerged that categorized strategies of resistance to being powerless, silenced, and isolated as highlighted in Figure 3.2 (refer to chapter 3) entitled "Conceptual Model of Adult Incest Survivors' Resistance to Childhood Oppression." The "Assessment of Resistance Strategies to Childhood Incest" presented in Appendix D translates this conceptual framework into a 24-item assessment to be used with an individual as she reviews her childhood incest experiences. Major constructs of the conceptual model are highlighted in bold; however, to simplify the assessment form (and thus not discuss the conceptual model) one might only include the 24-item list of resistance strategies for clients.

The following dialogue highlights how the worker helps the client reconnect with her own power initiated in childhood as she defended herself from her perpetrator. The worker helps the client to externalize the problem of depression and to use the ways she resisted her perpetrator to resist the depression. The client, Deborah, is a 38-year-old woman who experienced childhood incest between the ages of eight to twelve. The abuse stopped after Deborah refused to visit her father (i.e., the perpetrator) after he and her mother divorced. She continues to have an estranged relationship with him. Deborah defines her problem situation as "a lack of control" in her life. Essentially, she is feeling powerless to resolve her depression. The aftereffects of her childhood incest continue to plague her and in a sense she has become oppressed by the problem that she is seeking resolution for. The worker and Deborah have discussed the conceptual model of oppression and resistance as it relates to incest. Additionally, she has completed the assessment of resistance strategies. The following dialogue between Deborah and the worker focuses on translating these childhood strategies into her present circumstances as she opposes and stands-up to "the depression." The worker uses solution-focused exception questions (see Appendix A) to help Deborah connect her childhood acts of resistance to her present situation.

Worker: Deborah, you have talked about different childhood examples of your resilience such as defying your father, exercising your self-determination, disclosing the abuse, and accessing social support. I'm wondering if some of these resistance strategies may be further accessed to oppose, fight, or defy the depression. For example, let's start with item number one that you marked as using, "frequently" or a "4". Which is "I purposely did not do everything the abuser demanded of me." Let's instead, substitute "the depression" for "the abuser." So, it would state, "I purposely did not do everything the depression demanded of me." How would you rate yourself now on this item?

Client: A "2"—rarely.

Worker: So defying your dad you rated a "4" but defying the depression you rated a "2." How do you think you might apply the courage, determination and creativity used as a child to fight the depression?

Client: I don't know.

Worker: You have some hard-earned battle scars and have survived and persevered. How can you prepare to do battle against the depression?

Client: I don't know. That's what I need your help with.

Worker: Okay, um, depression can make it hard to step outside of yourself and look at it from a distance. So, I'm going to ask you some "exception" questions that will help you to look at when the depression is not a problem or less of a problem. For instance, you rated yourself a "2" and not a "1" why? Are there times when you do stand up to the depression?

Client: I guess so. I hadn't thought of it as defying it though. But sometimes I make myself do stuff that I don't feel like doing. Like coming here, I really wanted to stay in bed all day, but I remembered what you said about when I really want to avoid coming to counseling is probably when I really need to show up for it.

Worker: That's amazing that you stood up to it and not only got yourself ready to come but then followed through with it. You didn't let the depression get the best of you today. Let's look at another item that you marked as "frequently" used during childhood to resist powerlessness, "I fantasized about having more power than the abuser." Again substitute, "the depression" for "the abuser" and how would you rate yourself?

Client: A "3," occasionally.

Worker: So occasionally you dream or fantasize about having power over the depression. Tell me have you done this today or maybe this week?

Client: Yeah. I don't want the depression to win. I mean that's why I'm in counseling to try and defeat it. I can't keep living this way, so I either have to get better or end my life. And I don't want to end my life.

Worker: So you're not only standing up to the depression but to suicide as well. Deborah, you deserve to have a life where the depression is no longer a frequent visitor and there is no reason this cannot happen.

Client: I'm sick of the visitor. It has stayed way too long.

Worker: So you don't want it as part of your life anymore.

Client: Not at all. And if it has to visit, then I want to be able to kick it out or shorten its stay.

Worker: Sounds good. So how might you shorten its stay or kick it out? This relates somewhat to item number five in resisting powerlessness, "I tried to divert the abuse from happening." You were very creative in doing this as child, how might you use this talent to divert the depression?

Client: Not open the door and let it in, or kick it out the door when it has stayed too long.

Worker: That's amazing. How will not open the door and let the depression in?

Client: When I feel it getting worse, I won't leave the door wide open and welcome it with open arms.

Worker: Meaning?

Client: Usually when I'm depressed and have a bad day, I figure the day isn't going to get any better so why even try and deal with it. And I start thinking my life sucks and it's never going to get any better, so why try. So, I just give up. Once something goes bad in my day, it just keeps getting worse.

Worker: That's good insight. So how will you stand-up to the depression because it has tried to visit you for most of your life and likes to tighten its grip when you are having a bad day and bad thoughts.

Client: I'm stronger than it. Like I said, it hasn't won. I'm still here. Just because my day starts off bad doesn't mean I have to let it continue to be that way.

Worker: You are stronger than it, but sometimes one does get battle weary because the depression likes to keep you isolated and make you feel that you are all alone. So, you might consider bringing in reinforcements at times. Just as you resisted isolation as a child, you will need to continue to do this as an adult. Through letting others know about the depression and asking for support, it also takes its power away.

Client: That makes sense. Although I hadn't made the connection of what I went through as a kid, and how that can be similar to what I'm going through now, being depressed.

The dialogue between Deborah and the worker focused on her resourcefulness, allowing for an exploration of her childhood survival strengths as oppose to her deficits. Helping clients to see their active resistance is important because they often blame themselves for the social problems they experience; they believe they are passive in fighting it. Often they have cast their strategies of resistance in a pathological light. For example, Deborah resisted her perpetrator, such as with verbal challenges or physical struggle, although she was usually told to keep it a secret or was threatened with terrible consequences if she did not. In spite of this, she continued to demonstrate strength and determination repeatedly. As in Deborah's case, individuals' resistance may serve as a catalyst for survival and perseverance and for the subsequent development of strategies that promote resilience and recovery. In addition, building on resistance may serve as a stepping stone in taking effective action on one's behalf and in the service of social justice (Wineman, 2003). Practitioners can support clients by encouraging them to express the details and implications of their resistance to oppression.

Assessment of IPV Childhood Survival Strategies

This exploratory study (Anderson & Danis, 2006) included in-depth interviews with 12 women who during childhood were exposed in some way to their mothers being battered by their male intimate partners. Although previous research has focused on the negative consequences of exposure to domestic violence, this qualitative study looked at the strategies female children use to overcome this oppressive environment. Inquiry included exploring individuals' perspectives on the personal qualities and social conditions (i.e., psychosocial processes) that enhanced their ability to survive exposure to domestic violence and persevere throughout their lives. The key finding included uncovering the roots of their resilient capacities (e.g., breaking the cycle of violence) that were forged in resistance to their childhood adversity and its consequences, particularly the violence perpetrated by fathers toward their mothers. Participants were determined and creative in their efforts to resist despite being exposed to extreme forms of domestic violence. The interaction between these strategies demonstrated the resourcefulness of these women as they negotiated the challenges of their childhood adversity (refer to Figure 3.3 titled "Conceptual Model of Children's Resistance to Batterer's Oppression" in chapter 3). The participants' used different protective strategies to "withstand" ($n = 48$ strategies) and "oppose" ($n = 27$ strategies) a sense of powerlessness due to the batterer's oppression of their mothers and of themselves (refer to Appendix E for the 75-item list of childhood strategies).

Although the continued study of negative consequences of abuse exposure is important by focusing on the negative consequences, we may miss a more complete picture of the impact that exposure has on children and their ability to cope with and resist abusive environments. For helping professionals who work with adult daughters of battered women it is also important to help women recognize how their strategies of resistance led to their resilience. For instance, the form entitled "Assessment of Intimate Partner Violence Childhood Survival Strategies" in Appendix E may be used in a similar manner as Appendix D for incest survivors to highlight and make connections between childhood strategies of resistance and how these may be used to address their present circumstances. In this study, participants' strategies of resistance began as spontaneous reactions to their childhood adversity and its consequences, and evolved into strategies that were utilized throughout their lives. "Persons continue to resist, prudently, creatively, and with astonishing determination, even in the face of the most extreme forms of violence" (Wade, 1997, p. 31). Resistance to the batterer's oppression can be a catalyst for strategies of survival and perseverance and serve as a foundation for resilience among children exposed to domestic violence.

Assessment of Adult Recovery Strategies from Intimate Partner Violence

This qualitative study aimed to elicit women's ($N = 20$) perceptions of what helped them to recover from domestic violence. Despite the harmful consequences such exposure can produce, the present findings suggest that an individual's struggle to heal can, in some ways, also lead to a positive transformation. This study's findings underscore how recovery is possible including transformative growth where the trauma assumptive world of shame and blame is altered to one of personal strength, purpose, and a greater appreciation of one's life. Focusing on the survivor's resourcefulness draws on her resilience and allows for alternative ways to work with clients that honors their strengths as opposed to their deficits.

Participants inevitably experienced the trials and tribulations of recovery. They shared their moments of triumph along with the challenges they faced over time. In the aftermath upon leaving the abusive relationship, the stressors participants faced while healing from their victimization included posttrauma symptoms (e.g., depression, anxiety) and the batterers' persistent attempts at controlling them (i.e., stalking, breaking into their homes, and harassing the women's employers, friends, and family). Participants were persistent in pursuing help and determined to heal from domestic violence. Regardless of one's course of adaptation, each participant's story served as an exemplar of determination and, ultimately one of resilience and resolve.

Recovery strategies developed as a way for participants to resist their post-trauma stressors. They were determined to "get on top" of their lives and to not let their trauma dominate it any more. Although each participant's recovery process was distinctive, a restructuring of their view of themselves, the meaning of their trauma, and their purpose in life were key markers of their posttraumatic growth (see Figure 3.4 in chapter 3 entitled "Conceptual Model of Women's Recovery from Domestic Violence"). Appendix F titled "Assessment of Adult Recovery Strategies for Intimate Partner Violence" provides several key strategies (39 items) of domestic violence survivors' transformation process including: exercising one's personal tenacity ($n = 14$), developing social supports (14 items), and transforming one's suffering through giving back to others (11 items).

The following dialogue between the worker and Ginnie highlights how the aftereffects of her domestic violence, particularly her relationship with the abuser, continue to trouble her. Ginnie is a 48-year-old woman formerly in a 10-year verbally abusive relationship. Her former abusive partner, John, has initiated contact and is interested in getting back together with her. Ginnie and John have gone out together a couple of times. Ginnie states that these occasions were pleasant and she is considering returning to John. She has not been with him in the past year and is feeling overwhelmed with being lonely and managing on her own. The worker uses the "Assessment of Adult Recovery Strategies for Intimate Partner Violence" to help Ginnie get back in touch with her strengths and resources that she has used to achieve a life free of abuse.

Worker: Ginnie, you said that you are struggling with whether or not to get back together with John.
Client: Yeah, we've been out a couple of times and it has been pleasant. It's making me realize how much I missed him.
Worker: What is it that you miss about him?
Client: I miss having someone in my life. A companion.
Worker: Anything else?
Client: It's just easier being with someone. You don't have to make all the decisions yourself. You don't always have to go out alone and do

stuff. My friends all have somebody, so I'm always alone when we get together. They can't imagine that I'm not with a man, because it's been a year.

Worker: Is there anything you don't miss about John?

Client: I knew you were going to ask me that. Well, I can do anything I want without him constantly checking up on me, monitoring what I'm doing, checking my cell phone calls, my emails, my bank account.

Worker: What else don't you miss?

Client: The name-calling. The accusations.

Worker: Ginnie, I'm not judging you as I think you are the person who knows your situation best. I'm just curious because you have stood up to John before when he has wanted to get back together with you, what is different now?

Ginnie: I'm tired. I'm worn out. I don't know. I'm 48 and I don't want to be alone for the rest of my life.

Worker: Sure, that's understandable. Is there any reason in particular that it needs to be John rather than someone else?

Ginnie: I don't know.

Worker: You have worked hard on your goal to live a life free of violence. How does John fit into that goal?

Ginnie: I'm not sure if he does.

Workie: So what is it you would like me to help you with in regard to maintaining a life free of violence?

Ginnie: I guess to help me decide whether or not to get back together with him. Although I already know you're thinking I shouldn't.

Worker: No, I wasn't thinking about whether or not you should get back with him; I was thinking if you were changing your goal of having a non-violent life, since you don't know if John can be a part of making that happen or not.

Ginnie: I've been thinking that maybe it could be both.

Worker: So, you've been considering if you can have a violence-free life with John? And this has been more on your thoughts because you have felt more tired, worn out, lonely, and just thinking that life is too hard?

Ginnie: Yes.

Worker: Ginnie, would it be okay at this moment if we took a step away of thinking about whether or not John should be a part of your life and instead look at the work you've done in the past year to get to where you are now? I'm just thinking you've lost connection to your strengths, particularly your courage, determination, and resourcefulness.

Client: I know I've worked hard, but I don't feel like things have changed much.

Worker: Well, let's see what is different now from a year ago when you completed your "Assessment of Adult Recovery Strategies from Intimate Partner Violence." (Worker gets the assessment from the client's file.) I want you to look through it and see how you rated yourself back then and also rate yourself now on each item. So, by filling this out again, I want you to notice what changes you have made in exercising your tenacity, accessing supports, and in giving back to others. (Gives the client her former completed assessment form.)

Client: (She reviews her initial ratings and rates herself again on the assessment form.) Okay. I'm done.

Worker: What did you learn in regard to how you saw yourself then compared to now?

Client: Lots of 2s, 3s, some 1s. And now I am mostly 4s and 5s.

Worker: So, although you feel that things haven't changed, in reviewing your initial assessment and comparing it to where you are now, your situation has changed significantly. Let's start with looking at how you've changed in regard to your tenacity to survive and persevere. In reviewing these 14 items what strikes you as the biggest changes?

Client: Having a future. Looking forward to it and planning for it. I use to have such a hard time making decisions about my life and what I wanted but I've made a lot of decisions over the past year.

Worker: Such as?

Client: Going to counselling, getting my own place, finding a job.

Worker: Those are major decisions that you followed through and made happen. And it wasn't easy on you, but you didn't give up. How did you rate yourself on "I try and not let the abuser, John, control my life"?

Client: A 4, frequently. Once I left for good, he was so persistent calling me all the time, showing up at work, calling my parents, that was so hard.

Worker: Yes, I remember, and you just kept confronting him and saying, "No." You also had to reach out to your parents and your co-workers to help set up a safety plan when he would show up.

Client: Yeah, I'm glad it's better and I don't have to do that with him anymore.

Worker: Yes, but it didn't just happen, you made it happen. And you were even more worn out at that time.

Client: Yeah, I was so stressed and upset all of the time.

Worker: But you kept going. How do you think that made you a stronger person? Number 11, on the questionnaire?

Client: I guess I kind of won. I mean I didn't go back with him and I really wanted to.

Worker: And it took much courage to do that because John made your life miserable the more you set limits with him.

Client: God, I don't want to go back to that. I just wish I knew if he has really changed.

Worker: Well, things don't tend to change on their own without working to make it happen. You know how much work you've put into making changes not only with counselling but getting a job etc. I don't know that John has done the work to make changes in his life. So, it seems like you need more information from John beyond him stating, "I've changed" and having a couple of pleasant dates. Such as how did he make the changes? What work has he done? Who has he worked with to make the changes and then check out with these people what their thoughts are on whether or not he's changed. You are very resourceful and thoughtful so use those skills to collect some data on John's changes. If he has changed then he should be open to this, if he hasn't then maybe he hasn't changed as much as he wants you to believe. Has he been in counselling for his anger problems, especially the way he mistreated you?

Client: Not that I know of. Maybe a few times when I got the restraining order against him. I don't know. I guess I need more information.

Worker: That's how you have made life decisions in this past year, collecting information, weighing the pros and cons, and looking at the consequences. You also accessed social supports much more to help you in your decision making.

Client: Yeah. I talk more to my parents, friends, and to my minister.

Worker: Have you done this yet in regard to your decision making about John?

Client: No, I've not wanted to because I'm afraid they'll judge me. They'll think I'm crazy for wanting to get back together with John.

Worker: Okay, and yet, these are key people that you have sought their advice on for many important life decisions; I guess I'm not clear on why you would suddenly not include or trust them on this. They can disagree with you, but that doesn't mean they don't support you.

Client: True. They have seen me at my worst and have been there for me.

Worker: The final area of the assessment is giving back to others. You have done this, particularly in group with the other women who have been with abusive partners, by being encouraging, caring, and giving them advice. What would you say to one of the group members who is in a situation that is similar to yours, where she wants to go back with her abuser after being out of the relationship for a year?

Client: Don't go. Run.

Worker: What do you think about your advice?

Client: I should consider it. But I do want to get more information too.

Worker: That's understandable. So is that your next step? To get more information on John's changes, to talk to your friends and family, and what do you think about bringing it up in group?

Client: Yes, I would like to do that too.

Worker: Okay, so I want you to take a copy of your assessment with you to remind you of the changes you have made to achieve your goal of living a non-violent life. You have much courage, determination, and the ability to make decisions that are good for you. You know what is best for you, remember to listen to your voice, and consider the voices of others who have your best interest in mind, also.

Client: I will and thank you.

The dialogue between Ginnie and the worker assists her to reconnect with the changes she has made over the past year. It is easy for Ginnie to lose track of this, particularly, when she is feeling more vulnerable to John, although she has worked hard at putting the pieces of her life together, she is still struggling with feeling lonely. The worker did not recommend what Ginnie should do in regard to whether or not she should get back with John; instead, she helped Ginnie to see that she has the skills to make this decision and believes that she knows what is best for her. Ginnie feels she already knows what the worker, her family, and friends will say about it but has not checked this out beyond her assumptions. She is encouraged to gather more information from John on his changes, and to also ask for input from others. Even if her supports systems disagree with her, it does not mean anyone is right or wrong; instead, it is more about collecting information for her to consider rather than solely focusing on her reaction of feeling lonely and John's statements that he has changed. Ultimately, it is Ginnie's decision; however, it can be an informed one that draws on her foresight, data, and social support.

PSYCHOMETRIC MEASURES OF RESILIENCE, COPING, AND POSTTRAUMATIC GROWTH

The author's assessments may be used as clinical instruments in mental health practice. Additionally, one might use psychometrically validated scales to capture clients' resilience, coping, or posttraumatic growth despite enduring traumatic events. These measures may be used as a conceptual framework for helping professionals and adult survivors to assess areas that need strengthening along with uncovering personal and environmental resources that could be called upon in their recovery. Such knowledge could contribute to interventions that encourage well-being by building on one's strengths and resourcefulness. Additionally, these tools may be used as a pre- and post-test to assess the effectiveness of an intervention (e.g., cognitive-behavioral therapy) in promoting growth and change.

The Connor-Davidson Resilience Scale

The Conner-Davidson Resilience Scale (CD-RISC) is a 25-item scale in which individuals are asked statements regarding their resilient capacities (Conner & Davidson, 2003). The scale consists of a four-point Likert Scale (0 = not true at all, 1 = rarely true, 2 = sometimes true, 3 = often true, and 4 = true nearly all the time) and is rated based on how the person has felt in the past month. Total scores range from 0 to 100, with higher scores presenting greater levels of resilience. For instance, scores of "3" or "4" for each of the 25 items would yield a range of 75–100. The CD-RISC scale discerns between those with greater and lesser resilience. It was administered to participants in the following groups: two clinical trials of posttraumatic stress disorder (PTSD) (each with an $N = 22$), clinical trial of generalized anxiety ($N = 25$), general psychiatric outpatients ($N = 43$), primary care outpatients ($N = 139$), and a community sample ($N = 577$). The mean scores for PTSD patients was 47.8 (+ = 19.5), generalized anxiety was 62.4 (+ = 10.7), psychiatric outpatients was 68 (+ = 15.3), primary care was 71.8 (+ = 18.4), and the general population was 80.4 (+ = 12.8). The CD-RISC is a well-validated measure of resilience, has good internal consistency, and is simple to use.

Factor analysis of the CD-RISC indicates a multi-structural nature of resilience. The five factors identified include personal competence (8 items, e.g., "I take pride in my achievements."); trusting one's instincts and tolerance of negative affect (7 items, e.g., "In dealing with

life's problems, sometimes you have to act on a hunch, without knowing why"); secure relationships (5 items, e.g., "I have at least one close
and secure relationship which helps me when I am stressed"); personal
control (3 items, e.g., "I feel in control of my life"); and spiritual influences (2 items, e.g., "When there are no clear solutions to my problems,
sometimes fate or God can help"). The CD-RISC provides a means of
measuring individuals' overall strengths and abilities which may also
be applied in working with survivors of family violence (Conner &
Davidson, 2003).

The Intimate Partner Violence Strategies Index

The Intimate Partner Violence (IPV) Strategies Index (Goodman,
Dutton, Weinfurt, & Cook, 2003) is a 39-item scale developed to assess
the range of strategies women use to halt, escape, or resist violence in
their lives. These strategies were developed through focus groups with
domestic violence survivors and advocates, as well as existing literature
on battered women's coping tactics, and the researchers' clinical and
forensic experiences. The strategies were determined based on the following criteria: 1) the purpose for stopping the violence or escaping the
situation; 2) the way of handling it, in terms of confronting the abuser
or avoiding him; and, 3) level of involvement of others including both
formal and informal support networks. The index was administered to
406 battered women who were recruited from either a domestic violence
shelter ($n = 68$), a District Court, Civil Division ($n = 220$), or a District
Court, Domestic Violence Criminal Docket ($n = 118$).

The IPV Strategies Index includes six categories. Placating strategies (5 items) include attempts to change the batterer's behavior without challenging his sense of control (e.g., "I did whatever he wanted to
stop the violence"). Strategies of resistance (7 items) intend to challenge
the batterer's sense of control and possibly the balance of power in the
relationship (e.g., "I ended, or tried to end, the relationship"). Safety
planning includes strategies (10 items) for escape or protection against
a future incident of violence (e.g., "I worked out an escape plan"). Legal
strategies (4 items) include the use of an outside regulator, the legal
system, to change the batterer's behavior (e.g., "I called the police").
Formal network strategies (i.e., 9 items, nonlegal public agencies) range
from accessing medical to religious resources to change the batterer's
behavior and/or options for escape (e.g., "I stayed in a domestic violence shelter"). And, informal network strategies (4 items) are options

or resources for protection or escape against a future incident of abuse (e.g., "I talked to family or friends about what to do to protect myself/ children").

For each of the 39-items, participants are asked if they used the strategy by answering either "yes" or "no". The total score is calculated by summing the ratings for the "yes" responses. For items where participants answered "yes" they are then asked to score perceived helpfulness by indicating on a five-point Likert scale ranging from 1 (not at all) to 5 (very helpful) on how helpful each strategy was in coping with the violence. A score of 3, 4, 5, on any item is considered an indicator that the strategy was helpful. The sum of scores range from 39 to 195 with higher scores (range of 117–195) indicating more perceived helpfulness. Preliminary findings of the IPV Strategies Index demonstrate some evidence of content and convergent validity, but further psychometric testing is needed (Goodman et al., 2003). The IPV Strategies Index provides a way to highlight the nature and extent of battered women's responses to violence including public help seeking and the more private attempts to deal with the violence. Consequently, survivors may become more aware of how active they are in stopping, preventing, or escaping from violence and, thus, challenge those inner dialogues of shame and blame stemming from their beliefs that they did not do enough to protect themselves and their loved ones.

The Posttraumatic Growth Inventory

The Posttraumatic Growth Inventory (PTGI) (Tedeschi & Calhoun, 1996) is a 21-item scale that measures growth for those who have been through traumatic events (e.g., loss of a loved one, chronic or acute illness, violent or abusive crime, accident or injury, combat, job loss, and so forth). It is a five-point Likert Scale that ranges from "0" = "I did not experience this change as a result of my crisis" to "5" = "I experienced this change to a very great degree as a result of my crisis." Total scores range from 0 to 105, with higher scores presenting greater levels of posttraumatic growth. The PTGI has good internal consistency and over a two-month interval, the test-retest reliability is .71. The items were developed based on a literature review of perceived benefits from the result of negative events including changes in self, relationship to others, and philosophy in life. Factor analysis of the PTGI indicates a multi-structural nature of posttraumatic growth. The five factors include: 1) improved relating to others (7 items, e.g., "I have a greater sense of closeness with others"); 2) new found possibilities (5 items, e.g., "I established a new path in my life"); 3) acquired personal strength (4 items, e.g., "I have a greater feeling of self-reliance"); 4) enhanced spiritual change (2 items, e.g., "I have a better understanding of spiritual matters"); and, 5) an increased appreciation for one's life (3 items, e.g., "I have a great appreciation for the value of my life").

The scale was initially administered to groups of undergraduate students (199 males and 405 females) who were recruited from psychology classes at a large university and had experienced a significant negative life event in the last five years. Additionally, the PTGI has been empirically examined in a wide range of major life crises including rape, domestic violence, and breast cancer; each demonstrating posttraumatic growth in these survivors. Although we are becoming more knowledgeable in all areas of trauma, minimal research has been undertaken in regard to positive outcomes related to how individuals recover from these situations. Consequently, clinical work with individuals experiencing posttraumatic growth stress disorder typically does not take into account the potential for stress-related growth (Linley & Joseph, 2004). Yet, it is in the reevaluation, modification, or rebuilding of one's general assumptions about, and view of, adverse experiences that posttraumatic growth may be more readily addressed in the agency setting. Consequently, helping professionals can find ways to support this process of growth, even if they cannot create it.

SUMMARY

Because traumatic experiences and their consequences are overwhelming, survivors of family violence may lose sight of their resources and aspirations. Thus, to optimize well-being, the practitioner may assist a client to uncover these submerged areas of strength and potential through the author's assessment measures and the psychometrically validated scales highlighted in this chapter. Helping professionals can assist survivors of family violence in reflecting and construing meaning from their victimization experiences (Gillum, Sullivan, & Bybee, 2006). The survivor's development of this narrative and what has happened is a necessary basis for the individual to discover meaning in her struggles with adversity (Tedeschi & Calhoun, 1995). For some individuals, this may include recognizing positive outcomes that evolved from their struggles.

Practice that seeks to understand women's survival experiences in their own words gives voice to their observations about how traumatic events have shaped their lives and how their own unique resilient capacities are related to these events. By identifying their strengths and successes, abuse survivors may begin to transform their life narratives in a positive and affirming manner.

6 Creating a Self-Narrative of Strength, Purpose, and Possibility

A central task in adapting to difficult life experiences, such as family violence, is incorporating the traumatic events into one's ongoing life story. Survivors' trauma-related narratives include a collection of stories created to describe and make sense of their abuse experiences (Docherty & McColl, 2003). These survivors' stories about the self are the basis of personal identity and self-understanding and thus provide answers to the question "Who am I?" Answering this question is particularly challenging in the aftermath of trauma, as previously held assumptions about an invulnerable self (e.g., "I'm a good person, so bad things won't happen to me") are shattered. Family violence creates feelings of shame due to the insult on one's self-image and often blame because one feels responsible for the abuse. As a result, new assumptions develop to make sense of why one was victimized, such as, "I'm a bad person, so bad things happen to me." Survivors' life stories then may become dominated by a victim identity thus influencing how they perceive and interact with the world.

Constructing a narrative reflects efforts to cope with adversity through developing a sense of coherence, continuity, and meaning, which is difficult for survivors who no longer have a positive view of self. Or, in severe and prolonged cases of violence, the victims may no longer have a sense of self at all. Yet, the self is complex and constructed, and allows individuals to have choice in their identity formation (Docherty & McColl, 2003). Survivors possess differing self-concepts, and some are schemas of vulnerability, strength, or a combination of both. Some self-concepts may be more familiar, such as shame and blame, consequently, orienting them toward more problem-saturated rather than strengths-based life stories (Bhuvaneswar & Shafer 2004; Rappaport, 1995). Depending upon what self-concepts are activated, therefore, will guide what information individuals take in, process, and act upon in their lives (Polkinghorne, 1991). Recovery from family violence, then, may include stories about the self that serve to integrate diverse self-concepts (e.g., victim/survivor/thriver) and traumatic events into unified and understandable wholes.

This chapter underscores how narrative therapy provides an opportunity to support each person's unique attempt to explore, sequence, and advance her life story with the subplot of family violence as a theme to be contained, integrated, retired, or re-directed (Wrenn, 2003). The sharing of victimization experiences is the first step toward the painful process of integrating traumatic memories into a functional life story (Mossige, Jensen, Gulbrandsen, Reichelt, & Tjersland, 2005; Norman, 2000). When survivors tell the story of their abuse, it transforms their recent and traumatic memories so that they are incorporated into their self-narratives. Due to the horrifying and overwhelming nature of family violence, an individual may split off one or more aspects related to the abusive experience including one's thoughts, memories, perceptions, or feelings (O'Hanlon & Bertolino, 1998). Strengthening a self at these broken places, consequently, involves integrating parts of the self that are devalued, disowned, or dissociated as a result of the harm perpetrated on one's physical and psychological being. Upon integrating these self fissures, a view of self as broken may be transformed to one of wholeness (Cohler, 1991). And, a view of self as damaged may be transformed to one of strength and purpose. Essentially, these two processes are intertwined: putting the pieces back together for an integrated self while transforming the pieces into a new self inclusive of the past, present, and future. Digital storytelling, the practice of using computer-based tools to tell stories (an intervention discussed more fully in this chapter), provides a novel and innovative means of assisting survivors with this dual process.

A NARRATIVE MEANS TO THERAPEUTIC ENDS

According to several narrative researchers and therapists concentrating on words, phrases, and language can serve as a "narrative means to therapeutic ends" for both the client and the professional (Bhuvaneswar & Shafer, 2004; Weingarten, 1998; White & Epston, 1990). Narrative therapy is distinguished not only by its attention to the content in people's stories but to the form and structure of their stories as a reflection of their personal identities, position of power in the world, systems of meaning, and the cultural and social contexts in which the individual is situated. The goal of the helping process is not for clinicians to impose alternative interpretations onto survivors' life stories (Docherty & McColl, 2003). Instead, the role of the helper is to support individuals to find "space" within their narratives for a different understanding (Gasker, 1999).

Narrative principles offer guidance about how to listen to survivors' accounts without interference from one's professional theories, personal beliefs, expectations, or reactions (Chase, 1995; Clandinin & Connelly, 2000; Cooper & Lesser, 2005; Lieblich, Tuval-Mashiach, & Zilber, 1998; Riessman, 1993). Narrative therapists enact a not knowing stance, respectful listening, and a belief in the client as the author/expert of her own narrative. Language is used to build on client strengths and not to correct pathology or cognitive distortions (Cooper & Lesser, 2005; Wrenn, 2003). The practitioner, then, is the learner and the facilitator of new stories that are more empowering and hopeful then the problem-saturated story that presently dominates the client's life. As a result, the client reclaims her voice and develops a more inclusive self including the many possibilities of who she might become.

The socially constructed life story is increasingly being viewed as a legitimate vehicle for healing (Cooper & Lesser, 2005; Ridgway, 2001). By sharing personal narratives, people create or construct themselves while reviewing and reflecting upon their lives, beliefs, and actions, in dialogue with someone else. Survivors of family violence often live the stories of their perpetrators; instead of living stories more in keeping with their own voices and preferences. Thus, individuals think of themselves as damaged and live in a problem-saturated story. Narrative therapy helps clients rewrite their identity stories into ones that are less oppressive and undermining (O'Hanlon & Bertolino, 1998). For some survivors, this may include the helping professional activating self-concepts of courage, survival, and resiliency as a way of creating alternative meanings to a problem-saturated self-narrative. Once survivors of family violence realize that they can formulate their life stories any way they choose, they can then find ways to change the meaning of the past, to alter its grasp on the present, and to mark out a future life course (Gasker, 2001; Harvey, Mishler, Koenen, & Harney, 2001).

"Externalizing conversations" is a narrative approach that encourages clients to objectify the problems they experience as oppressive (White & Epston, 1990). In this process, the problem becomes a separate identity, such as "the depression," "the craving," or "the procrastination." Thus, the problem becomes "the problem" and external to the person or relationship that was attributed the problem. Clients are encouraged to talk about the effects of the problems in their lives and notice their own resources used against their difficulties. In deconstructing the problem, consequently, it changes its meaning and therefore its grip on people's lives. For instance, in the case example of Deborah (chapter 5), the worker helps her to externalize the problem of depression by applying the methods she used to resist "the perpetrator" to also stand-up to "the depression." Essentially, Deborah is helped to defy the aftereffects of her incest experiences (i.e., the depression) much as she did during her childhood in opposing her perpetrator. In doing so, she creates a self-narrative that not only encompasses her trauma and its consequences, but also includes her acts of courage, determination, and resistance. The example of Deborah highlights the means by which reconstructed experiences of the past are interpreted as useful in turning present adversity into opportunities of growth.

In an effort to make sense of negative life events, one's life story is reformulated (Cohler, 1991). Reclaiming an identity of strength, courage, and resilience requires analyzing survivors' stories for moments of triumph in an attempt to encourage the person to "reauthor" her life emphasizing these positive experiences. These are then plotted into a new or different story that focuses on the meaning of these successes in relationship to how survivors define themselves. Mental health practitioners may assist survivors of family violence in the facilitation of a functional life narrative through helping individuals create stories that feature them as "thrivers," "overcomers," or "resisters" rather than as "victims" (Gasker, 1999). "Reauthoring" or "restorying" thus helps to externalize one's pain and suffering and, therefore, move from a problem-saturated personal narrative to a strengths-based one. The clinician aids the survivor to recreate a narrative that includes positive outcomes from one's struggle to overcome the trauma, but not from any loss or changes that may have occurred as a result of it (Tedeschi & Calhoun, 1995). One must be careful to not minimize victimization and its often devastating consequences as a person is not better off, for instance, because she was sexually abused and thus lost her childhood innocence. Rather, individuals may redefine themselves by their struggles to transform and prevail despite their victimization (Norman, 2000). Because survivors cannot change the past but can influence how it is interpreted, they can choose whether or not victimization becomes the center piece of their identities.

In a supportive atmosphere, survivors of family violence extend invitations to others to enter into their narratives to create opportunities for new turning points, increased story cohesion, and coherence, and to generate alternative meanings for change. Sharing one's story plays a central role in survivor self-help and therapeutic groups. The group process allows participants to not only talk about the meaning of their own stories, but contribute to what meaning they gain from listening to others' stories. The shared experience, where others are speaking the same kind of truth, can produce a powerful normalizing effect that can help reverse and overcome feelings of shame. Additionally, multiple shared accounts help group members to go beyond familiar (e.g., problem-saturated) life stories as the interactive process allows for others to enter into the storytelling and participate in the creation of new meaning (Bhuvaneswar & Shafer, 2004). By helping group members to value and support their personal stories and their collective narratives, a context with multiple accounts emerges to create meaning, organize the past, explain the present, and consider options for the future (Gasker, 1999).

Although survivor groups help individuals tell stories about themselves, the professional literature is lacking in the range of ways that narratives can be used during the group process to open up a story to new possibilities, new meanings, and new information (Dean, 1998). The group process provides opportunities to react, question, and explore each others' stories on recovery. Yet, the group setting also may interfere with survivors "restorying" their lives in a manner that externalizes their victimization and its effects. A challenge includes finding "space" during the group process for providing alternative meanings, as members are often reluctant to shift from problem-saturated life stories (i.e., because it is what they know) to strengths-based ones. They have difficulty imagining a future with possibilities; where their trauma minimally or no longer interferes with their lives. They are often stuck in stories of blame, invalidation, and impossibility. Therefore, group experiences that highlight members' strengths, resilience, and acts of resistance may allow those survivors who have become trapped in problem-saturated life stories to consider alternative meanings and thus alternative futures (O'Hanlon & Bertolino, 1998).

Whether in a therapeutic dyad or a group format, survivors of family violence often do not speak plainly about their trauma as the experiences are often fragmented, difficult to understand, and associated with overwhelming emotions (e.g., anxiety, fear, depression). An additional challenge of integrating a traumatic event into one's self-structure is the constriction or numbing of emotions to manage unbearable pain (Herman, 1997; Yama, Tovey, & Fogas Teegarden, & Hastings, 1993). Integrated functions such as cognition, memory, and emotion become disconnected, particularly in the cases of prolonged exposure to trauma. Contributing to forgetting or protective blocking is the pressure for secrecy (Courtois, 1993). Therefore, many have to find alternative avenues, other expressions, to discover their voices. Digital storytelling provides such a means as it integrates narration, images (e.g., photographs), and music to help "tell" one's story of trauma and recovery. Additionally, this intervention fits well with evidenced-based practice in trauma recovery that recommends staying focused on the expression and discussion of traumatic experiences and memories and their associated thoughts and feelings (Whiffen & MacIntosh, 2005).

USING DIGITAL STORYTELLING TO HELP SURVIVORS SPEAK THE UNSPEAKABLE

Digital storytelling, as the name implies, includes some mixture of digital images, text, recorded audio narration, and music. Typically, digital stories are created in intensive 2 to 3 day workshops with 8 to 10 participants who share personal stories and offer feedback to each other within the context of a "Story Circle" (refer to *Digital Storytelling*, by Lambert [2002], for the structure of these workshops at www.storycenter.org/memvoice/pages/cookbook.html). Additionally, group members simultaneously revise their stories, create voiceover narrations, gather photographs or other still images, and select accompanying music while editing these materials into a 2 to 5 minute film. Workshops are concluded with a viewing of the completed stories. Digital storytelling workshops have been used with people of all ages to develop stories of individuals—including those impacted by violence—in ways that improve their lives. (Refer to The Center for Digital Storytelling at www.storycenter.org for a more in-depth explanation of the California-based arts organization dedicated to the art of personal storytelling. Additionally, refer to Silence Speaks at www.silencespeaks.org, an organization that provides digital storytelling workshops with victims of violence.)

Digital storytelling enables individuals without a technical background to produce stories using "moving" images and sounds. As one's story is created and saved, one can view it, edit it, and add to it until the final version is completed. The digital story, including all the pictures, narrations, and music, is saved as a video file that one can view in increments or in its entirety. The stories usually are brief, including a script of approximately 500 words, with accompanying images and music that is then translated into a video. Digital storytelling allows for gradual exposure to one's life experiences through the use of storyboards—a means of planning out and telling one's story in a compelling and emotionally engaging form. This intervention embodies the narrative approach of "emplotment," which involves arranging temporal elements into a whole by connecting them together and directing them toward a conclusion or ending (Polkinghorne, 1991). Essentially, storyboarding transforms a sequence of disconnected images juxtaposed with narration into a unified story with a point or a theme. In planning out one's story, then, one interacts with different images and narration in pieces allowing for immersion and disengagement of story material.

The remainder of this chapter illustrates the author's use of digital storytelling within a group format for adult survivors of childhood incest, which may be translated into other groups for survivors of family violence (e.g., domestic violence). A central aim of group work is to help individuals narrate their experiences, particularly events that are difficult to share with others. A group environment consisting of participants who have similar experiences offers safety and support for telling stories that all too often remain unapproachable and thus unspoken. Thus, the group process reduces feelings of stigma, isolation, and humiliation, while allowing opportunities for observation, modeling, and developing new skills (Chard, 2005; Knight, 2009; Roche & Wood, 2005). Additionally, bearing witness to other people's stories allows group members to take a stand against silence and invalidation of their victimization experiences, which have often been denied by family members and society in general.

DIGITAL STORYTELLING WITHIN A GROUP THERAPY CONTEXT

The author has adapted the digital storytelling process to a six-week group format for survivors of childhood incest. Each group consists of six members plus a group leader who meet for an hour and a half on a weekly basis. To describe the group content and process, the case example of Jasmine (chapter 4), is used to highlight the creation of her digital story of trauma and recovery from sibling incest. Jasmine has processed her trauma through different mediums including "talk" therapy, journaling, and art activities (i.e., painting, drawing), all of which have failed to alleviate her depression, mend a fractured self, or help her to move beyond a problem-saturated life-story.

When the author introduced her to the concept of digital storytelling, she commented, "I see. So it's not about finding your self. It's about creating yourself." In other words, by using stories to create meaning in our lives, to organize the past, and explain the present, we in effect create ourselves. This powerful insight (along with creating her digital story) helped Jasmine get "unstuck" from her depression as she ceased to look at the past to find herself, and, instead turned to her future to create the person she wanted to be. She acquired a sense of agency and integration that did not exist with prior interventions, which often left her feeling more depressed and helpless.

Pre-Group Session

Each prospective member meets individually with the group leader for a pre-screening session to cover the group purpose, its time-limited structure, attendance policy, and responsibilities of members including the facilitator. Additionally, for each member trauma triggers are discussed and ways of coping are explored. The group leader asks the following question to ascertain each member's individual goal(s), "How will you know in six weeks that the group has helped you?" Jasmine's response included, "I won't be stuck in my past. I'll feel better about myself." Next, Jasmine is asked about what story she wants to tell in regard to her trauma and recovery and how it will help in achieving her goals. Jasmine talks about integrating her past, present, and future self including: 1) the "me" during the abuse (past self); 2) the "me" after the abuse (present self); and the "me" without the abuse (the future self). In doing so, she hopes to have closure on her past and move on with a new "me" where the trauma and its effects no longer dominate her life.

In order to move her problem-saturated story (i.e., one sustained in the grips of her depression) to a strengths-based one, the group leader asks her to consider moments of her strength, resilience, and resourcefulness as she creates her story. To help shift a negative view of herself to a more positive one, she is given the "Assessment of Resistance Strategies to Childhood Incest" (see Appendix D) as a guide for reviewing her past. Upon completing the assessment, the group leader asks Jasmine about the strategies she used to defy her perpetrator and protect herself and how those may be incorporated into her life story.

Next, digital storytelling is introduced and Jasmine is given a USB flash drive with Photo Story 3, a widely used software program, to create digital stories on PCs. Photo Story 3 is explained as a free, easy-to-use program from Microsoft that lets individuals create slideshows using digital images including one's own photos, those downloaded from the Internet, or scanned images. (Note: Photo Story 3 is only available for Windows XP and Vista, and the stories created with the program can only be played back with Windows Media Player on PCs running Windows not on Macs.)

Photo Story 3 is capable of touching-up, cropping, or rotating imported pictures. One can add text, transitions, voiceovers, and music to the images. Additionally, one can custom pan and zoom effects to one's digital story to make it more unique and personal. It is further explained to Jasmine that during group sessions each member uses Photo Story 3 to create storyboards where images (e.g., photographs, drawings), narration (e.g., verbal, written), and music (e.g., original, commercial) may be modified as one's story unfolds. Thus, the process involves assessing and making decisions regarding how the story develops in regard to the interacting images, narration, and music. Once one's story is created and saved, one can view it, edit it, and add to it until the final version is completed. Saving the photo story, all the pictures, narrations, and music are compiled into a video file that one can work on during and between sessions.

Jasmine, along with several of the other participants, has a PC laptop computer that she brings to the pre-screening session, so the group leader can demonstrate Photo Story 3 and allow Jasmine an opportunity to work with the different features of the program. For those group members without computers, the group leader demonstrates it on her computer and also allows individuals time to work with the various program aspects. Those without access to computers are encouraged between group sessions to visit school/university or public libraries to work on their digital stories; however, this is not required as the work can be done within group sessions where all members have access to the Internet, computers, and a scanner.

For the first group session, Jasmine is asked to prepare a story idea or a script to present to the group. The script is further explained as a brief narrative, approximately 500 words. Parsimony is a challenge for Jasmine as she has not had a limit or structure to her writing, which often consumes numerous pages. Consequently, it is explained to Jasmine how digital storytelling allows for two tracks of meaning, the visual and the auditory, thus with the juxtaposition of images and narrative, less words are needed to "tell" her story. Additionally, Jasmine is reminded of the old adage, "a picture is worth a thousand words." Therefore, she is encouraged to begin gathering images in addition to formulating her script. Although there is no right or wrong in regard to the sequence of what should come first, the script or the image, one often starts with the script and then the pictures are added to complement the story.

Additionally, Jasmine is encouraged to think about background music that will interact with her images and script as a means of enhancing the story integration. It is stressed that instrumental music is often best as it does not compete with the voiceover. Jasmine is hesitant about creating a voiceover because she is reluctant to listen to her voice. She would prefer to only use images and music rather than recording a voiceover. The group leader encourages her to consider the use of her voice as a gift and that it may be time to take her voice off mute and turn up its volume.

Initial Group Session

During the initial group session, members are introduced to each other and group guidelines are reviewed. Members share their individual goals with each other in answer to the question, "How will you know in six weeks that this group has helped you?" Common group goals include increasing self-esteem, being less isolated, and moving on with their lives. Each member is asked to connect how creating her digital story will help her accomplish her goals. Some group members are in the stages of presenting their ideas, while others have scripts prepared. Group feedback and support is encouraged in regard to helping each group member "tell" her story and make her point.

The group leader role models respectful listening and supportive feedback by not commenting on the content (e.g., wording, sentencing, what to include or not include). Instead, the group leader focuses on the impact of the story and its connection to the point the member wants to make, including one's transformation. The transformative piece often gets neglected upon the initial telling of one's story and thus the leader begins to create space and offer alternative meanings for members to also consider this aspect of their stories.

Jasmine presents her story, which centers on her experiences with childhood incest perpetrated by her brother. Her script is about 250 words long and she reads it in a rapid fashion. Jasmine tearfully reports that while writing her script she became more despondent as she realized that there is no transformation because her whole being is centered on what happened to her. Jasmine has developed certain ideas about who she is based on messages she has gotten from others, particularly her perpetrator, and thus has made conclusions that her purpose in life is to be abused. Jasmine's feelings of blame and shame significantly impact the story. When group members highlight her strength and determination, she does not readily accept these views as she concludes that her perpetrator still has control of her life, as she continues to be defined by her childhood sexual abuse:

> My best friend told me that if I had a choice between taking the easy road or the hard road I'll always take the hard road. Taking the easy road would make me into the person others want me to be. Taking the hard road has made me the person I am. But maybe I didn't choose the hard road. Maybe it chose me because I am a survivor of childhood sexual abuse. It has shaped who I am, what I do, and how I act.

The group leader invites Jasmine to create an alternative storyline where her brother is not positioned as the central character; instead, she becomes the focus of her story. She is encouraged to think about her story's purpose and is asked, "Is the point of your story to emphasize that who you are is solely about being a survivor of childhood sexual abuse?" Jasmine replies, "No, there is much more to me, but the sexual abuse has shaped who I am." Group members, who have all completed the "Assessment of Resistance Strategies to Childhood Incest" (refer to Appendix D), inquire about what she did as a child to protect and resist her sexual abuse. She states, "I guess eventually I said, 'No.'" She is then asked about how saying "No," to her perpetrator, rather than the abuse experiences, has shaped her life. Jasmine replies, "I'm tough. I don't give up. I do my own thing regardless of what people think of me." She is asked to consider incorporating these strengths into her story: opposing her perpetrator, persevering, and being unique.

After the discussion of Jasmine's story, the other members share their scripts and also receive group advice and support. At the conclusion of the storytelling portion of group, each member is asked to reflect on her individual goals and report whether or not their developing stories help or hinder achieving such goals. The members then move into the "lab" portion of group where they work on computers and practice using the elements of Photo Story 3. The lab portion has an element of externalizing their trauma as group members interact with their story in a more technical manner through the use of computer tools to create their story. Throughout the lab portion of each group, members continue to interact with each other to provide support and advice along with technical help when needed. The group leader reviews the first step of Photo Story 3, which consists of importing pictures and editing them. An example is presented on how this feature works. For group members who have brought their own digital pictures, they spend time downloading them and trying the different editing features (i.e., cropping, rotating, enhancing color, and removing "red" eye). Group members, who have not brought images are provided with samples to practice editing.

Because a scanner is available for each group session, members may scan photos, drawings, and other still images that can also be imported into Photo Story 3. Additionally, group members are given Internet sites (e.g., www.flickr.com) that provide noncopyrighted photos to be downloaded. Although downloaded pictures from such sites are available, group members are encouraged to use these sparingly and instead to rely on their own images as they are more personal and representative of their experiences. Often, members have numerous images and they are reminded to economize, approximately using only 10 to 20 photos in creating their digital stories. At the conclusion of each group, all projects are saved on individual members' USB flash drives that they take with them and may continue to work on between group sessions. Additionally, the group leader makes back-up copies on her computer, so if members misplace or lose their jump drives, their work is still preserved. In the period between the first and subsequent group sessions, members are asked to continue to write and rewrite their scripts along with gathering photos and music to tell their stories.

Second Group Session

At the beginning of the second group session, members are asked to share their progress in developing their scripts. Those who did not share their scripts in the first session do so in this one. Additionally, those who previously presented are asked to share their script revisions. Jasmine reports that she has modified her script to highlight her resistance. She is unsure of how to portray this with images, but does know that she wants it as part of her story. Jasmine goes on to say that her story begins with what happened to her in childhood. For this part of the story, she selected childhood photos along with downloaded ones. Her story starts with, "My older brother told me not to tell anyone about what he was doing to me behind closed doors." With this sentence she has juxtaposed an image of a closed door with an antique lock and skeleton key. She states that images of closed and open doors is something that she wants to continue using when referring to her childhood. Jasmine also reports that she has selected a childhood picture of herself with her lips pursed shut to accompany the next sentence, "I didn't tell."

After all group members have revealed and responded to each other's scripts, they move into lab time where they further work on their storyboards in Photo Story 3. As in Jasmine's example, this involves sequencing one's images in relationship to her script. Additionally, the group leader demonstrates different effects that may be added to the images, such as turning a color photo into black and white or sepia. They are also shown how to add text (which may be modified in font type, style, size, color, and location) to their images. Throughout the lab portion, group members offer support, advice, and technical assistance to each other as they further develop their digital stories. At the end of group, all projects are saved.

Third Group Session

In the third group session, members are asked about their progress in the last week regarding revisions and updates to their scripts. Jasmine reports that her story has evolved into using repetition with particular sentences including: "I didn't tell," and, "I said, 'No.'" For each "I didn't tell," she uses the same childhood image of herself with her lips pursed shut. She has downloaded several images of the word "resist" (in different font style and format) to accompany "I said, 'No.'" Additionally, Jasmine has further developed the idea of her resistance in regard to opposing authority figures, trauma experts, and helping professionals who told her she would not succeed in life or heal from her childhood sexual abuse.

After members present and reflect on each other's work, they move into the lab portion of group. The group leader demonstrates how to use Photo Story 3 to add motion within and between their images. Since the program has a default custom motion, group members can decide to leave their images as is or they can modify the motion. For instance, they can alter the start and end position of the motion on each image. They also can increase or decrease the number of seconds the image is displayed (the default is 5 seconds). Jasmine decides to alter the custom motion on a childhood picture of herself and her two brothers. She starts with the entire picture and then zooms in to end with just a picture of herself and the perpetrator. On another childhood picture, she alters the motion to start with a close-up of her face and zoom out to end with a full picture of herself. Additionally, Photo Story 3 has a default motion between images, referred to as "cross fade," where one image fades into the next one. Jasmine leaves this default option rather than customizing the motion between images as she prefers how it looks. At this point, group members are able to preview their digital story with the added motion. As in the prior group sessions, members interact with each other throughout lab time to offer guidance, assistance, and feedback.

Fourth Group Session

By the fourth session, group members finalize their scripts and images. After members touch base with each other on their progress, they spend the majority of the time in lab as the group leader works with each member to fine tune her digital story. Jasmine's script is concise and needs only a few editing suggestions. However, some of her selected images add confusion when juxtaposed with the script. Jasmine, as many beginners do, selects images to mirror her words exactly. So, if she talks about a bedroom, then the accompanying image is a child's bedroom. Consequently, she ends up taking out many pictures of herself and replacing them with other images as, for example, with her statement, "I also knew I was slipping away." She replaces a childhood picture of herself, a brown-eyed, dark haired girl, with a picture of a blue-eyed, blond girl "fading away." Additionally, she uses images such as a leather chaise lounge and a picture of Sigmund Freud, a psychoanalyst, to portray the statement, "Trauma experts said that I would never heal from my childhood." Essentially, her image selection has become less personal. She is encouraged to go back to using pictures of herself to portray her story rather than getting caught up in the process of mirroring pictures with her words. She also is asked to consider reducing the number of images to make her point as the rapid succession of several pictures makes it difficult to process the juxtaposition with her script and thus diminishes the meaning of her story.

Upon reviewing each member's script and image sequence, the group leader then asks for volunteers to do their voiceovers, an audio recording of their scripts in concert with their images. Three members volunteer; Jasmine does not. One at a time, the group leader works with each of the volunteers in using the microphone to record her voiceover in a quiet space separate from the group room. Upon completing their voiceovers, each member may play it back and modify it if needed. Most often, this involves listening to their voiceovers several times as they work on the timing of the narration and image sequence. As the group leader works individually with each member, the others are in lab time and provide feedback and assistance to each other.

Fifth Group Session

The fifth session is the final time for members to work on their digital stories as the sixth and final session is dedicated to revealing their completed projects. Jasmine, and the others who did not previously do their voiceovers, do so in this session. For Jasmine listening to her voiceover is difficult; however, she becomes more comfortable as she repeatedly plays it back to modify her pace and thus not rush her sentences. Additionally, group members work on the final element of their digital story, which includes adding background music (e.g., classical, contemporary, jazz, blues). Members discuss and share selections with each other as they have brought downloaded music and compact discs. Photo Story 3 also provides different instrumental styles to choose from. Most group members select one musical number for their digital story; although some choose two instrumental pieces. Jasmine chooses the following classical piece as it is simple, repetitive, and slow-placed: "Concerto for Oboe and Strings in C minor: Adagio" to complement her story. Once group members complete this step, they are able to preview, and thus modify, the juxtaposition of narration, images, and music. This involves each member working with headphones as to not disturb or distract others in the final editing of their videos. Additionally, group members process their feelings regarding the upcoming final session, particularly the viewing of each other's videos. Group members want to celebrate their hard work and volunteer to bring snacks, while the group leader will bring beverages. The group leader informs them that their videos will be viewed on the big screen through the use of an LCD (i.e., liquid crystal display) projector, a type of projector that is connected to a computer to display videos or images. Group members express excitement regarding the completion of their projects and sadness that the process is ending.

Sixth Group Session

For the ending session, each member works on the final touches of her digital story including developing a closing caption. Jasmine selects a black background with white letters for her closing caption: "In Honor of Child Sexual Abuse Survivors. No Act of Resistance is Too Small." Upon completion of their projects, they are then saved in a final video format. Members prepare for viewing the videos, including setting out snacks and beverages, while the group leader sets up the LCD projector. Throughout the six-week group process members have shared their stories with each other; however, this is the first time they actually view the videos in their entirety. One at a time, each group member introduces her video, the point of her story, and how it has helped in achieving her goals. The following is Jasmine's story with accompanying images. Her video opens with the title "I Said No" in white letters on a black background.

I Said No

- "My older brother told me not to tell anyone about what he was doing to me behind closed doors." (A color picture of a closed door with an antique lock and skeleton key.)
- "I didn't tell." (A black and white picture of Jasmine as a child with her lips pursed shut.)
- "My younger sister walked in on us in the bedroom." (A color picture of a door slightly open.)
- "I didn't tell." (The same black and white picture of Jasmine as a child with her lips pursed shut.)
- "My sister told my mother and when she asked me about it." (Same color picture of a door slightly open.)
- "I didn't tell." (Same black and white picture of Jasmine as a child with her lips pursed shut.)
- "My mother told me she'd put an end to it." (A different color picture of a door wide open and light shining through.)
- "When he didn't stop, I didn't tell." (Same black and white picture of Jasmine as a child with her lips pursed shut.)

- "He told me if anyone found out again he would be sent away. Although I feared for what could happen to my brother." (Black and white childhood picture of Jasmine and her two brothers which zooms in on her and her brother, the perpetrator.)
- "I also knew I was slipping away." (A black and white childhood picture of Jasmine staring blankly into the camera as it zooms away from her face.) "I told him, 'no more' or I would tell."
- "Saying 'No,'" to my brother has shaped my life." (A color picture of the word "resist" with spray-painted white letters against a red brick wall.)
- "It's defined who I am, what I do, and how I act." (A color picture of Jasmine as a young teenager smiling.)
- "Authority figures said that I would not succeed in life." (A color picture of the word "resist" scratched into a gray wall.)
- "I said, 'NO.'" (A color picture of an adult Jasmine smiling with two of her students at a school graduation.)
- "Trauma experts said that I would never heal from my childhood." (A color picture of the word "resist" sprain-painted black on the side of an abandoned building.)
- "I said, 'NO.'" (A color wedding picture of Jasmine and her husband smiling and walking down the aisle.)
- "Helping professionals labeled me an adult survivor." (A color picture of the word "resist" spray-painted blue amongst other graffiti on a bridge.)
- "I said, 'NO.'" (A color picture of Jasmine smiling and sitting outside.)
- "I am not defined by what was done to me."(A black and white childhood picture of Jasmine as a child looking away.)
- "Instead, I define myself by how I resisted." (A color picture of Jasmine as an adult in her graduation robe with her husband hugging her and giving her the thumbs-up.)

At the conclusion, group members applaud and process with Jasmine her progress and final product. As her last two statements highlight, Jasmine no longer defines herself by what happened to her but instead by how she resisted. She reports that she is ready to retire her storyline of being a sexual abuse survivor and would like to move on with a new and different identity. She feels a sense of power, control, and has a voice in defining who she is. In essence, she has metaphorically and literally created an integrated, strength-based story of her past, present, and future.

SUMMARY

The identity stories that people live by can either restrict or open up possibilities. An unavoidable connection exists between what persons achieve and what they think they can achieve. Opening "space" within adult survivors' narratives to encompass both integration and transformation provides a good fit with a strengths-based helping paradigm that recognizes and appreciates one's potential for growth in the face of adversity (O'Hanlon & Bertolino, 1998; Saleebey, 2006). The intent is not to deny the real trauma of family violence; however, helping survivors reformulate life stories that restore hope and possibility does refute that people who endure such hardships are incapacitated for life or are unable to achieve their potential. Reclaiming a positive identity from a "damaged" self-definition are neither simple nor straightforward tasks. Consequently, it is necessary to have interventions, such as digital storytelling, that tap into and honor the inherent healing abilities that people possess as a means of helping them construct stories of trauma, recovery, and ultimately triumph.

7

Spirituality: Finding Meaning and Purpose in the Midst of Suffering

There are places in the heart that do not yet exist; suffering has to enter in for them to come to be.

—Leon Bloy, French novelist and poet

Many survivors of family violence find it challenging to put their traumatic experiences into a meaningful framework, as well as it serving a purpose in their lives (Gillum, Sullivan, & Bybee, 2006; Senter & Caldwell, 2002; Shantall, 1999; Silver, Boon, & Stones, 1983). Just as trauma shatters assumptions about an invulnerable and efficacious self, it also alters individuals' beliefs in a Higher Power and notions about a safe, orderly, and just world. Thus, individuals may experience conflicts and questions regarding spiritual and existential matters. Spiritual concerns such as the sources of faith and doubt, hope and despair, belonging and isolation are relevant in many survivors' lives (Gotterer, 2001). Consequently, they are not likely to separate psychological from spiritual issues when obtaining mental health services. As survivors try to understand the purpose and meaning of their lives, they seek answers for the "why" of suffering. Thus, helping professionals cannot discount the spiritual dimension so long as clients question injustice and seek spiritual responses to it (Asher, 2001; Chandler, Holden, & Kolander, 1992).

In the author's research (see chapter 3), most participants during childhood were involved in organized religion, including formalized rituals, symbols, doctrines, and places of worship. Additionally, these women discussed how participating in an organized expression of faith provided beliefs and moral codes shared and followed by its members. During adulthood few survivors continued to affiliate with a particular religion; instead most associated with spirituality: a personal quest for meaning, a reason for being, and union with a Higher Power (Canda, 1988; Sahlein, 2002). Detailing the differences and similarities between religion and spirituality is beyond the scope of this volume. Instead, the focus of this chapter is on the function of spirituality in survivors' lives as it relates to learning about self and finding meaning in traumatic life events, including answering the "why" of suffering.

Throughout this chapter, survivors' quotes (from the author's research) serve as examples of how these women found meaning and purpose in the face of immense suffering. As a result of their struggles, they were more able to clarify inner knowledge of themselves, develop fulfilling relationships with others, and find a life purpose. Victor Frankl, Auschwitz survivor and existential psychologist, aptly states, "In some way, suffering ceases to be suffering at the moment it finds a meaning" (Frankl, 1984, p. 135). Finding meaning, unfortunately, is more elusive for individuals victimized by a trusted family member whose violent acts compromised beliefs about truth (e.g., Who can I trust?), justice (Why was I abused?), and freedom (e.g., Will I be free of suffering?). This chapter underscores how survivors of family violence find meaning and purpose by answering the "why" for their suffering including an enhanced relationship with a Higher Power and one's true self.

SPIRITUAL PATHWAYS TO ANSWERING WHY ME?

Spiritual beliefs can and do shape the meaning of life experiences for many clients, including survivors of family violence (Bent-Goodley & Fowler, 2006; Ganje-Fling & McCarthy, 1996; Giesbrecht & Sevcik, 2000). Yet, relatively few studies have integrated spirituality into trauma practice and research. Thus, when individuals raise spiritual questions such as "why do bad things happen to good people" (Kushner, 1981), mental health professionals might feel ill-prepared (e.g., have minimal or no experience regarding such matters) in helping clients come to terms with beliefs about suffering and their purpose in life (Bergin, 1991; Sahlein, 2002). Yet, when survivors grasp meaning and see one's life as purposeful, their perceptions of esteem and control are likely to increase allowing for a sense of well-being (Tedeschi & Calhoun, 1996).

People are harmed by violence and one does not have to endure being choked, beaten, or raped to find meaning and purpose in life. Yet, even under these ominous conditions, life still holds meaning (Frankl, 1984; Kushner, 1981). Many would find ironic the idea of priceless value in a life marked by violence, but it is a striking outcome for many of the survivors in the author's research:

> It is what made me who I am and I no longer say, "I wish that it didn't happen to me." I now say, "I'm grateful that it happened because I wouldn't be who I am." I wouldn't be as strong. I don't think I'd be as intuitive. I wouldn't be as comforting to other people for having been through those things in life. I wouldn't have the courage to do what I do. I know that I wouldn't be who I am right now if it wasn't for that, this was an evolution of my life that had to take place. When I get faced with the very frustrating, I remember and say, "You can't change that, so you got to change yourself." (Jane, age 37, incest survivor)

> How I make sense of it is I wouldn't take it back for the world because it made me the person that I am now, and I think that everything happens for a reason and I think that eventually I'm going to help somebody and I know that whenever I run across people who are in a [troubling] situation, I know how to give them advice. (Moberly, age 32, survivor of childhood exposure to domestic violence)

Helping professionals often discuss the dynamics of abusive intimate relationships (e.g., power and control) with survivors providing them with important knowledge on the causes of violence; yet, it does not necessarily address or resolve the "why" of suffering for such individuals. Practitioners may be reluctant to enter into conversations with clients regarding the meaning and purpose of suffering as they may feel responsible for answering the "why" of violence. Instead, the helper's role is to assist the client to walk through, rather than around, her suffering and thus discover her own answer for "why me"? After the hurt has been dealt with, what remains is insight and special knowledge that many who are fortunate enough to not experience family violence may not have the benefit of. Consequently, each survivor may draw upon her intuition and wisdom to address the "why" of her suffering. As highlighted in the following quotes, the answer differs for each individual; however, some commonalities include an improved evaluation of self (e.g., stronger, more compassionate), a more profound understanding of the world (e.g., life is not easy thus to be human is to suffer), and a greater life purpose (e.g., breaking the cycle of violence, helping other survivors).

I still don't understand why it happened. And, I still have a hard time with God allowing it to happen, because I know He didn't make it happen, but He allowed it to happen, and so I struggle with that. But, I know that there must be a reason that it was to make me be a stronger person, because I've grown a lot in all the areas of my life since I've gone through treatment. I am able to tell my story more. I'm able to have more compassion for people who have gone through what I have gone through and I think just overall I've learned that life is not easy, but you have to keep persevering no matter what. I've learned more about having confidence in myself and I've learned that I can't let the incest break me, even though at times it seems like it has. (Jennifer, age, 35, incest survivor)

I have endeavored, though it was hard, to make ceaseless efforts to take the events of my life, often painful, sometimes unbearable, and transform them into meaningful experiences. So every time I went through something, it was difficult, but I tried to draw strength from it and learn something from it, instead of having it drop off as something that was really bad and then immerse myself in that and dwell on it and become worse. (Suria, age 35, survivor of childhood exposure to domestic violence)

Well it helped make me who I am, as crazy as that may sound. In childhood it took so much from me, but as I worked through it, in my adult life, it gave so much strength to me, so it's kind of a double-edged, bitter-sweet sword. There were many painful stumbling blocks and mountains and detours to take to get to where I am, but it made me more consciously aware of my surroundings. It made me be more determined to be open and honest with my child. And with everybody else around me. I don't mince words. I say what I think. If you ask for my opinion, be careful, because I'm gonna give it to ya. (Jackie, age 45, incest survivor)

I know that my purpose is to do whatever brings the glory of God and I feel like that is using my experiences that I've been through, whether it is through the domestic violence experiences that I've been through or just the experiences I've had with my dad in general. To just relate those to people so that they can realize that there is hope and I have God as my hope and so that is where my purpose comes from. (Joanna, age 22, survivor of childhood exposure to domestic violence)

Family violence is devastating and thus for many survivors they depend upon what's beyond them, a transcendent force, to rise above themselves and their suffering (O'Hanlon, 1999). In the authors' survivor studies, a relationship with God (or a Higher Power or Spirit) fostered a sense of meaning, purpose, and value in life for many of the participants; all heightened areas for these women in the aftermath of their trauma.

Additionally, a Higher Power was viewed as a source of strength, companionship, love and hope:

> I believe in God or a Higher Being, but I don't really connect with a particular faith. But I do believe that there is some Higher Power than us, and I've asked that Higher Power many times why this happened to me... I just think it all comes back to the test. I truly believe that. So, I figure I've been tested enough in my life. (Kathleen, age 26, incest survivor)

> I believe that there is a Higher Power, so I'm not agnostic. By that virtue I'm also not atheist. I don't think there's a dime's worth of difference between Buddha, Allah, Mohammed, Jesus Christ, God, the Trinity, Jehovah, I don't care what you call him/it/her, goddess... I think if we're limited to just ourselves and our own power, we feel very vulnerable, we feel very weak. So, we're hoping and praying that there's something out there greater than us that we can count on, that we can turn to. We all have this common need. We just all call him, she, or it by different names. (Donna, age 45, survivor of childhood exposure to domestic violence)

> The spirit was there for me. You can call it God, you can call is Jesus, you can call it Spirit, you can call it anything you want to, but it was there for me. It was there for me because I had gifts. Mother Earth was giving me gifts on a daily basis, even if it was just little things, a walk in the woods, a beautiful day, snowing heavily, coyotes singing. To me that was a gift... and that's how I maintained strength, is I looked for all the little gifts that came to me through a spiritual manner. Where they come from, who knows? But they came to me, and they were there for me, and they helped me through. (Ava, age 58, domestic violence survivor)

> I've always felt like there was something there that cared. In periods when I'm not practicing any form of spirituality, I don't do well. There has to be something there, organized or individual or what. I won't say that it saved my life, but it certainly got me through some of the tougher moments. That's right up there with the strengths that I have. Somehow I was just born with this innate feeling that something higher than me loved me, and if you were going to pick anything that was different between me and my siblings, I would pick that one and that was a gift. (Mary Poppins, age 51, survivor of childhood exposure to domestic violence)

Many survivors of family violence have an uneasy relationship with a Higher Power as they view Him/Her as failing to protect them during the abuse (Bent-Goodley & Fowler, 2006; Ganje-Fling & McCarthy, 1996; Muller, 1993). Additionally, they find it challenging to relate to a Higher Power who is viewed in a similar light as their abusers: paternal and punishing. Thus, they fear and distrust surrendering control to something beyond themselves (Senter & Caldwell, 2002). Other concerns include one's spiritual value as survivors perceive themselves as "damaged" and thus not worthy of God's love, acceptance, or mercy (Bent-Goodley & Fowler, 2006; Hall, 1995). Yet, as demonstrated in the following survivor excerpts, working through these spiritual conflicts and crises of faith often leads to altering previously held assumptions about a Higher Power as neglectful, controlling, and judgmental:

> I got happier with religion when I decided that He wasn't this all powerful thing. I mean, He's very powerful. He's amazing, but He doesn't keep everything from happening. If you think that, and then stuff happens, then you think He did it to punish you or whatever. Even though He can't keep every bad thing from happening, He was there, He hadn't abandoned me. (Chelsea, age 37, incest survivor)

> I've always believed in God, but during this turmoil, it was like God had abandoned me. And I come to find out, I come to realize God didn't abandon me, I walked away from him. So it took from my pastor, the support from my family, to help me get where I am. I still have a ways to go, and I'm not going to stop 'til I get there. (Angel, age 42, domestic violence survivor)

> I always knew that there was a God and that He had somehow let me survive. And even though it seemed like at times He had turned His back on me, I still felt like if it wasn't for God, I would be dead. I would have committed suicide and done it successfully. But my faith in God really gave me a source of strength and it just is vitally important in my life. (Jennifer, age 35, incest survivor)

> Over the last eight years, my relationship with God has waxed and waned, and I look at it as there were times when God was in my life, and there were times when alcohol was in my life. And so I had a hard time with both working in my life at the same time. But if alcohol wasn't there, God was, and if He wasn't, alcohol was there. And so, it's been through AA that I've realized that I am powerless over alcohol, that God is in control, and so I've just had this continued growth and a stronger relationship, more prayer, more meditation, and more church participation. (Trista, age 33, domestic violence survivor)

TO FORGIVE OR NOT FORGIVE

Mental health professionals often underscore how survivors are not responsible or at fault for their victimization (Bussey & Wise, 2007;

Herman, 1997; Saakvitne, Gamble, Pearlman, & Lev, 2000); yet, in the author's experience, many do indeed continue to blame themselves. Thus, it is necessary to enter into a dialogue with clients regarding how to forgive themselves whether the recrimination is justified or not. The practice of compassion and unconditional love needs to begin with survivors themselves as they work toward embracing their "broken places" with love and gentleness rather than judgment. The helper can be a catalyst for this process by asking, "Instead of your usual self-criticism and harsh judgment, what kind and accepting words, phrases, or actions could you use with yourself?" Essentially, the client is asked to extend mercy to herself as she would to others (O'Hanlon, 1999). Self-forgiveness for many survivors, as highlighted in the following quotes, includes choosing to not be destructive to self or others while moving beyond attaching their worth and identity to their victimization:

> I will never forget. There is no way I can forget. The memory is just too huge and to painful, and I cannot forget. But I do forgive. I guess it's a self-ish act, for my sake. I forgive, so I can move on. (Suria, age 35, survivor of childhood exposure to domestic violence)

> I've realized that forgiveness is letting go of my right to hurt other people. You know, because I have a right to be angry. I had a lot of right to be angry. But, I had to forgive in order to let that go, so that I couldn't hurt other people. If I didn't work on forgiving myself and the perpetrator, then it would affect my children. To me forgiveness just meant, kind of letting it go and giving it to God and realizing that it was something evil that happened to me. But that doesn't mean that's part of me. I just felt like the abuse could affect me in some positive ways. I could go and help other people. But it didn't have to affect my children. It didn't have to affect my marriage. I really don't like to be called an adult survivor. I just felt that it was something that happened to me. It wasn't a part of me. Kind of keeping it separate helps. (Shirley, age 30, incest survivor)

Many faiths embrace the concept of forgiving those who have harmed others, which is difficult for some survivors, particularly in regard to their abusers, because they feel that they are not holding them accountable for their violent acts (Bergin, 1991; Freedman & Enright, 1996; Giesbrecht & Sevcik, 2000; Hall, 1995). In the author's experience, forgiveness of one's perpetrator does not necessarily provide wholeness and resolution in the same vain as self-forgiving. It is helpful to shift self-blame to its appropriate owner, the abuser, and hold him accountable particularly as family and legal systems often fail to do so. Additionally, survivors are just in having anger about being victimized by their "loved" ones. Asking an abuser about why he chose to commit harm may explain his motives, but does not necessarily provide a resolution to one's suffering. A perpetrator owning responsibility and giving an explanation for his hurtful actions is important to healing; yet, it does not necessarily yield answers to the meaning and purpose of one's suffering or address the question of "How do I move on from what happened to me?" Additionally, inferring that one has to forgive her family assailant in order to fully heal replicates the abuse dynamics of coercion and control and narrowly defines the healing process:

> Anytime I hear anybody say you have to forgive, it's kind of like a control thing. I think the healing from incest is real different for people, so I think it's just going to take different shapes, but it narrowly defines the healing process to say you have to forgive. (Madison, age 37, incest survivor)

> From what I get like from the church, forgive is like, it's not okay what they did, but you just kind of like move on. And, I'm not ready to move on. I'm just not ready to have him [her perpetrator] part of my life. I really don't think it [religion] has helped. I have a real hard time with wondering. Because if God is so loving, then why would he continue to put me through everything? (Ann, age 25, incest survivor)

FINDING A REASON FOR BEING: BREAKING THE CYCLE OF VIOLENCE

There is much about abuse within the family that is paradoxical and thus difficult to understand. For example, Becky, age 40, who during childhood was exposed to domestic violence, asked, "Why would you beat the hell out of somebody that you love?" Nonetheless, one has choice over one's existence and with it comes the responsibility of what one will do with the hurt and suffering (Frankl, 1984). Many survivors, consequently, choose to be different from their abusers, a resolve that serves them well as they learn to live lives without hatred or malice. Additionally, they turn their struggles with adversity into a means of action to help, rather than hurt, others. The subsequent survivor excerpts underscore their commitment and responsibility for breaking the cycle of violence:

> Honestly, incest is just absolutely the most senseless thing that could happen to a human being. It cannot be condoned. And I have the responsibility

to not pass on the harm to other people. I have the responsibility to no longer be destructive to myself or other people. The sense of knowing and being and taking responsibility. I have responsibility as a human being to take care of what I know. (Lori, age 52, incest survivor)

The first time I made a real, solid, life-changing choice was when I was 8 years old, and my dad beat my mom up, and my mom beat my older brother up, and my older brother beat me up, and I beat my little brother up. This all happened like in 15 minutes. Just total insanity. Just violence to the max. When I hit my little brother in the face, I seen [sic] this brokenhearted, pain-filled look on his face, and I, at that moment in time, dropped my hand, I turned around and I walked out the front door. I made a decision in my heart that I would never hit anybody again, that I would never violate a person to the best of my knowledge for the rest of my time alive. (Sally, age 38, incest survivor)

Just as there is a purpose for life; there is a purpose for suffering and for some survivors of family violence it includes a mission to give back to others. The strengths they forge, such as courage and compassion, in regard to their adversity is thought to be of benefit to others who might be struggling to persevere. As a result, they are drawn to situations or experiences where they can make a difference. Survivors, therefore, hope that something good can come of the harm they endured; thus, they are motivated to reach out and offer understanding, faith, and support to others who have been similarly abused (Cobb, Tedeschi, Calhoun, & Cann, 2006; O'Hanlon, 1999). During the author's research process, many participants discussed how it was helpful for them to talk about what had happened to them, but what was more important was sharing their experiences in an attempt to help others. These women had a strong desire to give back to others, as evidenced in their participation in the family violence studies. Additional examples of wanting to make a difference included entering a helping profession, doing volunteer work, being an advocate for others, and/or contributing in survivor support groups:

I think, too, that coming into the field of social work just isn't on a whim. It's a real calling. It's a spiritual calling that I know that I have, and it's also a gift that I know that God's given me through all of the stuff that I've been through, to be able to take the adversity and turn that adversity into something that I can give back to somebody...God has given me an incredible gift of patience and empathy and understanding that a lot of people never get to have. (Sally, age 38, incest survivor)

We don't have degrees, but I've been to the school of hard knocks, as my mom would say. And I can talk more knowledgably about the pain and the hurt and witnessing those things than people who've read about it in books. So that's what I have to offer, and that's what I would like to be able to do. I'd like to either give talks or whatever that I could to help people. As I've finally seen, you are bigger and you come out better for what happened to you. You can blame them [abusers] all day long, but in the end, you've come out a better person, because you're still alive. And that supersedes anything else that could have happened. You're still alive and you could have been killed easily, or killed yourself many, many times. So that's what I want to contribute. I think that I have a lot to offer. (Maggie, age 45, survivor of childhood exposure to domestic violence)

I feel like I wanted to give back when I heard about this study. I felt like I wanted to give back somewhat of the things that I have been given and to help other survivors. I've often thought that one day I might write a book or something. But at this point, the way I'm giving back is through my group therapy. I just really try and help encourage other survivors. (Jennifer, age 35, incest survivor)

PARTNERS WORKING TOWARD COMMON ENDS: SPIRITUALITY, RELIGION, AND MENTAL HEALTH PRACTICE

Religion and spirituality are pervasive and beneficial aspects in many clients' lives, one with direct relevance to mental health and quality of life issues (Fry, 2001; Hodge, 2001; Pellebon & Anderson, 1999; Washington & Moxley, 2001). Resiliency research, posttraumatic growth literature, and strengths-based social work practice (refer to chapter 2) has stimulated practitioners interest in people's resources, including the spiritual dimension, and has underscored how clients' personal and environmental strengths are central to the helping process (Saleebey, 2009; Wolin & Wolin, 1993). Overlapping goals and values of mental health practice, spirituality, and religion include helping individuals to manage life's difficulties, find meaning in life, develop inner knowledge of self, form supportive networks, and provide avenues for transformation (Furman, 1994; Gotterer, 2001). Helping professionals, thus, may think of themselves as partnering with spirituality and religion in working toward common ends.

  Psychosocial assessments, traditionally, involve clients' religious and spiritual involvement as possible resources to be tapped into on behalf of their well-being. For example, in Appendix B the "Person Centered Strengths Assessment" includes questions such as: How important is religion, church, or spirituality in your life? Would you like to strengthen your spiritual life? Additional probes of the past (e.g., Have you ever had or followed religious or spiritual beliefs and practice?); present (e.g., Do you have any spiritual or religious figures or activities that you think would be helpful to you in this situation?), and future (e.g., What would you like to do in the future in regard to spiritual or religious involvement or activities?) may also assist clients in uncovering spiritual solutions to help with their current problems (O'Hanlon, 1999). Such assessment instruments also provide fruitful information regarding resources for clients to draw upon to find meaning in what was thought to be meaningless (e.g., suffering).

Helping professionals who work within clients' spiritual schemas allows for individuals to find meaning in suffering and, thus, an avenue for psychological growth. However, if practitioners operate more within their own personal/professional schemas, such as viewing spirituality as only connected to an organized religion or theism, then they risk minimizing or discarding significant client content that does not fit that definition. For example, some survivors' relationship with a God or a Higher Power is troubled or nonexistent; yet, they do have unity with a transcendent force. A continued dialogue, then, regarding the client's relationship with a Higher Power would be insensitive and thoughtless; consequently, exploring other spiritual constructs that capture what is "beyond the self" would be more fruitful. For instance, survivors may connect more with the idea of a Higher Self: one that knows the essence of who a person is without all of the defenses (e.g., distrust, fear) and images (e.g., damaged) one has created. Thus, the Higher Self is both transcendent and a part of the person. Essentially, a person is connecting to beyond what can be seen, heard, or touched; thus moving into a deeper experience of one's true self. As one of the author's clients fittingly stated upon a conversation regarding her Higher Self, "So in avoiding life experiences I'm avoiding my true self. So when I don't want to try something new or different, I'm dodging my true self." "Fear arises when we believe we will not be strong enough to handle the pain we will be given" (Muller, 1993, p. 25). Yet, the Higher Self knows that the darkness will pass and again there will be light. Consequently, rising above one's self requires approaching one's fears (e.g., hope, trust, love, peace) and accepting that whatever the future brings forth can be handled. The Higher Self, then, ultimately has the answers for the "why" of suffering, a reason for being, and how to fulfill one's needs of love, compassion, acceptance, and inner peace (O'Hanlon, 1999).

Additionally, clients may draw upon religious beliefs and doctrines to put their suffering into a meaningful framework. Yet, helping professionals may perceive organized, dogmatic religion as being harmful to clients as extreme religious beliefs have contributed to social injustice and inequality, such as religious precepts used to justify child abuse, the subjugation of women, and the condemnation of homosexual behavior (Asher, 2001; Bergin, 1991). Additional professional obstacles when dialoguing with clients about the purpose of religion in their life, include a lack of experience and knowledge in such matters, being uncomfortable in one's own beliefs, limitations of one's professional code of ethics, and restrictions by an individual's organization (e.g., separation of church and state). Consequently, as underscored in the following survivor's quote, conversations regarding religion are preempted by practitioners and thus minimized as a possible client resource for strength, support, and meaning:

> Never say that faith isn't the answer. I had counselors telling me that my faith wouldn't get me through. I had counselors telling me that my religion wasn't going to save me, and I can look back, and that's what did save me. It was my church community; it was these people at "Women to Women." They are all Christian-based women who have been through this [domestic violence] and have come to know the Lord through these situations. People say that He's not around. I always thought God had abandoned me. When I look back, He was right there by my side every step of the way. He put people in my path that He knew I would need to strengthen me, to guide me, before I even did. And that's the advice I would give to counselors is just don't put faith and religion in a box because sometimes that is the greatest blessing. I mean, it was like divine intervention that me and my daughter got out of our situation. (Daisey, age 31, domestic violence survivor)

Mental health practitioners can assist survivors of family violence in reflecting and construing meaning from their victimization experiences through providing a safe place for them to explore their spiritual beliefs and values (Gillum et al., 2006). Often clients feel despair not because of their suffering, but because of the struggle to find meaning for their suffering (Frankl, 1984). The human desire to find meaning is a primary motivational force for most individuals. Thus, helping professionals need to carefully listen rather than avoid individuals' stories of suffering to uncover meaning potentials. Using narrative therapy (as discussed in chapter 6) can help practitioners focus on the client's presenting problems along with assessing their spiritual perspectives. The following questions may be used to identify any dominant themes that emerge in relationship to spiritual issues, including clients' views on the meaning and purpose of their suffering:

- What sustains you? What keeps you going in troubling times?
- Have you ever felt connected to something beyond yourself (e.g., a Higher Self, a Higher Power or God, nature, humanity, or the universe)? How does this connection give you a sense of meaning and/or purpose in life?
- What are the lessons learned from enduring suffering in regard to positive changes in yourself, relationships with others, and the beyond (e.g., a Higher Self, a Higher Power or God, nature, humanity, or the universe)?
- How, if any, have you found meaning in your suffering?
- How, if any, does your suffering provide you with a greater life purpose (e.g., breaking the cycle of violence, wanting to make a difference for others)?
- What is the legacy you want to leave? How can you start making your legacy happen?

SUMMARY

For the survivors in the author's research, "the places in the heart that came to be" as a result of their suffering included: wholeness, acceptance, courage, patience, honesty, faith, hope, unity, generosity, and compassion. Spirituality for them ultimately involved connecting with a Higher Power that provided a sense of meaning and reason for being. "To live is to suffer, to survive is to find meaning in the suffering" (Frankl, 1984, p. 11). For these women, their understanding of their suffering and their responses to it developed over time. Their desire to act on that knowledge was associated with wanting to make a difference in the lives of others similarly harmed by family violence. Thus, answering the "why" of suffering allowed these survivors to not only experience psychological relief but to develop a greater life purpose.

8   Recommendations of Survivors of Violence to Other Survivors

This chapter provides advice from participants in the author's research and exemplifies their desire to give back to other survivors. These women are committed to making a difference for those who are suffering and hope that their advice will help individuals believe that their lives can improve. This points to the essence of their conversion of pain to compassion, rooted in their process of gaining understanding and resolution. The participants' 10 recommendations reflect the ups and downs of their own healing experiences. Their hard-earned wisdom provides a source of support to be drawn upon for other survivors. Thus, mental health practitioners are encouraged to share this chapter with survivors of family violence as it underscores that no one is doomed by the past and that each of us possesses the right and the ability to make our own choices and, therefore, destinies no matter what has come before.

Lesson One: Hold on to Hope, Life Does Get Better

Participants want survivors to understand the importance of persevering in the healing process. They know what it is like to feel as if one's life will never get better, but they are proof that it ultimately does. In fact, the majority of participants have reached a point where their past trauma is no longer a dominating issue in their lives. They understand that suffering does not have to be useless as it can further develop self-awareness and compassion. These women do have struggles; however, they are now able to accept their limitations as part of the human experience rather than the legacy of an abused person. Essentially, life does knock them down on occasion but they are able to bounce back and carry on. Because they have lived it, participants know that it is possible to not only endure but to prevail in ways that are hard to imagine, particularly at the beginning of one's healing journey. Participants highlight that enduring the violence itself is a much greater challenge than stepping out of the darkness and embracing a hopeful attitude.

> Based on my experiences, I would say, even though sometimes it looks very bleak and you see no way out, there's always a glimmer of hope, and you've got to continue to persevere and know that you will get through it even though it seems like it's endless. I guess I've always had this innate sense of wanting to survive. And I think what has really helped me is that I've felt like the perpetrators would be winning if I gave up. And I don't want to give them that satisfaction. (Jennifer, age 35, incest survivor)

> You just have to encourage yourself half the time; you can't expect people to come up and encourage you. You have to just know that you deserve better, know that you can get better or you can do better, and feel it in your heart. If you believe it's so then it will be so. That's the best thing I can say. Because when you do everything with love in your heart then you know you're gonna do what is right. (Corinthia, age 46, survivor of childhood exposure to domestic violence)

> There is hope. And it does get better. There is a light at the end of the dark tunnel. And I am so much happier now, and I would never be where I was at right now if I had stayed in that [abusive] relationship. It's like you're a robot when you're in that position and you're always on egg shells and you're never able to relax, to just feel what it's like to relax; and it's amazing to just chop off your hair or just not vacuum or just not make your bed when you've been made to do all these things like a robot for years. And so, there is hope. I'm not saying that you're not gonna struggle because I still struggle daily; but it gets better. (Katie, age 30, domestic violence survivor)

Lesson Two: Choose to Heal

Participants stress the importance of moving toward healing rather than remaining "stuck" in suffering. They recognize there is a choice in one's healing. To be miserable is not comfortable; however, one may remain "stuck" out of despair, doubt, and fear that her life can improve. The dichotomy for survivors often includes feeling powerless over their circumstances; yet, also feeling responsible for everything that goes wrong. Consequently, the past serves as a catalyst for one's present misery as it continues to shape one's actions, thoughts, and feelings. Thus, survivors end up with a high tolerance for suffering and an attachment with this state of being. Yet, despite these struggles, survivors are not necessarily doomed to repeat the mistakes of the past. As underscored in the following participants' quotes, such struggles provide building blocks for the future. As a result, one has the ability to shape her current reality, including choosing to heal rather than relinquish herself to a victim identity.

> Believe in yourself. The other thing is to be willing to look at the fact that you have a choice to stay stuck or have a better life. There is a life that can be so much better and not be stuck in that place. There is a choice. We don't have to be attached to it and let it own us. (Holly, age 58, incest survivor)

> I would say sometimes we have to let go because a lot of times we hold on to all this stuff and it's like you sit around and create your own pity party. Everybody has had something. Trust me, we all hurt. But now how do you get over it? It's time to wise up and say, "I'm not gonna do that anymore." You have to make some solid decisions to not accept that pain. You've got to let go, I'm not saying that I'm 100% just perfectly healed. I'm not. I'm still human, and I've still got feelings and emotions but I don't let it consume me. And that's what I'm saying. Don't let it consume you. Just know that there is always tomorrow. (Corinthia, age 46, survivor of childhood exposure to domestic violence)

> It's like you have to be willing to not be a victim and be suffering all the time. That took me a long time to really own that. I can make myself miserable all the time, but to choose not to do that, and for me now not to have to be in that stuff all the time and know that that's okay. It's okay to be feeling better. It's okay to have good days. You don't have to stay stuck. (Em, age 37, incest survivor)

Lesson Three: Find Meaning and Purpose in the Suffering

As addressed in chapter 7, it is possible for survivors of family violence to find meaning and purpose in the midst of their suffering. As a result of their struggles to heal, participants were more able to appreciate their strengths, to be empathic to others' victimization, to recognize commonalities in suffering, and to develop a reason for being. In essence, they learned that everyone endures pain, albeit in different doses, and to be fully human is to encompass all life experiences including the ones that hurt, sadden, and dishearten. In doing so, one becomes more whole and thus more able to transform suffering into gains that can benefit self and others. An important connection for the majority of participants was their relationship to God or a Higher Power to guide them through their suffering. Additionally, this spiritual relationship helped these women see their life purpose in a different light, including giving back to others who are suffering.

> I've always believed that things happen for a reason. I mean, what doesn't kill you always makes you stronger, that's just what I think. I've been through a lot. I've been through things that a lot of people can't make it through, and I ask myself, how can I be so forgiving to people for what they've done to me, and how did I manage to make it this far? And the only answer that I come up with is by the grace of God; I don't know how else to explain it. (Jill, age 32, domestic violence survivor)

> And my spirituality has evolved over time. It had to evolve, and I think that that was where the 12 steps came in really helpful. It evolved from the fire and brimstone sin-based thing to drop all of the religious dogma about everything and figure out what is the meaning of life. Without all the other bullshit around, you know? I don't think that if I couldn't get in touch with that spiritual place, I would be able to do what I do [social worker]. I don't think I would be able to get up, I don't think I would be able to be effective. (Becky, age 40, survivor of childhood exposure to domestic violence)

> I've always been what I would consider a person of faith. I believe in God. Without Him we wouldn't be here. So there is a God, and have faith in Him, and He will help you through. There's always obstacles that are put in our way. We have to face those obstacles, and when there's a closed door, there's always another one to open, and things happen for a reason. (Susie, age 56, domestic violence survivor)

Lesson Four: Break the Silence, Heal the Hurt

Participants broke their silence regarding their victimization and in doing so found the help, connection, and encouragement necessary to heal from their experiences. These women learned that building a life in spite of, or around, silence can become overwhelming and pervasive.

Essentially, their silence kept them isolated in their misery. Therefore, telling someone about their victimization was a courageous act that often provided emotional relief along with a connection to others similarly hurt. Yet, not everyone can bear witness to stories of suffering and thus may minimize or avoid it when survivors choose to break the silence. In the participants' experience, this does not necessarily mean people do not care; instead, they just cannot face the human cruelty that was perpetrated. Thus, these women stress that survivors have to keep reaching out to find those people who are safe, accepting, and trustworthy to support them as they step into and walk through their suffering. Telling someone dispels the shame, acknowledges the truth of what happened, and may ultimately unite one with other survivors who also no longer suffer in silence.

> I think advice for other people, is find somebody that believes in you, and you trust them, and talk about it. Because keeping it inside doesn't help anybody at all. (Becky, age 50, domestic violence survivor)

> Don't hide it. Remember and learn from it. Talk with your friends probably they've went through it. There's probably a lot more that went through it than have not went through it at some point or another, on a different level. It seems like if they've gone through anything even close, they can relate with you, talk with you, and it helps. I've never known so many people that went through problems. But you know what, it all winds up being just about the same boat at some point or another. Maybe it's they didn't get abused physically, maybe it was just mentally. You're dumb, you're stupid, you're a hillbilly, you're fat, you're skinny, you're ugly, you're tall or short, you know? It helps to talk to somebody else who can relate. (Diane, age 27, survivor of childhood exposure to domestic violence)

> I really think a lot of it is just admitting it, or realizing it, and then talking about it, whether it's just sitting around in a group of friends talking about it or something. But I think sometimes the more you do talk about it, the more you can kind of come to grips with it and hopefully deal with it or that you could go and get more help if you needed to. So, I think the first thing is just talking about it with somebody that you trust. (Deb, age 56, survivor of childhood exposure to domestic violence)

Lesson Five: Cultivate Your Support Systems

Participants encourage survivors to not isolate themselves and to risk reaching out to others to ease their burdens. The first step toward empowering oneself is asking for help and breaking the silence regarding one's victimization. These women underscore how not all responses may be immediate or helpful; yet, if one perseveres, each survivor will find the support necessary for recovery. Participants talked about the significance of individuals in their lives who offered encouragement, direction, and affirmation during their healing journeys. They renewed or developed relationships with natural helping networks such as friends, family, co-workers, and neighbors who helped them to understand a world without abuse. Additionally, these connections often led them to formal resources such as clergy, attorneys, health and mental health care providers. Participants highlight how survivors do not need to suffer alone because as they seek out help they will find compassionate people who will accompany them in discovering the violence-free life they deserve.

> If I hadn't had people support me, I never would have made it. I've got like a couple of really good friends that put up with me, and if they hadn't been there, I don't think I would have made it . . . You have to have a support system. If you don't have a support system, forget it. (Lola, age 40, incest survivor)

> I think my advice would be that it's really up to your personal relationships, to just pour out some of the things inside of yourself because if you just keep talking to yourself in your mind—and I talk to myself a lot in my mind—you get to the point where you're just running around that same circle; and it's not until you allow yourself to enter into other deep and loving relationships that that circle gets bigger and you can actually sort through some of that stuff. And it's definitely a process that takes time. I just don't think that there is any worldly substitute for allowing a close personal relationship to help with your self-development. Actually that would be my advice, that you need some of those relationships in your life. (Heather, age 37, survivor of childhood exposure to domestic violence)

> Find those people who are safe and cultivate them. I cultivated that support because I needed it around me. And I think that to do that and not wait for them to come to you and to really cultivate it. Talk to people who are really truthfully going to be safe for you. Learn how to be your own protector. (Chelsea, age 37, incest survivor)

> Probably asking for help is one of the hardest things a person can do, but it's one of the best things a person can do. 'Cause you can find out that there's something else out there and that you don't have to hurt all the time. You don't have to be demeaned in various ways. You don't have to be in the hospital with a broken arm and say you fell down the stairs. There is another way to live and they can help you find that way to live and show you how to live. (Ruby, age 24, domestic violence survivor)

Lesson Six: Seek Professional Help if Necessary

Participants thought counseling was invaluable in helping them address their family violence experiences. However, they also caution survivors to find a competent therapist in the area of trauma. They want to affirm that "good" help is available and to keep looking for the right person who is safe, accepting, trustworthy, and knowledgeable. Additionally, several participants recommended joining survivor support or therapy groups because they provide a sense of connection, affirmation, and validation of one's experiences. Groups also provide an opportunity for one to give back through offering advice and support to others.

> There is nothing that caring people can do like a qualified professional. I have lots of people who love me and care about me, but all the love and all the caring in the world didn't help me get through all those shoeboxes I'd put away. And to really know yourself and be comfortable with who you are, you've got to empty all those out. It's a lot of baggage, and you just can't carry it around forever. I think it's absolutely essential that you spend a long, long time with a good counselor that you trust. There are so many things that I had put in a shoebox, tied a nice string on top of, opened the closet door, put it on the top shelf of the closet, and closed the door, and didn't process, didn't want to deal with, didn't want to think about, didn't want to remember, and I had no idea how those things affected me until a crisis in my life made it necessary for me to go digging. I don't think it's anything that you can overcome alone. I think it takes a qualified professional to help you get through that. (Donna, age 45, survivor of childhood exposure to domestic violence)

> Counseling, I think, is very, very, very important. I think that without knowledge and without understanding what happened, people tend to repeat the same pattern over and over and I've seen that so many times. So, I would think one of my biggest things I would say to people is seek help and that's probably my biggest thing because really people don't know. I mean, they just don't know and they don't understand, and sometimes it takes somebody wiser than you to gain that understanding. (Melinda, age 35, survivor of childhood exposure to domestic violence)

> I think, for me, some of the important things that kept me goin' was believing that I was worth it. Believing it when other people told me that or just innately drawing on that knowledge that I was worth it. And that there was good help out there. When I finally connected with that person that felt really safe to me, felt really right to me, then I was able to do the work, and something kept me goin' during that time. And for me it was to keep persevering and keep going because I wanted to live differently. Perseverance is a good trait and an important trait. It's like you got your bayonet and your

war fatigues on, and you just keep goin' through the terrain until you find it. (Becci, age 34, incest survivor)

I share the same thing in my group. Because many of them will say, "I can't wait until I get to where you are." What they don't realize is that, it's not going to just happen. That's what I tell them, and I know they don't want to hear it, but it doesn't just happen. And they may not get to where I'm at. They've got to want it, for one thing. A lot of them in there don't seem like they do. They make excuses..."Oh, he beats me with a 2 x 4, but I love him." I don't understand that. I'll tell them that. I don't understand it. (Trish, age 37, survivor of childhood exposure to domestic violence)

Lesson Seven: Accept and Let Go of the Past

An important component to participants' healing process included acknowledging the realities of their victimization and accepting the fact that what happened to them could not be changed. Generally not experienced as a moment of epiphany, the path to a new consciousness and better life began for these women with the need for closure and the freedom to focus on the future rather then the past. Thus, living a life free of violence included no longer repeating a history of self-destruction or involvement in harmful relationships. The simple, yet complex, act of coming to accept the past and the life they were given was a necessary step toward participants' transformation.

I have looked forward to getting better and better, and not to look back and dwell on the past because it doesn't get you anywhere. That was her [counselor] strong words of advice to me, and I have really lived by those words, actually, just to keep on plugging ahead and to know that you are worth something and no matter what someone else tells you that you are worthy and that you are an individual person and you are able to make your own decisions and know that they are right, even if someone else disagrees with you. (Sally, age 64, domestic violence survivor)

Today, I can honestly say my feelings, my emotions, I don't let the past control me anymore. When you get those flashbacks from the past, you've just got to tell yourself, "No, you're not going to steal my joy. No, you're not gonna take away this moment." (Daisey, age 31, domestic violence survivor)

A lot of people think that this is their destiny, that they're meant to go down the same path because it's what they're use to. They're meant to be an alcoholic. They're gonna hit people, they're gonna abuse people because it's instilled in them. So, my advice to others is you don't have to go down that same road that you've been on. You've gotta try something different. Just don't think you have to follow in those footsteps. You have choices. There is help out there. (Lea, age 48, survivor of childhood exposure to domestic violence)

When you get out of it [abusive relationship], it's miserable. It's real miserable, you think about going back, but it gets better. Get a teddy bear, get a doll, hug the doll. And don't jump into another relationship. You set yourself up for another fall. Because it's dangerous, 'cause the guys you end up attracting are the guys like the guy that you left, if not worse. (Thelma, age 37, domestic violence survivor)

Cope in whatever way you can and get past it and just learn from the experience and try not to perpetuate it in the future I guess would be a huge piece of advice that I would give. Knowing what you know, having been through it, just don't do it again. Don't let it happen again. (Danielle, age 37, survivor of childhood exposure to domestic violence)

Lesson Eight: Rise Above Shame

As the participants became more aware of what happened to them, they also became more conscious of their shame. These women recognize that individuals may have gotten messages from their abusers or significant others that blamed them for the violence. Yet, they want to raise survivors' awareness that those messages were distorted and inaccurate. Participants want other survivors to know that one does not have to carry the shame for the violent acts committed by their perpetrators. Thus, these women believe that letting go of blaming oneself through assigning responsibility to their abusers is essential in moving forward in one's healing process.

A lot of people are ashamed about what happened, but when you realize it's not you that caused it [domestic violence], there's nothing to be ashamed of, then you realize "I'm okay. It wasn't me. I have nothing to be ashamed of. I overcame." You can overcome, too. You rely on your strengths, your values, your core, you never lose sight of that, because that's what's going to bring you through it all. That's what it's about, and a lot of women need to know that you're okay, it wasn't you. (Daisey, age 31, domestic violence survivor)

The main advice I can give is if you are in a [domestic violence] relationship, realize that no matter what he says it is not your fault. You are not the one to cause them to lose their temper. Don't let them put the blame on you, because maybe you have said something wrong to set it off, but for them losing their temper there is no excuse. And to get to the point I am now don't close your future off. Don't just back down from your future. Don't hide yourself. Because there's other ways in this world to be safe that you don't have to lock yourself away. (Angel, age 42, domestic violence survivor)

Try and remember that it's not your fault, even though it feels like it and you got those messages from long ago but they're not valid. And, one thing that keeps me going is to always remember that I'm not gonna let my dad [perpetrator] win. I'm gonna be the one who wins. (Tracy, age 44, incest survivor)

They [batterers] make you think that they are the only person there for you, and that no one else will understand you as well as they do. And they bring you down. They let you know that you're nobody, and that you're nothing, and get you down so low that you can't see the top. But it's all what that man has done to you. It's not you. You are not the lowest life form on earth like he likes to make you think you are. All you have to do is have some support. These men hold you down and grasp you so tight that there's no way to get out of it without help. Whether it be from the law, from your parents, from anybody. From a complete stranger, go banging on doors. (Cher, age 24, domestic violence survivor)

Lesson Nine: Honor Your Strength, Courage, and Determination

Participants inevitably experienced the trials and tribulations of healing. Even though these women endured trauma, they did not give up on themselves or their survival. They highlight that prevailing over adversity provided sources of strength, particularly tenacity, courage, and resourcefulness. These women lay claim to the dignity and honor of emerging stronger for having endured suffering. Throughout their healing process, participants drew upon these survival strengths to face the challenges of reshaping their lives. Consequently, they want other survivors to recognize their strengths and honor the courage that evolves from enduring and ultimately overcoming adversity.

It does make you a survivor and things that come along in your life that you don't think you can handle, you can. Because you've survived something much greater than what that challenge may be. (Kathleen, age 26, incest survivor)

The pain, I say, is like wisdom coming against our will. We can take from it and obtain strength, optimism, courage, like I did, proactivity, spirituality, humor, altruism, we want to give back, and love, and thus transform them into meaningful experiences. I also ask them not to look at themselves as victims, because when you emerge from it, you're actually a survivor. (Suria, age 35, survivor of childhood exposure to domestic violence)

Woman to woman support is so important. I guess I would say to other incest survivors there is hope when we talk about it with each other and care about each other and help each other find healing and affirmation, the gifts that we have to give each other and to society in general, because we have survived, and we can bring all of that to a world that has been raped and tortured and abused. (Rosie, age 56, incest survivor)

Lesson Ten: Turn Your Struggles into Helping Others

Not only a source of pride but a blueprint for their future, participants express determination for a better life for themselves and for other survivors. They understand the devastating effects of family violence and, thus, are committed to helping those who may be struggling in their healing process. These women learned that facing their suffering allowed them to gain wisdom, tolerance, and compassion. Additionally, participants found that giving back to others offered renewal of self and resolution of anguish.

I do feel the need to pay it forward. I've been helped by a lot of people in their own different ways. I am not involved in any organized activity, but I do help all who come my way. I don't memorize who I've helped or how I've helped, but I certainly try my best to do what I can. (Suria, age 35, survivor of childhood exposure to domestic violence)

You have to overcome it [suffering]. You have to put it to use. You have to take what you've learned and put it in your everyday life, going forward is more important, because I think so many people focus on survival—that's the baseline. You have to get to the point where you say, "Okay, I survived it, but now how do you overcome it and then put it into some positive aspects in your life to move forward." And they become a source of strength instead of what feeling like right now a source of weakness. This is very empowering. (Jane, age 37, incest survivor)

SUMMARY

In this chapter, participants in the author's research shared their moments of triumph along with the challenges they faced over time. These women held onto the belief that they deserved a better life and were worth the battle to obtain it. They know the depth and reality of what they have experienced in their healing journeys and thus are aptly equipped to give advice to other survivors. Further, it is possible that these 10 lessons will help other survivors to look toward the future, armed with the knowledge, motivation, and tools needed to make informed decisions and create self and life according to these enhanced understandings, values, and perspectives.

9   Recommendations of Survivors of Violence to Helping Professionals

This chapter presents survivors' recommendations (from participants in the author's family violence research) for building therapeutic rapport and improving mental health practice. These women note how working through one's trauma requires a safe, accepting, and trustworthy therapeutic environment. Fostering a positive rapport between the client and helper provides the foundation for the counseling process. Unfortunately, for several participants their suffering was exacerbated by unsupportive, judgmental, and controlling mental health professionals. Therefore, these women underscore how within the therapeutic relationship one's victimization needs to be validated without taking away the survivor's power. Participants' seven suggestions center on supporting and honoring client strengths, competencies, aspirations, expertise and self-determination. They also want to raise awareness of negative mental health influences (e.g., managed care) that often thwart the healing process and risk recapitulating the power imbalance of family violence within the worker-client relationship. Ultimately, participants hope that their advice may prevent inadequate, inappropriate or even unethical practices from affecting other survivors reaching out for help and services.

Lesson One: Support Client Strengths, Competencies, and Resourcefulness

Participants recommend that mental health professionals not treat survivors as people who are "different" or "damaged." They already feel

143

stigmatized because of their family violence experiences so they do not need additional judgment from helping professionals. When practitioners view clients as "different" and "damaged" then it is more difficult to see survivors' strengths and to trust that they know what is best for them. Additionally, many helpers lack the ability to understand the full meaning of family violence and its consequences. For instance, participants' mental health experiences often included practitioners who interpreted their pain and hurt as evidence of pathology. Consequently, their resourcefulness was frequently minimized, invalidated, or ignored during the helping process.

> These people I babysat for I was really close with the mom. I said [to the therapist], "Well, I'm thinkin' about telling her about what happened [childhood incest]." And my counselor said, "Don't tell her." She said, "Because she may think you're doing something to her kids." I would say if they [survivors] want to talk about it, don't tell them not to. She goes, "Don't tell her until you've stopped babysitting for the kids." And that's what kind of put in my mind, "Well, people are going to think I'm doing this [to kids] or I'll do this to my kids." (Ann, age 25, incest survivor)

Participants underscore how the professional role is to nourish, encourage, assist, support and stimulate the strengths within clients. The life experiences of survivors provide numerous examples of their resourcefulness; yet, they may need help rediscovering such assets as their self-concepts are regularly clouded with problems, failures, and missteps.

> Have the skills to guide them [survivors] through the pain. And have the skills to help them come to an understanding about what that pain means and look at the strengths that they bring with them from that pain, so they can put that pain to rest. It's not all of who they are, but it also isn't all of the ugly—that there was something positive that came out of that ocean of pain, and take that and let that be the seed that you plant and let it grow. (Jackie, age 45, incest survivor)

> Battered women really do have endurance. However, we don't realize that we do, because someone else told us that we didn't have it, but we do have it. It's just that we have to discover that. We have to know deep inside our hearts that we can move along and we can do it without a man's help. I grew up in a society where women were always subservient to men, and I think that was a lot of the problems that I had during my lifetime. Not until I got older did I realize that there are things that women can do without men, and do it just as well if not better. And I think that professionals have

to realize that we do have endurance. We just don't realize that we have it. (Sally, age 64, domestic violence survivor)

Lesson Two: Listen, Accept, and Honor Stories of Suffering

Participants found that when they explicitly brought up their victimization experiences some professionals negatively responded by: ignoring or "forgetting" that it had been mentioned; minimizing its significance in relationship to current problems, or changing the subject. Additionally, a few of their counseling experiences included helpers who blamed them for the abuse. These women, therefore, stress the importance of creating a safe, accepting, and respectful space for survivors to tell their stories of victimization. Disclosure is difficult for many survivors as they fear their experiences will be minimized or ignored. Thus, acknowledging the significance of family violence once the client brings it up is crucial to the therapeutic relationship. If the professional communicates openness and acceptance when the survivor breaks her silence, sharing the details of her story is more likely to follow.

> I had determined very early on in the relationship with the psychiatrist—he had his own agenda, and it wasn't mine, and it wasn't addressing what was wrong with me. And when I would broach a subject that was coming close to what was bothering me, he would go off on another tangent. Evidently, he was more uncomfortable with it [incest] than I was, because I desperately wanted to do well. (Kelly, age 58, incest survivor)

> As far as the things that have gotten in the way of my recovery, it's been about lousy therapists. I had started seeing this therapist. He did some work on anger with me, and I told him about the sexual abuse, I think it was the first time I saw him, and his question was, "Well did any intercourse take place?" I said, "No." And that was it. I needed to talk about my childhood with him. I tried to do that, and it was like he didn't help me do it, so it kind of petered out after awhile. (Pan, age 45, incest survivor)

> I think the one thing that never, ever, ever needs to be asked is, "Why did you stay with him [the batterer]?" Because that blames the person who already knows that they shouldn't have stayed. Ask questions that don't leave the person feeling more defeated, because if you're going to ask things that are condescending in any kind of way, as a person who's gone through it, some of these questions can feel very condescending. Then you start the whole process again of covering it up. "Well, it wasn't that bad." And so ask

questions, but ask in a way that's not condescending. (Lou, age 50, domestic violence survivor)

I've had some therapists that I went to once and never went back. Because the minute I feel that blame is being placed on me, they're not doing their jobs, and they're not being effective to me, and I'm not wasting my time. But I know for other women who maybe it's the first time they've gone to a therapist, they don't know; and so, those kind of therapists can be more harm than good, and so I think if women are seeking counseling and they go to a therapist and they leave there feeling worse than they did when they walked in the door, don't go back. Don't go back, 'cause it's not your fault. There is nothing that you did wrong to make this abuse occur. They think, "They're a therapist, they're gonna help me. They got a degree. I'll keep going back." Well, it does more harm than good. (Katie, age 30, domestic violence survivor)

Participants' narrative construction reflected attempts to understand the purpose and meaning of their lives as they sought answers for the "why" of suffering. Pursuing spiritual answers allowed several of these women to come to terms with their suffering, including "God's plan" for them to become stronger, wiser, and more compassionate.

However, when these women broached spirituality as a source of support, self-worth, and a reason for being, helpers often minimized or inadequately addressed the topic. Their mental health experiences highlight how professionals may fail to explicitly address spirituality and keep it as a subject of discussion in their work with clients.

Even though my self-esteem was low, there was still a part of me that knew that somebody loved me and that somebody was God, and even if I couldn't feel Him or see Him or touch Him, it still just kept a little spark, to keep me going, to give my life purpose, even when it felt like everything was really black. (Erika, age 38, incest survivor)

Lesson Three: Convey an Outlook of Hope and Possibility

Participants want to caution helpers from casting a shadow (from the past) on survivors' abilities to survive, persevere, and eventually thrive. Thus, they advise mental health practitioners to let clients know that healing can occur for anyone regardless of one's history. These women learned firsthand how acquiring a life-affirming attitude and being possibility-focused allowed them to grasp on to hope and believe their lives could get better. Participants know based on the trials and tribulations of their healing journeys that change is happening all the time as individuals are always "in process". In other words, nothing ever happens the same exact way in the same exact manner even with what may be considered a "setback". These women want helpers to understand the strength and courage it takes for clients to show-up for services, as in their case it often was six months (or more) of sessions before they "wanted" to come to therapy. They know that working with survivors can be frustrating as progress seems slow or nonexistent. Yet, when a survivor attends her counseling appointments, she is already "in process" of change. The healing flow is unpredictable and taking "breaks" from addressing the trauma was part of participants' therapeutic process. Additionally, these women highlight the necessity for helpers to be patient and not rush into "fixing" survivors; instead, they recommend providing them with hope and reassurance that they will discover the answers for "fixing" themselves.

> I'd say [to counselors] don't give up. That's the main one. Don't give up, because anything you can do is going to be appreciated in the long run, I know it was for me, with the professional help that I was able to receive. Don't give up, no matter what you do, because the clients you have in the long run are going to appreciate you even more. (Angel, age 42, domestic violence survivor)

> Whoever works with survivors needs to be really patient and tolerant. And I know it's not always easy. I felt like some therapists I've had in the past wanted me to really move faster than I was ready to move or they felt like I was just dragging my feet on purpose. And I felt like one therapist that she was very pushy. She would show me videos to try to trigger things with me and that wasn't helpful either. (Abby, age 40, incest survivor)

> Some of the things that helped me, where I just go at my pace, taking my steps, no matter how small, and what I often sensed with counselors was that you've got to do a certain amount of work in a counseling session. But I remember this one she was so busy trying to fix things for me, I had one session with her, and she was like, "Have you tried this and have you tried that?" And I remember she was interning, and she really wanted to work with me, and it would have been free, but I remember telling the agency, "I am not coming back." They asked, "Would you at least let us know why, so we can help her [the counselor] understand?" I said, "Because she's too busy trying to fix me. I don't think I need fixing. I want to process things, I want to work through things, and I don't want simple answers. There are no simple answers to these things." (Pearl, age 50, domestic violence survivor)

Lesson Four: Communicate Empathy, Acceptance, and Compassion

Participants advise helpers to identify with clients in some way as it shows a willingness to understand the worlds they navigate in and thus allows for accompanying them in their healing journeys. These women caution that taking an "all knowing I'm the expert" professional stance revolves more around a need to fix rather understand the client. Instead, mental health practitioners who communicate an empathic attitude are more likely to open up opportunities to align with clients' perspectives, skills, and experiences. Consequently, they recommend professionals who observe from within the relationship rather than outside of it. Participants suggest letting go of professional expectations, assumptions, and the desire to judge a person's behavior/motives as this will allow for accepting the client as the expert regarding her ideas, feelings, and memories. Additionally, these women underscore the necessity for professionals to convey compassion through bearing witness to clients' suffering and expressing a desire to relieve it. Ultimately, participants found that working with empathic, accepting, and compassionate mental health professionals significantly helped to decrease the effects of betrayal and harm experienced as a result of family violence.

> If you [counselor] can't identify in some way with the person that you're trying to help, you can't help them. It's just impossible. Because you'll end up making them feel less than whole, not worthy, more ashamed, wanting to hide it more, ostracized. And I just know that that doesn't work. So that's my advice, whether it's children or adults, if you're going to try to work with them, you have to be able to identify with them in some way, and I can absolutely guarantee you that if a therapist will go outside himself just for a moment, he will find one thing that he has in common with that person, and that is true for everybody on earth. You'll have at least one thing in common with that person. And if you can tap into that one thing, you're golden, and if you can't, you might as well just not even start. (Maggie, age 45, survivor of childhood exposure to domestic violence)

> She [counselor] never judges. She always encourages me. I think that's got to be number one. Never judging or acting disappointed in us, I know how hard it is to leave them [abusers], and it's frustrating, knowing what I know now, to see someone that might go back to stay with them, but I totally understand why. There are so many reasons. But I think the not judging us and just being a positive support system is the way to be. (Lisa, age 46, domestic violence survivor)

I would recommend that they [counselors] really need to know that it's very important for a survivor to feel compassion and survivors naturally feel like they're different from other people, and it helps when somebody just takes time to really listen. You spend so much time fighting so many different things in the course of your life that it's nice to know that there is someone who really cares. (Jennifer, age 35, incest survivor)

Lesson Five: Demonstrate Humility

Participants recommend eliminating professional arrogance that one knows more and thus is superior to the client. Demonstrating humility by mental health practitioners may be more difficult for those who believe survivors are too "damaged" to know the reality of their situations. Consequently, an agenda that takes into account the worker's rather than the client's experiences is more likely to occur. A collaborative helping relationship, on the other hand, involves drawing equally from the knowledge and expertise of both the client and the professional. In other words, building therapeutic rapport is a two-way street where the worker and client can both learn from each other. Furthermore, acknowledging professional limitations and errors demonstrates one's humanness and can enhance the clinical relationship rather than detract from it.

Participants also want to caution helpers that it is not effective to tell clients, "You're the expert" without also offering professional guidance, input, or information. Obviously, professionals do not need to discard their background, skills, or knowledge; in fact, this expertise is essential in helping and supporting clients in their healing journeys. These women highlight how receiving professional input and advice created additional ways of understanding themselves and their situations. Thus, participants emphasize that both the professional and the client's expertise are crucially important in guiding the helping process.

I think they [counselors] should always be careful, consider the other person, and not ever be condescending or disrespectful to another person, well, for one thing you should never do that anyway, but for another thing, if you do that to someone who's experienced this [family violence], it's just gonna perpetuate how they feel about themselves. And you should always elevate the other person. 'Cause I have been to some professionals who weren't that helpful and who were elevating themselves just for their sake and they weren't helping the person that they were suppose to help. (Lisa, age 50, survivor of childhood exposure to domestic violence)

Just listen. I've had a lot of people think they can help me with psychobab-
ble, and that's not what I need. I just need someone to listen and just hear
me out. I guess just make judgments lightly and I guess my main critique
is don't have a pity factor on the person that you're listening to 'cause that's
the last thing that I would want. (Kairi, age 20, survivor of childhood exposure to domestic violence)

And for providers, you just really need to remember that humans are so judgmental, and we have to categorize everything, and find a reason for everything,
and just to remember that victims are human beings, they have this complex
life and you don't have any idea. You don't have any idea what they've done,
you don't have any idea what they're doing, you just need to be completely
open to what she's [the battered woman] saying to you, because she knows
best. She knows what's happening, she knows what's going on, and if she says
to you "I can't leave" [an abusive partner] because of this, that and the other,
then she cannot leave. So your job is to do something else for her. And if she
tells you "I can't do an ex parte," then she can't, and you need to not tell her
she has to, you just need to find some other way to help her, because she
knows what she can do. That's hard as an advocate, even as someone who
has been through it, not to say "just do the ex parte, just do it, it's going to fix
everything for you." It's really hard not to do that, we have to keep reminding
ourselves that she knows best, and our job is to do what she needs us to do,
not what we feel like what's best for her. But that's what a lot of the professionals need to remember. (Claire, age 31, domestic violence survivor)

Additionally, participants advise being up front about the professional's
skills, knowledge, and practice orientation, particularly in the area of
trauma. Several participants were treated by mental health practitioners
who did not fully understand the reality of trauma and its aftereffects
including rage, numbness, disjointed thoughts, memory loss, hypervigilance, hyperactivity, and internalized worthlessness. Because of such
persistent symptoms, these women were often misdiagnosed (particularly
with personality disorders), and thus misguided in their healing process.

If you don't know your stuff, if you're in over you head, for God's sake,
please, go read some more, go do the research, go talk to someone who
might have experience with this. Don't play it by ear. Don't fumble along.
Don't go along with the boss or the supervising psychologist or whatever
just because you think they must be right, because I've seen first hand
when they were dead wrong. (Donna, age 45, survivor of childhood exposure to domestic violence)

It's just that you need to be experienced to work with people who have
a lot of pain and stuff. I would encourage therapists to know more about

traumatic memory and about PTSD and what it does to a person. (Tracy, age 44, incest survivor)

I'm watching [the counselor] and saying okay, are you going to say the same typical phrases, like, "What brings you here today?" I mean, there are typical counselor phrases and when people start using them, I'm like, you know what, I could ask myself those same questions. I could do that too. I want you to do something more than I can do. Please don't do the typical things, because I'm going to recognize it, and I'm not going to react the way you want me to. But that's just me. (Pearl, age 50, domestic violence survivor)

I guess to learn about it [domestic violence] yourself. I think that it's obvious a lot of people haven't lived it. I think that especially professionals, you might have learned about it like in a text book where some things are like very cut and dry and generic. But I think that the more you can talk to people, and just have conversations about their experiences the more you can kind of learn from that. I think that would make you a better professional obviously. I still feel like there's a perception that domestic violence only happens in certain kinds of families or certain races or certain SES. And so I think that being open and realizing that it can happen across, all races, all ethnicities, and all cultures, you know? So I think just being more open to that. It'll make other people kind of let their guards down. (Elise, age 24, survivor of childhood exposure to domestic violence)

Lesson Six: Support Client Self-Determination

Participants strongly recommend that mental health professionals believe in clients' abilities to direct their own therapeutic agendas so they are not giving over their authority to professionals. In other words, they do not want other survivors to feel "forced" into having to perform for their counselors who may have preconceived ideas of what and how healing should take place. Obviously, not having control is a significant issue for survivors, so these women advise helpers to validate clients' expertise, competency, and insight. Thus, they want professionals to support each survivor in discovering her own point of view, her own choices, and her own vision for the future. Additionally, participants underscore how survivors' self-worth is often lacking and thus they often need support and encouragement within the therapeutic relationship to take ownership for their helping process.

From my experience, it was me coming up with the answers. It shouldn't be the therapist guiding the therapy. It should be the one seeking the therapy, and they are just helping you through that process. (Kathleen, age 26, incest survivor)

Let the client lead. This one therapist has been the reason—I credit him with the reason why I've been able to heal to the extent that I have—he let me lead pretty much. I knew what I needed. I knew what I needed in that relationship with him. But others [therapists] would resist as far as they thought they knew better. (Toby, age 49, incest survivor)

Don't discredit what clients say. Really give them a voice, empower them. Give them that knowledge that they have a voice that they've come so far, so keep going, you do have strength. Even if it's just a little bit, feed that flame 'cause that's eventually gonna break the cycle. (Jenni, age 37, survivor of childhood exposure to domestic violence)

A lot of counselors in my past taught me to be reliant upon them, so I never fully learned how to rely on my inner strength; I never really learned how to rely on my self-worth. Even now, at times, I feel like a little girl. I still have this little girl immaturity. At times I come off as not like a full-grown adult, because of that. Don't have people be reliant upon counselors; it doesn't do any good if you keep a person locked in as a young child. (Daisey, age 31, domestic violence survivor)

Therapy felt like there was a performance factor, and that if you beat the pillows hard enough and if you yelled enough, then the therapist had done a good job, and if you didn't then you weren't working through your stuff, and you were holding it in, and it felt like it was just like the incest energy, where somebody is forcing you to do what you don't want to do. Though there wasn't any force, there was a demand there that this is the way you do it. And I'm wanting to say, "No" to the therapist, but they're in control, and it was that similar type of relationship and the power balance was unequal, and they're telling me to do something and I'm not wanting to, but I can't say, "No." (Madison, age 37, incest survivor)

Lesson Seven: See the Person, Not the Diagnosis

Participants understand that individuals will receive a diagnosis as the medical model pervades mental health treatment. Unfortunately, managed-care exposes professionals to too much emphasis on symptoms, deficits, and diagnoses and not enough on clients' competencies, capabilities, and desires. Thus, helpers are likely to over attend to client symptoms and under attend to client strengths. Participants caution that a diagnosis should never be viewed as the crucial feature of clients' identities. Additionally, these women stress that if diagnostic categories are the central focus of practice, then helpers do not see survivors' resource-fulness (to the same degree as the problems) and thus are likely to miss the total picture of clients and their life situations.

> I know you have to have a diagnosis for your treatment or whatever, but don't always just think that's the whole person. Don't be rigid in what you see. (Erika, age 38, incest survivor)

> I feel like there is a rush to judgment. In the medical field, there's cattle call medicine. How many patients can we circulate through the office to get enough reimbursement back from the insurance? I think that mental health professionals can be the same way. I have seen personally so many erroneous diagnoses made too quickly, that were then proven false with just a little more time, a little more counseling, a little more digging, and they were proven false. It's scary to think that you can be branded. You can change people's lives too easily and too quickly. (Donna, age 45, survivor of childhood exposure to domestic violence)

> I think there are a lot of problems in our mental health care system in general, and it really bothers me. People who have been through trauma have difficulty navigating life in a healthy manner; therefore, they have few resources, and unfortunately doctors and counselors and all these things take money. And very often people just don't have that money, and our society doesn't help, there are mental health clinics that have a sliding fee scale or whatever; but the problem there is so often they are completely understaffed, the counselors are immensely overloaded, and very often they don't know what they're doing because you get a lot of students who are working on their psych degree or whatever and so they're practicing on somebody else's life. And I kind of have an issue with that. (Melinda, age 35, survivor of childhood exposure to domestic violence)

The healing journeys for several of the participants included lengthy treatment periods. Thus, they are troubled by current mental health policy changes that limit the type and duration of services because they fear it will thwart the recovery process for survivors of family violence. Yet, if managed-care policies cannot be changed, they recommend being upfront with clients regarding restrictions (e.g., number of sessions) placed on therapeutic services.

> With the managed care model of mental health when you're talkin' about sexually abused people, and you're trying to do something with a 90-day, solution-focused therapeutic intervention, that ain't gonna get it. And these

insurance companies and doctors need to hear that 90 days is not gonna cut it. It's detrimental, in my opinion, to a lot of individuals, particularly women. (Jackie, age 45, incest survivor)

I would be honest with my clients, and I would say "Do you know how long your insurance has given me to work with you?" Some clients it is 30 days, some 60, some 90. How can we lay this out, what's comfortable for you? Where do you see yourself versus where does the insurance see you as being? And so, with managed care, if counselors could just be honest, and say, "I have this amount of sessions that I can do with you, and how much can we accomplish?" And then I could say, "Well, you know, it's going to take me at least three sessions to even decide to tell you anything worth telling." (Pearl, age 50, domestic violence survivor)

SUMMARY

Interestingly, participants' seven recommendations parallel assumptions and principles of strength-based and solution-focused mental health practice. Their advice guides helpers to tap into, elucidate, and build on the strengths, competencies, and resourcefulness of clients. Additionally, they request that professionals honor rather than avoid clients' stories of suffering. These women underscore how survivors know firsthand the realities of family violence and thus their expertise, insight, and determination should be respected during the therapeutic process. The healing journey is arduous; yet, mental health practitioners who convey hope, possibility, empathy, acceptance, and compassion helps to ease the burden. Ultimately, participants' advice to helpers challenges the premise that survivors who have suffered family violence will remain wounded or become less than the persons they might otherwise have been.

10 The Compassionate Helper

In client outcome studies, the quality of the therapeutic relationship is consistently shown to have the greatest impact in the change process (Skovholt, 2001). Thus, the professional's use of self has a significant impact on lessening or aggravating the suffering of clients. As highlighted in chapter 9, survivors of family violence who interact with unsupportive, judgmental, and controlling mental health professionals often experience negative outcomes and premature termination of services. Helpers who fail to convey an open, trusting, and collaborative helping relationship may lack essential knowledge and skills to work effectively with the profound anguish of clients. Additional reasons for inadequate practice may include the occupational stressor of bearing witness to the pain and suffering of clients, referred to as *vicarious trauma* (VT) (McCann & Pearlman, 1990), *secondary traumatic stress* (STS), or *compassion fatigue* (CF) (Figley, 1995). These terms, often used interchangeably, depict the phenomena of professionals' own distress as a result of helping those who are suffering and is perhaps the single most common personal consequence of practice (Kottler, 1992). An empathic, accepting, and compassionate helper indirectly experiences the client's world, including the reality of violent experiences in their lives. This work-related stressor is different from *burnout* (BO) (Maslach, 1996), which may occur in any job setting and is related to negative work conditions (e.g., high workload, negative work culture, job dissatisfaction) that may spill over to one's work with clients but is not the result of it. Therefore, the construct of burnout alone does not fully capture the effects of experiencing secondary traumatic stress as an occupational risk for helping professionals.

In the author's teaching experience with graduate social work students, they often report fears of burnout (their use of this term includes everything job related including secondary trauma) as professional literature, practitioners, and educators have repeatedly told them it is an inevitable occupational hazard. Thus, they fear and expect it to happen particularly if they work with survivors of family violence. Students often aspire to make a difference in the lives of others; yet, this is often prefaced with their major concern of burnout. The legacy thus being instilled in future helpers is that if you care enough you will eventually stop caring because the compassion well runs dry. Yet, not every professional who works with traumatized individuals experiences burnout or secondary traumatic stress; in fact, some are continuously rejuvenated rather than depleted from their work.

Working alongside clients as they transform their lives to ones of strength, purpose, and possibility provides fulfillment and pleasure for many practitioners. A term that captures this phenomenon is *compassion satisfaction* (Stamm, 2002). Professional literature, however, does not highlight the concept of compassion satisfaction as much as it does the hazards of practice. As a result, additional study on what helps practitioners be resilient in the midst of client suffering is necessary (Radey & Figley, 2007). More research is needed regarding the personal (e.g., a life-affirming outlook) and environmental (e.g., supportive supervisors) protective factors that promote professional compassion satisfaction (Stamm, 2005). Just as helping paradigms have shifted from problem- to strengths-based practice with clients; such a change is also necessary in regard to helpers.

This chapter identifies both the challenges and benefits clinicians face in their work with traumatized individuals. Additionally, the causes and consequences of job distress (i.e., VT, STS, CF, and BO) are delineated. As the causes are different for each type of stress, the solutions to alleviate them also vary. Working with victims of violence is challenging, thus to prevent helpers' compassion wells from going dry we must ensure that their needs are adequately addressed (Bride & Figley, 2007). For example, if a professional is experiencing secondary traumatic stress, a remedy may include changing the worker's caseload to reduce one's exposure to family violence cases. In contrast, if the cause is burnout, a remedy may include changing the worker's job responsibilities. The

Professional Quality of Life Scale (ProQOL) is introduced as an instrument for practitioners to use in their professional development as a means of differentiating types of stress and thus solutions. Decreasing job stress does not automatically lead to (although it helps) increases in compassion satisfaction. Therefore, the ProQOL also measures compassion satisfaction as a separate construct. Additionally, this chapter underscores ways to support and enhance professional fulfillment that go beyond stress reduction (Bride & Figley, 2007; Skovholt & Jennings, 2004).

WHEN THE COMPASSION WELL RUNS DRY

Mental health practitioners are exposed to client stories of suffering on a daily, if not hourly, basis. Facilitating the healing process involves sharing clients' emotional burdens and bearing witness to the devastating and cruel events in their lives (Baird & Jenkins, 2003). It is nearly inevitable that professionals will absorb some of the anguish that accompanies such stories of suffering. Survivors of family violence often experience emotional release and relief when breaking their silence to a compassionate helper. As clients become desensitized to the horrors of their past, helpers may become more vulnerable as they accumulate a litany of painful stories that they bear witness to and as a consequence take in. Thus, a professional may begin to over identify with a client's feelings of helplessness, hopelessness, and entrapment resulting in emotional exhaustion and manifesting itself in negative attitudes toward self, work, and life itself (Baird & Jenkins, 2003; Kottler, 1992).

Professionals can only give away what they have, in terms of empathy and compassion, and when the well runs dry one's functioning is impacted. Research shows that caseloads dominated with trauma survivors increases aversive physical, mental, cognitive, and social effects in helpers. Additionally, workers exposed to human-induced trauma (e.g., family violence) tend to suffer more harmful consequences than those who deal with natural-induced trauma (e.g., natural disasters) (Salston & Figley, 2003). When helpers' coping methods are overwhelmed, they may experience employment dissatisfaction and eventually burnout (Maslach, 1996). The following list of symptoms/consequences does not infer that helpers are destined to endure them or that their causes are always related to the professional's work life. Yet, it does provide a framework for understanding the professional bio-psycho-social-spiritual costs to bearing witness to clients' experiences of cruelty and horror (drawn from the work of Adams, Boscarino, & Figley, 2006; Dutton & Rubinstein, 1995; Figley, 1995; Lahad, 2000; Pearlman & Saakvitne, 1995).

1. Physical symptoms: fatigue (physical exhaustion), sleep disturbances, hypertension, headaches, and somatic symptoms (sweat-
   ing, rapid heartbeat, breathing difficulties, and dizziness).
2. Emotional symptoms: rage, numbness, irritability, anxiety,
   depression, guilt, fear, sadness, helplessness, hopelessness, and
   decreased self-esteem.
3. Behavioral symptoms: aggression, callousness, pessimism, defen-
   siveness, impatience, boredom, cynicism, substance abuse, social
   withdrawal, elevated startle responses, hypervigilance, physically
   or verbally acting out, and an increased sensitivity to violence.
4. Cognitive symptoms: diminished sense of competence, changes
   in identity and world view, paranoia, rigidity of perceptions,
   decreased concentration, intrusive imagery, and dissociation.
5. Interpersonal symptoms: perfunctory communication, social
   withdrawal, sarcastic/caustic humor, mistrust, disconnection
   from loved ones, decreased interest in intimacy, and increased
   relationship conflicts.
6. Spiritual symptoms: increased questions regarding the meaning
   and purpose of life, loss of purpose, anger at God or a Higher
   Power, doubt regarding prior religious beliefs, and greater skepti-
   cism about religion and spirituality.
7. Work-related symptoms: low morale, low motivation, evad-
   ing work tasks, apathy, negativity, poor client interactions,
   increased absenteeism, avoidance of clients, withdrawal from colleagues, poor work performance, and risk-taking (e.g., breaking
   confidentiality).

Various constructs denote the negatives effects experienced by workers
exposed to traumatic populations including vicarious trauma (VT), secondary traumatic stress (STS), and compassion fatigue (CF) (Steed &
Bicknell, 2001). While these terms are not entirely synonymous, they
do have a great deal in common in understanding the mental exhaustion of helpers. They draw from trauma theory as a framework to better
understand how helpers exposed to significant suffering (albeit indirectly) experience stress that impacts their coping (Horwitz, 1998). Such
psychological stress may negatively alter the clinician's physical, emotional, cognitive, behavioral, spiritual, and interpersonal functioning.

The elusiveness of "success" with traumatized individuals, who often have needs greater than social service, educational, or health systems can meet, creates additional strain (Skovholt, 2001). Ultimately, professionals may lose their sense of empowerment, well-being, and purpose when assisting survivors of family violence (Figley, 2002).

VICARIOUS TRAUMA

Oppression, violence, and injustice are devastating for victims, as well as for helpers who bear witness to it. Professionals repeatedly encounter clients who have been tortured, raped, and beaten, and who routinely have not received justice. Being personally exposed to such human cruelty can take a toll on professionals' emotional resources and, consequently, may affect their perceptions and worldviews in fundamental ways. Vicarious traumatization results when the helper's self is negatively impacted by repeated exposure to clients' trauma histories and trauma effects (Cunningham, 2003; McCann & Pearlman, 1990). Essentially, the professional's personal belief and value systems are battered by continuously witnessing clients' experiences of torture, humiliation, and betrayal. Being repeatedly exposed to stories of suffering inevitably challenges helpers in the areas of their basic faith and sense of vulnerability (Pearlman, 1995, 1996; Pearlman & Mac Ian, 1995). Important assumptions that individuals hold about themselves, other people, and the world are disrupted (Guzzino & Taxis, 1995). They may question their spiritual beliefs as they experience new and more problematic feelings about the meaning and purpose of life.

Professionals' cognitive worlds are altered as a result of having regular and close proximity to wells of sadness and the intense anger their clients often exhibit. As professionals try to make sense of clients' stories, they are simultaneously integrating these stories into their own cognitive schemas (Canfield, 2005). During the process of integration, helpers may experience secondary traumatic stress reactions or compassion fatigue, which may include PTSD symptoms of intrusive thoughts (repeatedly replaying clients' traumatic stories); avoidance (minimizing or ignoring traumatic content), or hypervigilance (persistent arousal associated with traumatic material) (Figley, 1993; McCann & Pearlman, 1990a, 1990b). Additionally, helpers who have a trauma history may be more at-risk for cognitive disruptions if they themselves have not found meaning and purpose for the suffering they endured. Thus, working with clients' suffering may compound unresolved issues for helpers with their own personal histories of family violence (Cunningham, 2003).

Decreasing or preventing vicarious trauma requires a supervisor-worker relationship that is safe, supportive, and respectful where the worker is free to express her fears, concerns, and inadequacies (McCann & Pearlman, 1990; Pearlman & Saakvitne, 1995). Mentor and peer support are critical for helpers working with traumatized populations. This is particularly important for novice professionals and students who are often most at-risk for VT, as they often lack a framework for understanding the pervasive effects of trauma work on their identity, world view, beliefs, and memory systems. Thus, they feel overwhelmed with stories of suffering and have doubts about their professional efficacy. This negative transformation of the inner experience of the helper can be confusing, defeating, and saddening. Yet, VT can also occur with even the most seasoned professionals as bearing witness to numerous trauma stories can take a toll on one's beliefs and values about justice.

Vicarious trauma may be evident during supervision when workers comment: "I don't think I'm helping my clients as they continue to endure such intense suffering." "Just when I think I have seen the worst that can happen to a person, I get a case that tops it." "I don't know that I can keep doing this work because the human cruelty perpetrated on others is never ending." Thus, when workers are seeking assistance regarding the meaning of such cruelty in the lives of their clients and for themselves, a supervisor response that is *not* helpful includes, "Maybe you're not cut out for clinical work." During supervision, when clinicians report feeling overwhelmed and saddened in their work, they should not be further shamed or blamed for being "too sensitive" or "too involved" or, questioned about their motivation for doing trauma work (e.g., suggesting they may have unresolved issues in their personal histories). Instead, what is needed is a caring supervisor who provides a safe and confidential mentoring relationship that allows workers to express their fears, doubts, and concerns regarding their work with traumatized individuals.

Caring, competent, and committed leadership involves creating a supervisor-worker relationship that provides a means of building self-efficacy while exploring the meaning and purpose of one's work. It is creating an environment of hope for workers that can be transferred to their work with clients. The following is a mentoring example in which the worker, a graduate intern at a domestic violence and sexual assault center, is helped to address her trepidations regarding self-efficacy and whether or not she is meant to work with survivors.

Supervisor: What is on your agenda that you want to address today?

Graduate Intern: I don't know. This week has been tough. I've worked with a lot of clients who are suffering immensely and they do not think that things are getting any better for them.

Supervisor: What are your beliefs about whether or not the work you are doing together is helping?

Graduate Intern: I don't know that I'm being effective. I don't know if I'm helping.

Supervisor: In the last week or in general?

Graduate Intern: I really wanted to work in the area of domestic violence and sexual assault but I'm beginning to think that maybe I'm not cut out for it.

Supervisor: In what ways do you think you're not cut out for it?

Graduate Intern: I just feel terrible for my clients and what they have gone through. I worry about them a lot and what I can do to help them. Plus there doesn't seem to be any justice because for the most part nothing ever happens to the abusers. It's not fair that these women have to go through so much and yet nothing happens to the perpetrators. I have a hard time shutting it off.

Supervisor: Well, it makes sense that you would have a hard time shutting it off as your mind is trying to process or make sense of such violent events in the lives of your clients. You're trying to wrap your mind around such human cruelty, not something that is easy to do. You are also struggling with the concept of justice and why it seems so elusive for victims of family violence. I've been at this for 20 years and at times still have difficulty making sense of it also. When your mind can't let it go it usually means you're trying to place it in some framework for understanding your clients' suffering and injustice. It is referred to as vicarious trauma; where professionals who work with suffering may at times suffer themselves. It usually relates to changes in assumptions about meaning and purpose of one's work along with beliefs about one's personal efficacy.

Graduate Intern: I've never heard of vicarious trauma. So, it is okay to feel this way? It seems like all I hear from my professors and other people in the field is that if I can't learn to leave work at work then I'm going to burnout. So this is normal?

Supervisor: Yes, particularly for someone who is newer to the domestic violence/sexual assault field. But it can happen to seasoned professionals too. It is just difficult to make sense of why a person has to endure so much pain and suffering.

Graduate Intern: So, it just happens, there is nothing I can do about it?

Supervisor: No, you can impact it and it does diminish. Just like clients can't heal in isolation, you can't do trauma work in isolation. So, a first step is what you did today, and that is to share what you are going through as a means of working through your professional doubts and concerns. Secondly, is to not judge yourself so harshly for caring about your clients. Thirdly, is to connect not only to the pain but also the strengths of survivors. You are privileged to work with women who have not only survived but have prevailed in amazing ways. Believing in them and their strength will help you to feel less responsible for alleviating their suffering. You do not have to have the solutions for their suffering; instead, you are helping them find those answers for themselves. Additionally, maintain a connection to hope that clients' lives will get better. Change is happening all the time for these women, and you can never underestimate the power of providing a safe, accepting, and hopeful relationship in their healing process. You might not see it in the moment, the next day, or even the next month. But, just because you can't "see" healing, doesn't mean it isn't happening. Also, there is a reason we get into advocacy work and it is often about changing unjust systems for victims such as the legal system which you might want to consider becoming more active on macro-level issues.

Graduate Intern: I am consistently in awe of the wisdom, compassion and humor of these women who have often quite literally had the life beat out of them. They are truly inspiring and I'm honored to accompany them on their healing journeys. And it makes sense that I take my frustrations and anger and channel it into doing something that will have an impact not just with my clients but with survivors in general.

Supervisor: You are the only one who can decide if you're cut out for this type of work, but I would ask you to wait and not make that decision right now. Instead, give it some time and start keeping track, maybe in a journal, of the good work that is being done between you and your clients. Perhaps, you are too bogged down in their victimization histories to see the victories. Be reminded of these women's resiliency by also recording examples of their strength, courage, and determination. Additionally, you may want to have objects that serve as reminders of people, places, and beliefs that give your life meaning and purpose.

Graduate Intern: I will wait to make a decision. And thank you for your guidance. I honestly was at a point where I was giving up on my desire to help others. Just talking about my doubts and fears has helped immensely.

Supervisor: These professional struggles are how you develop. So, don't give up yet; you don't know what great things are yet to come in your career.

SECONDARY TRAUMATIC STRESS/COMPASSION FATIGUE

Secondary traumatic stress (STS) results from empathic and compassionate efforts by the helper with those who are suffering and, consequently, places them at risk for becoming traumatized in the process (Figley & Marks, 2008; Salston & Figley, 2003). A less stigmatizing and more normative term used in the work-stress literature and is synonymous with STS is *compassion fatigue* (CF). Bearing witness to suffering may result in fatigue and, consequently, reduce a helper's capacity or interest to further extend compassion to clients. Secondary traumatic stress or compassion fatigue refers to posttraumatic stress reactions in workers including reexperiencing client's traumatic histories, avoidance of reminders of traumatic events (i.e., the client), and persistent arousal (e.g., anxiety) associated with the client (Figley, 2002). The symptoms often show up suddenly and create a sense of helplessness, shock, and confusion in the worker (Figley, 2007).

In comparison to vicarious trauma (VT), compassion fatigue encompasses worker stress reactions rather than altered cognitive schemas. Although VT and CF may co-occur, they are not necessarily a cause or a consequence to each other and may emerge independently (Baird & Jenkins, 2003). Vicarious trauma and compassion fatigue originate primarily from repeated exposure to client trauma and thus their etiology is different from burnout, which stems from a negative work environment. Yet, both VT and CF may be complicated by a lack of support and satisfaction in the workplace (Bride & Figley, 2007; Bride, Radey, & Figley, 2007; DePanfilis, 2006).

Secondary suffering emanates from understanding and identifying with clients' anguish. Thus, the aptitude of the worker for noticing the pain of others (i.e., empathic ability), having a desire to relieve it (i.e., empathic concern), and making an effort to reduce it (i.e., empathic response) may give out to fatigue (Canfield, 2005). Similar to PTSD, helpers may experience the following traumatic reactions (Adams, Boscarino, & Figley, 2006; Bell, Kulkarni, & Dalton, 2003; Canfield, 2005; Figley & Kleber, 1995):

1. Re-experiencing the client's traumatic event resulting in an intrusive response by the worker such as taking on the role of the "rescuer" and thus crossing boundaries that ultimately disempower the client.
2. Avoiding both the client and reminders of the client's trauma resulting in professional distancing to the point of abandoning the client. Additional constrictive responses may include doubting or denying the client's reality, numbing, or dissociation.
3. Feeling persistent arousal (e.g., anxiety) due to intimate knowledge of the client's traumatic experiences resulting in inattentiveness and thus not being fully present for the client regardless if she shares something traumatic or ordinary.

Sustaining the professional self amidst client suffering can take an emotional toll on practitioners, putting them at risk for poor professional judgments (e.g., misdiagnosis), inadequate treatment planning, or abuse of clients (Bride & Figley, 2007). Thus, it is essential to prevent, address, and alleviate consequences of compassion fatigue as it is costly to both helpers and those who seek their services. Safety and comfort for workers can come from agency practices and policies that address the risk of secondary trauma such as the following (Figley, 2002; Pearlman & Saakvitne, 1995; Skovholt, 2001):

1. Diversify caseloads thereby limiting exposure to traumatized individuals. Helpers cannot avoid exposure to client anguish; however, overexposure to particular trauma cases such as sexual abuse or rape may be lessened.
2. Educate helpers on secondary traumatic stress or compassion fatigue to alert them to its causes, consequences, and how to remedy it.
3. Provide staff development opportunities in regard to professional self-care.

4. Provide helpers with adequate benefits of vacation time or personal days that offer time off for rejuvenation and replenishment.
5. Promote a caring, friendly, and welcoming work environment where helpers feel they can reach out to colleagues in their times of need.
6. Provide supportive supervision to all staff, even those that are more seasoned, which encourages professional reflection on one's work experiences.

The following supervisor-worker dialogue occurs in a nonprofit counseling agency and provides an example where the clinician is helped to develop "compassionate distance" from her work with a client who has experienced horrible violent events in her life, particularly, a gang rape at the age of 12 years old. *Compassionate distance*, a term used by the author (although she does not claim to be the originator of it), captures how one can care about their clients but also distance oneself from their suffering. In other words, one is compassionate and empathic to the client but does not overly attach to the suffering and, consequently, share ownership of it.

Supervisor: What is on your agenda that you want to address today?
Worker: I have a particular case that I don't know if I'm helping the person much. She has a history of trauma in childhood and adulthood. And it just seems that she isn't getting better.
Supervisor: Is the client saying that therapy isn't helping?
Worker: No, not at all. She finds our work together helpful; but I don't see it as she isn't changing; she still has problems with agoraphobia, and she is continuously and constantly triggered by everything around her.
Supervisor: What has been the focus of your work together?
Worker: Helping her to talk about what has happened to her. I've been exposed to numerous stories of sexual assault and violence in my work with survivors. Yet, this one experience that she shared I just can't seem to let it go. She was gang raped at age 12. And I can't get it out of my mind.
Supervisor: What can't you get out of your mind?
Worker: The assault itself. She hasn't even really shared that much about it, but I keep picturing her at age 12, being held down defenseless, and raped over and over again. I think what really got me was when she said that she pleaded for them to stop and cried for her momma and they laughed and spit on her. It haunts me.

Supervisor: How else is it affecting you?

Worker: I kind of dread seeing her, which sounds awful. I'm actually relieved when she cancels, so I don't follow up with her to reschedule. I just wait for her to make the next appointment. And when we do meet, I get anxious because of what she might share next.

Supervisor: Has it affected your life outside of work?

Worker: I sometimes have nightmares about it. It's odd as I don't really even know the details of the rape, but I dream about them anyway. Also, I'm driving my kids nuts because I'm so hyperaware now of where they're at, who they're with, I'm driving them crazy with my constant text messaging to check on them.

Supervisor: The reactions you're describing are similar to PTSD that we see in clients, but the difference is you are experiencing it secondary as a result of being exposed to your client's traumatic experiences. It often comes on suddenly and is referred to as secondary traumatic stress or compassion fatigue.

Worker: I've never heard of it. All I ever heard about in graduate school was burnout. I never knew I could get PTSD from my client's traumatic experiences, but it makes sense. Also, it explains why I'm constantly replaying what she told me and yet wanting to avoid it such as hoping she will cancel her appointment with me. Plus, the anxiety I have when we do meet and of course it explains the hypervigilance with my kids.

Supervisor: I know that you give your heart and soul to your work, but in doing so, at times, it may take a toll.

Worker: I just feel terrible about what she's gone through. I also have done something different with her than my other clients. She asked to be seen two or three times a week but I told her, "No," because agency policy doesn't permit seeing clients individually beyond once a week as they are referred to the drop-in groups if they need additional counseling. But, I've been going over our 50 minutes sometimes as much as an hour and a half if I don't have any one scheduled after her. I know I shouldn't do this but I'm doing it anyway. She's been through so much and I just don't want to be another person who lets her down.

Supervisor: So, what would you like to do differently?

Worker: I guess start with talking to her about staying within the 50 minute sessions.

Supervisor: I know it can be challenging to set boundaries after the fact but it is necessary to do so. This might be disappointing for her or she could be relieved that you are setting a limit. Either way it will help to address it. So, stick to 50 minutes even if she suggests paying for an hour and a half and offer her the drop-in group. Additionally, I want to talk to you about creating compassionate distance. This is what I refer to as being there for your clients and supporting them in their healing process but having emotional distance from their suffering. For instance, I care deeply about the clients I work with but this does not mean I own their suffering. I know that they will work through their suffering and perhaps even find meaning and purpose in it. It is not to say that it doesn't affect me but it is in a manner that allows me to be emphatic rather than sympathetic. So, how can you create compassionate distance with this client?

Worker: I guess to detach from the helplessness of the 12-year-old girl and instead to connect with the strength, survival, and perseverance of the adult. She is definitely a survivor and continues on her healing journey as painful as it is at times.

Supervisor: And how might having compassionate distance impact your work with her?

Worker: I'll actually be more fully present if or when she shares more traumatic experiences, because I won't be dreading it but instead will be hopeful about her recovery from it. Also, if she cancels, I'll follow up with her to set another appointment rather than hoping on some level that she chooses to not come back. So, I guess I will feel much less helpless and more hopeful.

Supervisor: I think you'll be surprised at how much strength she has if you can stop seeing her through her victimization.

Worker: I agree. I'll probably feel much less responsible for her recovery also.

BURNOUT

Vicarious trauma, compassion fatigue, and burnout overlap in the symptoms of emotional exhaustion, depersonalization (i.e., a dehumanized or impersonal attitude toward clients), and a reduced sense of accomplishment. Yet, burnout can occur within any job setting or with any client population where as the other occupational stressors are a result of working with traumatized individuals. Burnout is job stress related to role ambiguity (e.g., lack of clarity of one's work role), role conflict (e.g., conflicting demands related to one's work role), and workload (e.g., the amount of work performed on the job) (Maslach, 1982). Work stress can emanate from responding to people in pain and crisis; yet, characteristics of the organization can significantly contribute as well. Burnout is a condition that emerges gradually whereby workers who have heavy demands placed on their energy, strength, and resources become depleted of physical and emotional energy (Freudenberger, 1975; Maslach, Schaufeli, & Leiter, 2001).

Negativity in the work environment is easy to catch. At first, negativity is seductive because when you join in with others who are dissatisfied you feel better as you are not alone in your frustrations. So, venting with similarly situated colleagues provides a release initially; yet, if venting does not lead to solutions then the only action is more venting. Consequently, complaints without resolutions serve to validate workers' helplessness and hopelessness that they can impact agency change. Causes of work negativity include such stressors as staff shortages, inadequate compensation, unfair treatment, restrictive policies (e.g., managed care), long work hours, excessive paperwork, little opportunity for advancement, work overload, unresponsive and unappreciative leadership. Additionally, women are found to be more vulnerable to burnout, because they tend to have jobs of lesser status and thus acquire less power (Erickson & Ritter, 2001; Hochschild, 1983). Excessive stress or dissatisfaction is associated with low morale, reduced self-esteem, problematic coping (e.g., substance abuse), and withdrawal from work (e.g., increased sick days) (Baird & Jenkins, 2003; Stalker, Mandell, Frensch, Harvey, & Wright, 2007).

Burnout is a problem of the social environment in which people work (Maslach & Leiter, 1997). Operating in a critical, cynical, and pessimistic work setting makes it difficult to replenish one's resources such as the skills of compassion and empathy, critical to building rapport with clients. Consequently, ways to prevent such a work situation is necessary starting with preventing work stress from turning into burnout. Burnout appears to be moderated by certain factors, such as social supports and a sense of accomplishment (Koeske & Koeske, 1989, 1993; Schwartz, Tiamiyu, & Dwyer, 2007). For example, a helper who has a lower level of social support (e.g., supervisor, coworker) and reduced feelings of self-efficacy, is more likely to experience work stress, which may result in burnout (Stalker et al., 2007). Thus, seeking social support may help workers from depersonalizing clients and may contribute to a stronger sense of accomplishment (Schwartz et al., 2007). The following four types of agency support are instrumental in lessening work stress and thus burnout (Himle & Jayaratne, & Thyness, 1991):

1. Emotional support: coworkers or supervisors who are receptive and approachable when the worker has a problem.
2. Approval support: coworkers or supervisors who provide approval when a worker has done a job well.
3. Instrumental support: coworkers or supervisors who provide assistance to a worker when completing a difficult task.
4. Informational support: coworkers or supervisors who provide information to a worker when needed.

The following supervisor-work dialogue occurs in a public mental health center and provides an example where the worker receives all four types of support from the supervisor. The worker is agitated regarding restrictive agency policies, negativity of coworkers, a lack of resources for clients, and the mental health care system in general.

Supervisor: What is on your agenda that you would like to discuss today?

Worker: I don't think I'm helping my clients because I don't have the time to devote to them. I just feel that all we do here is put bandages on major issues. I'm really disillusioned with the mental health system—it seems like all we do is medicate people and no "real" change happens. I see the same people with the same problems day in and day out. Plus, I'm frustrated with our agency policy that I can't work with someone who is actively using drugs and/ or alcohol unless they are receiving substance abuse services; yet, there are no substance abuse services available. If I can get someone into inpatient treatment, they are there only a few days and are discharged once they've detoxed.

Supervisor: So you're frustrated with the agency policy on client substance use and provision of services along with the mental health care system in general.

Worker: It's ridiculous, aren't we suppose to be helping people learn new ways to cope? Well, until they learn them they're going to fall back to old coping behaviors like using drugs. Plus, if it's a client dealing with trauma, they may actually use more. So, to just say to them we can't treat you I think is irresponsible not to mention unethical.

Supervisor: I agree if agency policy said that we can't treat people who are actively substance abusing and then didn't give them resources to do so that would be irresponsible. However, you might recall that the agency policy states that after six sessions if the client is continuing to actively use and not following through on any type of referrals for substance abuse services or supports, such as Narcotics Anonymous and Alcoholics Anonymous, that individual therapy or case management services will not be provided. They are still able to access our crisis services and our drop-in support groups. And, they are able to reengage in individual services once they have chosen to address the substance abuse issues.

Worker: I know but when you have to be the one to set the limit and they are pleading with you for one more session it is difficult. It is much like our client no-show policy. If they no-show three times in three months because they have not cancelled within the 24-hour period before their appointment then I cannot see them any longer as an individual case.

Supervisor: It is frustrating that we can't meet the needs of all the people who access our services, including the 70 people on our waiting list, due to our limited resources. It can feel like you're in a no-win situation.

Worker: Exactly, and all I hear from our referral sources is how they can't get anyone into the mental health center because there is a four month waiting list. That's not a good reputation to have. And, I'm not the only one frustrated here; others are saying the same thing.

Supervisor: How would you describe the work environment here?

Worker: People are frustrated. Exhausted. Plus it seems like we always have to be adjusting to some new policy change whether it is managed care, Medicare, Supplemental Security Income. I just don't know how I can keep doing this work. I think I need out of this. I'm just exhausted and I don't feel that I'm accomplishing anything. It is impossible to make my 30 direct hours for billing because not all my clients show up and so then I have to schedule 35 clients, which means I'm usually working more than 40 hours a week. And I have had to start coming in on Saturdays to do my paperwork.

Supervisor: It does sound like you're exhausted and frustrated. And rightly so.

Worker: Who wouldn't be? Plus, I get tired of everyone complaining around here because then I do the same thing. I'm just angry and frustrated all the time and that generally is not my state of being.

Supervisor: No, it is not. You generally are not negative and are actually the opposite, often calm, cool, and collected. Not to mention your wonderful sense of humor. So, how can I help? What changes would you like to see happen?

Worker: Get rid of the negativity. Somehow get staff to create a work environment that is positive and hopeful. Also, I would like to lessen my case load and take on other administrative responsibilities, such as supervising student interns. I think I would be a good mentor and would welcome being connected with people who want to learn and grow. I also would like to improve my skills in working with substance abuse by getting credentialed in the area.

Supervisor: And your concerns about restrictive agency policies?

Worker: I'm wondering if we can revisit these policies during our staff meeting to see if their purpose is still viable.

Supervisor: Well, those are all doable recommendations and you've obviously put much thought into this. I think you would do a good job at mentoring students who could also share your cases, which would ease your workload. I can talk to the executive director about supporting your professional development in the area of substance abuse. So, get me information on credentialing such as the time investment and cost. Also, revisiting agency policy is always a good idea and I will put it on the agenda for the staff meeting along with asking staff about ideas to make the agency more about hope and possibility rather than negativity. Obviously, it's not comfortable for anyone to work in an environment when they don't feel appreciated or supported.

Worker: Thank you for hearing me out. I know I've been quite angry and frustrated and I appreciate you listening to my concerns and also helping me come up with some solutions.

Supervisor: Well, you made great suggestions that I think we should seriously take a look at. So, in the future, let me know about your concerns so it doesn't leave you so frustrated you're thinking quitting is the only way to solve them.

Worker: It feels good to take some kind of action rather than sitting around complaining all the time. Thank you.

COMPASSION SATISFACTION

Even though working with traumatized individuals is highly stressful it is also highly rewarding. Many professionals experience "compassion satisfaction": pleasure and contentment as a result of helping others (Stamm, 2002, 2005). Helping clients and making a positive difference in their lives is gratifying; yet, emotional exhaustion is a concern and fear for those in the helping professions. This chapter has reviewed elements of the work environment that contribute or deter from the helper's quality of work life. Work stress remedies include ongoing and enriching supervisor/colleague relationships that provide an essential stress buffer. Additional stress busters include individual protective mechanisms, such as having a sense of personal control and using effective stress relievers. Yet, less is known regarding what adds to compassion satisfaction and it cannot be assumed it is directly related to decreases in psychological distress. Instead, it appears to be a separate construct that encompasses the joy and pleasure derived from helping others (Radey & Figley, 2007; Stalker et al., 2007). Turning to research regarding the characteristics of highly competent and satisfied helpers provides essential information for maximizing compassion satisfaction and thus the quality of the professional work life.

Obviously, not all who are in the business of helping are negatively affected by their work. There are those helpers who rarely experience vicarious trauma, compassion fatigue, or burnout (Skovholt, 2001). Or, if they do, are able to effectively use their resources to refill their wells of compassion and empathy. Skovholt and Jennings' (2004) studied 10 "master" therapists and found specific cognitive, emotional, and relational characteristics of these highly competent and satisfied professionals. Their findings highlight the significance of key personality characteristics rather than specific skills or theoretical orientation in master therapists. The master therapists were found to have good coping skills, mastery and personal control, strong relationship skills, and emotional stability (Skovholt & Jennings, 2004). The authors' findings add to the occupational stress and coping literature and underscore how continued professional and personal development is not only essential for building professional expertise but for compassion satisfaction as well.

The participants in Skovholt and Jennings' (2004) research included six PhD psychologists, three masters-level social workers, and one psychiatrist. The 10 master therapists (seven women and three men) ranged in age from 50 to 72 years old, and their level of experience varied from 21 to 41 years ($M = 29.50$). Study participant criteria included being nominated by four or more peers as a "master therapist" (i.e., a therapist perceived by their peers as the "best of the best" including being knowledgeable, skilled, compassionate, and empathic). The theoretical orientations represented included psychodynamic ($n = 4$), family systems ($n = 2$), existential-humanistic ($n = 2$), and integrative ($n = 2$). Therapeutic mastery was found to involve persons who actively engage in improving their skills, are proactive in confronting professional and personal stressors, constantly acquire new knowledge, and maintain openness to experiences and feedback from others. Additionally, they nurture a personal life, construct fortifying relationships, and are involved in a variety of restorative activities. Interestingly, the following qualities of the 10 master therapists have much in common with the characteristics of self-actualized people (Skovholt & Jennings, 2004):

Cognitive Domain:

- Voracious learners who have a will to grow, are insatiably curious, and are continuously developing personally and professionally.
- Accumulated experiences and thus wisdom are a major resource.
- Value cognitive complexity and the ambiguity of the human condition. They have a profound understanding and acceptance of the human condition.
- Express a life-affirming outlook.

Emotional Domain:

- Preserve emotional wellness, thus insuring professional vitality.
- Attend to emotional well-being and how it affects the quality of one's work.
- Accept feedback and are non-defensive.
- Accept self and acknowledges limitations.
- Passionately enjoy life.

Relational Domain:

- Possess strong relationship skills. They are able to intensely engage others.
- Establish a strong working alliance with clients. They believe in a client's ability to change and heal.

PROFESSIONAL QUALITY OF LIFE SCALE (ProQOL)

Helpers may not be doing their job effectively as they are unaware of the causes, symptoms, and consequences of different types of work-related stressors. Thus, a place to start for professionals who are struggling in their work environments is to assess for secondary trauma/compassion fatigue and burnout. Yet, evaluating only worker distress does not give a complete picture of the professional's quality of work life and, thus, assessing for the positive qualities of the helper's work experience is necessary as well. The Professional Quality of Life Scale (Stamm, 2005) assesses the quality of life associated with one's chosen profession and includes both the positive (i.e., compassion satisfaction) and negative (i.e., burnout and secondary trauma/compassion fatigue) aspects of doing one's job. It is not a diagnostic test but instead is a resource for practitioners to assess and monitor their own levels of distress and satisfaction (see Appendix G for a copy of the scale, scoring instructions, and copyright information).

The ProQOL is a 30-item scale where helpers (e.g., therapists, nurses, humanitarian workers, teachers) are asked to indicate how frequently each item occurred during the last 30 days (Stamm, 2005). The scale consists of a 6-point Likert Scale (0 = Never, 1 = Rarely, 2 = A Few Times, 3 = Somewhat Often, 4 = Often, and 5 = Very Often). The ProQOL has three discrete subscales measuring compassion satisfaction (10 items), burnout (10 items), and secondary trauma/compassion fatigue (10 items) that are scored by summing the item responses for each 10-item scale. Higher scores indicate increased compassion satisfaction, burnout, and compassion fatigue. Thus, ideally one would desire high compassion satisfaction scores and moderate to low burnout and compassion fatigue scores.

For the ProQOL, compassion satisfaction is defined as the pleasure derived from being able to do one's work well. This includes feeling satisfied, successful, having a positive outlook, and believing one can make a difference. An item example is, "I feel invigorated after working with those I help." The average score on this subscale is 37 (SD 7; alpha scale reliability .87). Burnout refers to difficulties in coping with work or with doing one's job effectively and is characterized by feelings of unhappiness, exhaustion, being overwhelmed, and "bogged down". An item example includes, "I feel overwhelmed by the size of the caseload I have to deal with." The average score on the burnout subscale is 22 (SD 6.0; alpha scale reliability .72). Compassion fatigue is characterized as exposure to secondary trauma. Unlike burnout, CF involves negative feelings driven by fear along with a preoccupation with thoughts of people one has helped. An item example includes, "I jump or am startled by unexpected sounds." The average score for CF is 13 (SD 6; alpha scale reliability of .80).

SUMMARY

Professionals' empathic and compassionate reserves are at times exhausted, giving away to feelings of hopelessness and disconnection from their clients (Bride, Radley, & Figley, 2007). Helpers who work with traumatized individuals often are emotionally exhausted; yet, many experience compassion satisfaction in their work. Job stress is real, but the benefits of the work often overcome the challenges. The professional literature rarely addresses the resilient practitioner; the helper who is fulfilled and flourishes despite being exposed to client pain, anguish, and trauma. Consequently, Skovholt and Jennings' (2004) qualitative study on master therapists provides essential information on the protective mechanisms for those helpers who consistently replenish and restore themselves in the midst of working with client anguish. Additional research is necessary to explore the specific connections and pathways between vicarious trauma, compassion fatigue, burnout, and compassion satisfaction.

11

Implications, Cautions, and Future Directions

This book has offered conceptual frameworks, assessments, and intervention methods for practitioners to support and enhance resiliency in female survivors of family violence. The anguish clients experience from traumatic events should not be minimized. Yet, it does not have to be the centerpiece of individuals' identities. Incorporating a resiliency and strengths-based focus into mental health services with survivors assists in letting go of a pathology-oriented helping paradigm and instead centers on individuals' abilities to grow and heal in the midst of their suffering. Additionally, it embodies a philosophy of hope, underscores the resourcefulness of clients, and illuminates the many ways people prevail during, and in the aftermath, of family violence. This chapter addresses practice, research, and policy implications for future direction in identifying, encouraging, and honoring the resourcefulness of survivors. Practice cautions of implementing resiliency and strengths-based practice with survivors is also addressed.

CHALLENGING THE MEDICAL MODEL IN MENTAL HEALTH PRACTICE

Core concepts of the medical model prevail in mental health practice and policy, particularly the categorization of human distress in the form of a diagnosis. Mental health policies that rely on diagnosis of mental disorders, particularly when it is not guided by an understanding of oppression and trauma, may be less responsive to the needs and strengths of survivors of family violence (Dietz, 2000). Additionally, increased reliance on evidence-based practice and outcome measures may inadvertently lead to more ritualized interventions preventing helpers from seeking out or practicing alternative approaches to mental health treatment (Oko, 2006). Yet, as highlighted throughout this book, the ramifications of focusing on symptom reduction and client deficits—more so than client strengths, resilience, and posttraumatic growth—can impede the healing process and at times exacerbate client suffering. For example, Erika, age 38, (a participant in the author's research on incest survivors) experienced numerous mental health services that centered on her pathology resulting in several hospitalizations, a variety of prescribed medications, and many diagnostic labels. After nine years of little progress and revolving in and out of mental health treatment doors, Erika, out of desperation, summoned up the courage to choose a different life. She made the decision that she could no longer live life as a "mentally ill" person confined to psychiatric facilities. She became determined to no longer be in state care because she wanted to "do something" with her life.

> I never thought I even had choices. I felt like everything was so limited. Choice is a wonderful gift, and I think we forget how special it is until you don't have it. When I was 29, I woke up one morning and decided I had to make a decision. I had three choices: live my life like that [in institutions], kill myself, or get out and do something. I decided to do something. I did get out and have never been back to a long-term state hospital like that.

At the age of 32, Erika took further control of her life and decided to go back to college and earn a degree as a respiratory therapist. She was still affected by her trauma, particularly her dissociation, so she searched and found a therapist who could address her trauma's aftereffects while also supporting her dreams and aspirations (and thus not cast a shadow of the past on her future). Erika received her degree and now works full time as a respiratory therapist—something that her past helpers never imagined possible. Erika believes that her struggles with adversity helped her to be intuitive to the needs of others. She loves her job and feels that she has a positive impact on her patients because she can see their needs from a holistic perspective (e.g., bio-psycho-social-spiritual) rather than only acknowledging their respiratory (i.e., physical) issues.

> When I started to get better, as far as my self-esteem and believing that I was worth something, then I started to correlate the strengths that I used to survive the incest to the strengths that I was able to use [to move on in my life]. One thing I really learned is intuition. I pick up things quickly. I'm observant, and it helps me to prepare to problem solve and in my position at work—I'm a respiratory therapist—it's been very helpful because I see the whole person because I know that's important. I know my patients appreciate it because I hear it [from them]. It just makes me feel good to know that I was able to open my eyes enough to see what their other needs may be.

Erika's resolve to heal, along with finding a compassionate and understanding therapist, allowed her to address both her past incest experiences and her future ambitions of finishing college and obtaining full-time employment. Yet, even with her successes, she still wishes that she had not been sexually abused. However, she recognizes that her struggles to overcome her childhood trauma have shaped her into the person she is today. She continues to be determined to be the "best that she can be":

> The abuse part was really hard. But I learned a lot from it. It has made me the person I am, and in some ways, I don't think I would have the qualities I have unless I had gone through it. I'm not sayin' I'm glad [that I went through it]. [But] I believe that all things happen for a reason. It made me who I am, and that's okay, but I need to let it [the victimization] go more as this is my life, and I want it back [a life that doesn't center on victimization]. And I want to be the best that I can be.

Shifting helping paradigms (i.e., from a medical model to a strengths-based model) in mental health settings does not tend to happen simply as a result of changing agency policies or mission statements that underscore client strengths and resilient capacities. The presence of a clear and credible policy is important; yet, if a set of carefully defined program activities is lacking, workers are left without a means of how to deliver services in a strengths-based manner. As a result, mental health professionals may not embrace an alternative helping paradigm not because they are not interested, but because it is one more thing in which they are not equipped to do. Without the appropriate practice tools, a situation is set up where workers report that they address clients' strengths to meet agency expectations, but in practice may still operate from a deficit approach. Helpers who are bogged down in client symptoms, diagnoses, and deficits may overidentify with clients' feelings of helplessness and hopelessness. Therefore, viewing clients as having strengths and resources to cope with adversity provides a much better chance of helping clients find avenues to improve their situations (Cohen, 1999). Ultimately, using a helping framework that draws on client strengths and abilities allows for hope and the possibility that one's life can change regardless of what has come before.

SHIFTING HELPING PARADIGMS: MENTAL HEALTH PRACTICE IMPLICATIONS

Resiliency research, posttraumatic growth literature, and strengths-based social work practice contribute to a helping framework that optimizes well-being while counterbalancing a medical model in mental health practice. Integrating these cutting edge trends into work with survivors of family violence provides a different way of looking at individuals that highlights their capabilities, competencies, hopes, and possibilities however shattered or altered through oppression and trauma (Saleebey, 1996). Although addressing the consequences of family violence is an important treatment concern, it should not obscure the need to honor and develop women's resilient capacities. The following quote is from a former client of the author's that illustrates how focusing on resiliency allowed her to see herself in a different way and thus respond accordingly to her newfound view of herself as a resilient survivor:

> Although I had done some reading on my own about incest survivor recovery, most of what I found in self-help literature was grounded in a damage paradigm. I was not familiar with the challenge model or the concept of resiliency. Kim's [the author] ability to integrate her knowledge as a scholar into her work as a healer was truly life changing for me. I have become a better advocate for my school [place of employment], my staff, and our students and families because of my newfound understanding of myself as a resilient survivor.

As highlighted in chapter 9, survivors' recommendations for mental health practice centered on improving the quality of the worker-client relationship. The therapeutic connection provides an opportunity for survivors to experience bonding with another person while also healing from some of the effects of personal and social oppression (Palmer, 1991). For many participants in the author's research finding a connection with a caring helping professional, who believed in their ability to heal, was essential to their recovery. Survivors' advice to helpers is similar to assumptions and principles of the strengths perspective in social work practice. "The strengths perspective honors two things: the power of the self to heal and right itself with the help of the environment, and the need for the alliance with the hope that life might really be otherwise" (Saleebey, 1996, p. 303). Clients are motivated to change when their strengths are supported by professionals who believe in them and their possibility of a different future. Clients' skills, strengths, and competencies provide the foundation for moving on with their lives (Saleebey, 1996). Thus, the client's knowledge and lived experiences are of central importance in guiding the helping process.

PRACTICE CAUTIONS FOR IMPLEMENTING RESILIENCE AND STRENGTHS-BASED PRACTICE

Helping organizations may not operate from a strengths orientation, such as those where a medical model prevails, and thus centers agency policies and practice on the reduction of client symptoms. Consequently, practitioners that are possibility-focused rather than problem-based may be at odds with the agency and perhaps their colleagues who do not understand or oppose a capacity-based approach. In the author's experience with graduate social work students, they often enter into their internships with a strengths-based perspective, but quickly become disillusioned as they are told by more "seasoned" helpers that they are being naïve and too idealistic. The author often congratulates them on receiving such feedback. This generally leaves the students confused until it is further explained that these are actually compliments. In other words, being "naïve" means the student is starting where the client is, suspending disbelief, and offering acceptance. Furthermore, being "idealistic" means the student believes in clients' abilities to heal and transform their lives. Essentially, the author explains that they are practicing from a strength-based perspective, which is not wrong but may differ from their colleagues' view of clients' abilities. Although creating this awareness helps students to understand that it is not about their inexperience, but instead the helping paradigm they operate from, it is still challenging to work in this manner when it is not standard agency practice. Yet, the author reports to them that coworkers start to "come around" when clients, whom others generally have given up on—and thus believe to be beyond redemption—show progress, change, and transformation. As one student reported, "I've been assigned a 'multi-problem' family that staff has worked with over the years and, consequently, warned me about in regard to their 'resistance' to change. Yes, they do have problems, but I also see them as a 'multi-strength' family who continue to seek services because they want to have a different life." Interestingly, the student's "multi-problem" and "resistant" family made significant progress in their work with the "naïve" and "idealistic" student. They made so much change that her colleagues inquired about her secret for turning the family around. She replied, "There is no secret. I just supported their desire for change and we worked together to make that happen."

Clients generally seek mental services because of problems that are causing distress in their lives (McMillen, Morris, & Sherraden, 2004; McQuade & Ehrenreich, 1997). Therefore, identification of strengths is not likely to be relevant to clients initially if helpers do not also empathize with clients' suffering and offer avenues to lighten their burdens. Appropriate timing of highlighting an individual's strengths is necessary as clients quite often see themselves from a "damaged" or "vulnerability" perspective when they start services. The obligation for practitioners to focus on two targets (problems and strengths) is challenging but important for starting where the client is (McMillen et al., 2004). Thus, mental health practitioners may embrace the belief of survivors as experts; yet, they need to continue to validate the seriousness of their victimization. For instance, telling survivors who are overwhelmed and stressed that "you have the solutions to your own problems" (when they feel that is not the case and hence the reason they are asking for help) may leave them feeling rejected and doubtful that the worker understands their suffering. Working with clients who are not used to thinking of themselves in terms of strengths is hard work because enhancing resiliency in survivors is not simply a matter of reframing their problems. If that was the case, then clients would not have to actually work to make changes instead they would merely reconceptualize their problems as strengths (Saleebey, 1996). Instead, supporting their resiliency involves unraveling strengths, capabilities, and competencies intertwined with their problems and building on these in order for them to progress forward in their lives.

For survivors of family violence who seek mental health services, safety remains the number one concern, whether that is physical and/ or psychological safety. Allowing clients to endure unsafe situations without any type of safety planning is harmful and irresponsible. Putting the onerous task on them to bounce back from experiencing violence is not the intended purpose of encouraging resiliency in survivors. Clients are the experts; however, this does not mean that they have access to all the resources needed to affect their situations. The worker also brings skills, knowledge, and guidance to the therapeutic relationship to offer tools for addressing PTSD symptoms, safety issues, and restoring support networks. Upon establishing physical and/or psychological safety, survivors are then more equipped to transform life narratives centered on their victimization into ones of strength, purpose, and possibility.

Because survivors cannot change the past but can influence how it is interpreted, they can choose whether or not victimization becomes the centerpiece of their identities. Yet, the goal of the helping process should not be for clinicians to impose alternative interpretations onto survivors' life stories including ones of strength and resiliency (Docherty & McColl, 2003). The clinician must be careful to not minimize victimization and its often devastating consequences as a person is *not* better off, for instance, because she was beaten, raped, or sexually abused. Rather, individuals may redefine themselves by their struggles to prevail despite their victimization (Norman, 2000). Thus, the practitioner aids the survivor to recreate a narrative that includes positive outcomes from one's struggle to overcome the trauma, but *not* from any loss or changes that may have occurred as a result of it (Tedeschi & Calhoun, 1996). It is a natural impulse for helpers to want to sort, categorize, label, and weave disjointed or disconnected themes into an organized whole that moves survivor accounts into a progressive trajectory toward health. Yet, moving survivors' narratives toward a "storybook ending" rather than creating "space" for alternative interpretations of their suffering only serves the practitioner who perhaps is uncomfortable or unprepared to bear witness to the torture and horror that are a part of clients' life stories. Thus, helpers who listen and support survivors' stories of suffering without letting their agendas interfere validates clients' experiences and, consequently, opens up "space" for them to view their stories in a different light including any gains received from their struggles to overcome their trauma.

RESEARCH IMPLICATIONS

The intent of the author's research (see chapter 3) is to carefully explore the dynamics and consequences of family violence; particularly, regarding how individuals' survival abilities develop amongst chaos and pain. For these studies, participants were viewed as experts whose knowledge could assist in developing theory that would transform mental health practice. To elicit stories of oppression and resistance, the author used the qualitative method of in-depth interviewing to generate descriptions of areas of resilience in survivors of family violence and to build insight on how to mobilize these resources in mental health practice. Participants were actively involved in the theory building because they provided the data from which it evolved. Understanding how women interpret their survival is essential because it assists researchers and clinicians in gaining a comprehensive view of the many dimensions of trauma, trauma recovery, and resilience. Participants' stories demonstrate the depth of pain they experienced and the power of the human spirit to heal from such adversity. Their stories of courage and determination are truly inspirational for others facing similar hardship.

Qualitative inquiry focuses on the meaning of participants' subjective experiences, particularly by vulnerable groups such as traumatized persons. The personal and interactive communication offered through qualitative approaches may be best suited in researching such sensitive topics as family violence (Jansen & Davis, 1998). Open-ended interview research allows for the exploration of participants' views of reality while providing them control over what information they contribute, as well as control of the direction of the research. In studying the issue of family violence, survivors will not disclose information unless they feel comfortable with the research process. Their control is essential because they are being asked to give something so personal of themselves: their stories of vicitimization. Having survivors share their life stories validates their wisdom and, at the same time, helps to develop a deeper understanding regarding the many dimensions to healing from trauma.

A rich source of meaning is present in the stories of women who have experienced family violence. Naturalistic inquiry involves being immersed in the world viewpoints of the participants and is guided by the assumption that not all concepts related to the phenomena under study have been identified (Crabtree & Miller, 1992; Strauss & Corbin, 1990). Thus, such qualitative research provides an opportunity to develop concepts of resilience that go beyond preset determinants of "healthy" coping (e.g., the absence of psychological distress). Rather than focusing on survivors' damage, the author's research provides an alternative to existing research and clinical literature by recognizing the enduring strengths those individuals have as a result of findings ways to resist their subjugation and its aftereffects. The heightened focus on strategies of protection and resistance encourages researchers to get back in touch with the resourcefulness of survivors and provides a background for studying and applying additional strengths.

MENTAL HEALTH POLICY IMPLICATIONS

Managed care policies provide increasing pressure for practitioners to treat mental health concerns in a more cost-effective way. "Managed mental health care is defined as a variety of strategies, systems, and mechanisms, whose goal is the monitoring and control of the utilization of mental health and substance abuse services" (Riffe & Kondrat, 1997, p. 43). Under managed care, requests for initial services are reviewed including the diagnosis, the type and quantity of services provided, the reimbursement rate, and review of any additional requests for continuation of services (Claiborne & Fortune, 2005; Merrick, Horgan, Garnick, & Hodgkin, 2006; Reamer, 1997). Limitations on type and duration of mental health services may circumvent the healing process for survivors of family violence. Thus, it is imperative that clients' voices and experiences inform mental health policy as well as individual practice. A need exists to organize survivors and mental health practitioners to lobby for the regulations of managed care that will benefit clients healing process rather than restrict it (Deitz, 2000).

CONCLUSION

A former client of the author's stated that she did not want to be labeled as a survivor and that a new word should be developed to capture the experiences of individuals who prevail over family violence. She came up with the term *overcomer* to identify herself and others who have overcome despite experiencing immense adversity. This book contains numerous examples of overcomers. Their wisdom, courage, and determination highlight that healing is possible regardless of one's traumatic history. Addressing survivors' resourcefulness and resiliency helps those to overcome experiences that otherwise might threaten to render them powerless. A quote from a well-known overcomer, Helen Keller (a blind and deaf American educator), encapsulates the spirit and hope of this book for practitioners and survivors who seek their services: "Although the world is full of suffering, it is full also of the overcoming of it."

References

Ai, A. L., & Park, C. L. (2005). Possibilities of the positive following violence and trauma: Informing the coming decade of research. *Journal of Interpersonal Violence, 20*(2), 242–250.

Adams, R. E., Boscarino, J. A., & Figley, C. R. (2006). Compassion fatigue and psychological distress among social workers: A validation study. *American Journal of Orthopsychiatry, 76*, 103–108.

Aldwin, C. M., & Levenson, M. R. (2004). Posttraumatic growth: A developmental perspective. *Psychological Inquiry, 15*(1), 19–21.

Allen, J. (1995). *Coping with trauma: A guide to self-understanding.* Washington, DC: American Psychiatric Press, Inc.

Anderson, C., & Alexander, P. (1996). The relationship between attachment and dissociation in adult survivors of incest. *Psychiatry: Interpersonal and Biological Processes, 59*(3), 240–254.

Anderson, K. M. (2001). Recovery: Resistance and resilience in female incest survivors. Doctoral dissertation. University of Kansas, *Dissertation Abstracts, 62*(09), 3185A.

Anderson, K. M. (2006). Surviving incest: The art of resistance. *Families in Society, 83*(3), 409–416.

Anderson, K. M., Cowger, C., & Snively, C. (2009). Assessing strengths: Identifying acts of resistance to violence and oppression. In D. Saleebey (Ed.), *The strengths perspective in social work practice* (5th ed., pp. 181–198). Boston: Allyn & Bacon.

Anderson, K. M., & Danis, F. (2006). Adult daughters of battered women: Resistance and resilience in the face of danger. *Affilia, 21*(4), 419–432.

Anderson, K. M., & Hiersteiner, C. (2007). Listening to the stories of adults in treatment who were sexually abused as children. *Families in Society, 88*(4), 637–644.

Anderson, K., & Sundet, P. (2006). Making a mission statement a reality in child welfare: Resiliency and solution-focused therapy as core strategy. *Professional Development: The International Journal of Continuing Social Work Education, 9*(2–3), 54–64.

Anderson, J. C., Martin, J. L., Mullen, P. E., Romans, S., & Herbison, P. (1993). The prevalence of childhood sexual abuse experiences in a community sample of women. *Journal of the American Academy of Child and Adolescent Psychiatry, 32,* 911–919.

Anderson, G., Yasenik, L., & Ross, C. A. (1993). Dissociative experiences and disorders among women who identify themselves as sexual abuse survivors. *Child Abuse & Neglect, 17,* 677–686.

Asher, M. B. (2001). Spirituality and religion in social work practice. *Social Work Today, 1*(7), 1–5.

Armstrong, L. (1994). *Rocking the cradle of sexual politics*. New York: Addison-Wesley Publishing Company.

Baird, S., & Jenkins, S. R. (2003). Vicarious traumatization, secondary traumatic stress, and burnout in sexual assault and domestic violence agency staff. *Violence and Victims, 18*(1), 71–86.

Barnard, C. (1994). Resiliency: A shift in our perception? *The American Journal of Family Therapy, 22*(2), 135–144.

Banyard, V. L., & Graham-Bermann, S. A. (1993). Can women cope? A gender analysis of theories of coping with stress. *Psychology of Women Quarterly, 17*, 303–318.

Beardslee, W. R., & Podorefsky, D. (1988). Resilient adolescents whose parents have serious affective and other psychiatric disorders: Importance of self-understanding and relationships. *American Journal of Psychiatry, 14*(1), 63–69.

Beitchman, J., Zucker, K., Hood, J., DaCosta, G., & Akman, D. (1992). A review of the long-term effects of child sexual abuse. *Child Abuse & Neglect, 16*, 101–118.

Bell, H., Kulkarni, S., & Dalton, L. (2003). Organizational prevention of vicarious trauma. *Journal of Contemporary Human Services, 84*, 463–470.

Bent-Goodley, T. B., & Fowler, D. N. (2006). Spiritual and religious abuse: Expanding what is known about domestic violence. *Affilia, 21*(3), 282–295.

Bergin, A. E. (1991). Values and religious issues in psychotherapy and mental health. *American Psychologist, 46*(4), 394–403.

Bernard, B. (1996). From research to practice: The foundations of the resiliency paradigm. *Resiliency in Action, Winter*, 7–11.

Bhuvaneswar, C., & Shafer, A. (2004). Survivor of that time, that place: Clinical uses of violence survivors' narratives. *Journal of Medical Humanities, 25*(2), 109–127.

Blake-White, J., & Kline, C. (1985). Treating dissociative process in adult victims of childhood incest. *Social Casework, 66*, 394–402.

Blundo, R. (2001). Learning strength-based practice: Challenging our personal and professional frames. *Families in Society, 82*(3), 296–304.

Bogat, G. A., Levendosky, A. A., Theran, S., von Eye, A., & Davidson, W. S. (2003). Predicting the psychosocial effects of interpersonal violence (IPV). *Journal of Interpersonal Violence, 18*(11), 1271–1291.

Bolen, J. (1993). The impact of sexual abuse on women's health. *Psychiatric Annals, 23*(8), 446–453.

Bremner, J. D., & Marmar, C. R. (1998). *Trauma, memory, and dissociation*. Washington, DC: American Psychiatric Press, Inc.

Bride, B. E., & Figley, C. R. (2007). The fatigue of compassionate social workers: An introduction to the special issue on compassion fatigue. *Clinical Social Work Journal, 35*, 151–153.

Bride, B. E., & Radey, M., & Figley, C. R. (2007). Measuring compassion fatigue. *Clinical Social Work Journal, 35*, 155–165.

Briere, J., & Runtz, M. (1993). Childhood sexual abuse: Long-term sequelae and implications for psychological assessment. *Journal of Interpersonal Violence, 8*(3), 312–330.

Briere, J., & Scott, C. (2006). *Principles of trauma therapy: A guide to symptoms, evaluation, and treatment*. Thousand Oaks, CA: SAGE Publications.

Browne, A., & Finkelhor, D. (1986). Impact of child sexual abuse: A review of the research. *Psychological Bulletin, 99*(1), 66–67.

Byrd, R. (1994). Assessing resilience in victims of childhood maltreatment. Doctoral dissertation. Pepperdine University, *Dissertation Abstracts, 5503.*

Bryer, A., Bernadette, A., Nelson, B., Miller, J., & Krol, P. (1987). Childhood sexual and physical abuse as factors in adult psychiatric illness. *American Journal of Psychiatry, 144*(11), 1426–1430.

Burgess, A. W., & Holmstrom, L. L. (1974). Rape trauma syndrome. *American Journal of Psychiatry, 131,* 981–986.

Burstow, B. (2003). Toward a radical understanding of trauma and trauma work. *Violence Against Women, 9*(11), 1293–1317.

Bussey, M., & Wise, J. B. (2007). *Trauma transformed: An empowerment response.* New York: Columbia University Press.

Cadell, S., Regehr, C., & Hemsworth, D. (2003). Factors contributing to posttraumatic growth: A proposed structural equation model. *American Journal of Orthopsychiatry, 73*(3), 279–287.

Calhoun, L. G., & Tedeschi, R. G. (1998). Beyond recovery from trauma: Implications for clinical practice and research. *Journal of Social Issues, 54*(2), 357–371.

Campbell, J., Rose, L., Kub, J., & Nedd, D. (1998). Voices of strength and resistance: A contextual and longitudinal analysis of women's responses to battering. *Journal of Interpersonal Violence, 13*(6), 743–762.

Canda, E. R. (1988). Spirituality, diversity, and social work practice. *Social Casework, 69*(4), 238–247.

Canfield, J. (2005). Secondary traumatization, burnout, and vicarious traumatization: A review of the literature as it relates to therapists who treat trauma. *Smith College Studies in Social Work, 75*(2), 81–101.

Cavanagh, K. (2003). Understanding women's responses to domestic violence. *Qualitative Social Work, 2*(3), 229–249.

Ceresne, L. (1995). Reflections on resilience: Narratives of sexually abuse women's coping and healing strategies. (Doctoral Dissertation Dalhousie University). *Dissertation Abstracts, International, 35*(05), 2078A.

Chaffin, M., Wherry, J., & Dykman, R. (1997). School age children's coping with sexual abuse: Abuse stresses and symptoms associated with four coping strategies. *Child Abuse & Neglect, 21,* 227–240.

Chandler, C. K., Holden, J. M., & Kolander, C. A. (1992). Counseling for spiritual wellness: Theory and practice. *Journal of Counseling & Development, 71,* 168–175.

Chard, K. M. (2005). An evaluation of cognitive processing therapy for the treatment of posttraumatic stress disorder related to childhood sexual abuse. *Journal of Consulting and Clinical Psychology, 73*(5), 965–971.

Charmaz, K. (2006). *Constructing grounded theory: A practical guide through qualitative analysis.* Thousand Oaks, CA: SAGE Publications.

Chase, S. (1995). Taking narrative seriously: Consequences for method and theory in interview studies. In R. Josselson & Lieblich, A. (Eds.), *Interpreting experience: The narrative study of lives* (Vol. 3, pp. 1–25). Thousand Oaks, CA: SAGE Publications.

Chu, J., & Dill, D. (1990). Dissociative symptoms in relation to childhood physical and sexual abuse. *American Journal of Psychiatry, 147*(7), 887–892.

Claiborne, N., & Fortune, A. (2005). Preparing students for practice in a managed care environment. *Journal of Teaching in Social Work, 25*(3/4), 177–195.

Clandinin, D., & Connelly, F. (2000). *Narrative inquiry: Experience and story in qualitative research.* San Francisco: Jossey-Bass Publishers.

Cobb, A. R., Tedeschi, R. G., Calhoun, L. G., & Cann, A. (2006). Correlates of post-traumatic growth in survivors of intimate partner violence. *Journal of Traumatic Stress, 19*(6), 895–903.

Cohen, B. Z. (1999). Intervention and supervision in strengths-based social work practice. *Families in Society, 80*(5), 460–577.

Cohler, B. J. (1987). Adversity, resilience, and the study of lives. In E. J. Anthony & B. J. Cohler (Eds.), *The invulnerable child* (pp. 363–424). New York: Guilford Press.

Cohler, B. J. (1991). The life story and the study of resilience and response to adversity. *Journal of Narrative and Life History, 1,* 169–200.

Cole, P., & Putnam, F. (1992). Effect of incest on self and social functioning: A developmental psychopathology perspective. *Journal of Consulting and Clinical Psychology, 60*(2), 174–184.

Conner, K. M., & Davidson, J. (2003). Development of a new resilience scale: The Connor-Davidson resilience scale (CD-RISC). *Depression and Anxiety, 18*(76), 76–82.

Coons, P. (1986). Child abuse and multiple personality disorder: A review of the literature and suggestions for treatment. *Child Abuse & Neglect, 10,* 455–462.

Cooper, M., & Lesser, J. (2005). *Clinical social work practice: An integrated approach* (2nd ed.). New York: Pearson Education, Inc.

Corcoran, J. (1999). Solution-focused interviewing with child protective services cases. *Child Welfare, July/August*(4), 461–479.

Courtois, C. A. (1993). *Adult survivors of sexual abuse.* Milwaukee, WI: Families International, Inc.

Cowger, C., Anderson, K. M., & Snively, C. (2006). Assessing strengths: The political context of individual, family, and community empowerment. In D. Saleebey (Ed.), *The strengths perspective in social work practice* (4th ed., pp. 93–113). Boston: Allyn & Bacon.

Crabtree, B. F., & Miller, W. L. (1992). *Doing qualitative research.* Newbury Park, CA: SAGE Publications.

Cummings, J., Peplar, D., & Moore, T. (1999). Behavior problems in children exposed to wife abuse: Gender differences. *Journal of Family Violence, 14*(2), 133–156.

Cunningham, M. (2003). Impact of trauma work on social work clinicians: Empirical findings. *Social Work, 48*(4), 451–459.

Davis, L. (1986). A feminist approach to social work research. *Affilia, 1*(1), 32–47.

Dean, R. G. (1998). A narrative approach to groups. *Clinical Social Work Journal, 26*(1), 23–37.

De Jong, P., & Berg, I. K. (2002). *Interviewing for solutions* (2nd ed.). Pacific Grove, CA: Brooks/Cole.

De Jong, P., & Miller, S. (1995). How to interview for client strengths. *Social Work, 40*(6), 729–736.

Denzin, N. K., & Lincoln, Y. S. (1998). *The landscape of qualitative research.* Thousand Oaks, CA: SAGE Publications.

DePanfilis, D. (2006). Compassion fatigue, burnout, and compassion satisfaction: Implications for retention of workers. *Child Abuse & Neglect, 30,* 1067–1069.

Dietz, C. (2000). Responding to oppression and abuse: A feminist challenge to clinical social work. *Affilia, 15*(3), 369–389.

Dinsmore, C. (1991). *From surviving to thriving: Incest, feminism, and recovery.* Albany, NY: State University of New York Press.

Docherty, D., & McColl, M. A. (2003). Illness stories: Themes emerging through narrative. *Social Work in Health Care, 37*(1), 19–39.

Dutton, M. A., & Rubinstein, F. L. (1995). Working with people with PTSD: Research implications. In C. R. Figley (Ed.), *Compassion fatigue: Coping with secondary traumatic stress disorder in those who treat the traumatized* (pp. 82–100). New York: Brunner/Mazel.

Egeland, E., Carlson, E., & Sroufe, L. (1993). Resilience as process. *Development and Psychopathology, 5,* 517–528.

Erickson, R. J., & Ritter, C. (2001). Emotional labour, burnout, and inauthenticity: Does gender matter? *Social Psychology Quarterly, 64,* 146–163.

Everett, B., & Gallop, R. (2001). *The link between childhood trauma and mental illness: Effective interventions for mental health professionals.* Thousand Oaks, CA: SAGE Publications.

Everstine, D. S., & Everstine, L. (1993). *The trauma response: Treatment for emotional injury.* New York: W.W. Norton & Company.

Fantuzzo, J., Boruch, R., Beriama, A., Atkins, M., & Marcus, S. (1997). Domestic violence and children: Prevalence and risk in five major U.S. cities. *Journal of the American Academy of Child & Adolescent Psychiatry, 36*(1), 116–122.

Farber, E., & Egeland, B. (1987). Invulnerability among abused and neglected children. In E. J. Anthony & B. J. Cohler (Eds.), *The invulnerable child* (pp. 253–288). New York: Guilford Press.

Figley, C. R. (1993). Coping with stressors on the home front. *Journal of Social Issues, 49*(4), 51–71.

Figley, C. R. (1995). *Compassion fatigue: Coping with secondary traumatic stress disorder in those who treat the traumatized.* New York: Bruner Mazel.

Figley, C. R. (2002). *Treating compassion fatigue.* New York: Brunner-Rutledge.

Figley, C. R. (2007). An introduction to the special issue on the MHAT-IV. *Traumatology, 13*(4), 4–7.

Figley, C. R., & Kleber, R. J. (1995). Beyond the "victim": Secondary traumatic stress. In R. J. Kleber, C. R. Figley, & B. P. R. Gersons (Eds.), *Beyond trauma: Cultural and societal dynamics* (pp. 75–98). New York: Plenum.

Figley, C. R., & Marks, R. E. (2008). An introduction to the special issues, identification and applications of lessons learned by the Tulane University Community. *Traumatology, 14*(4), 4–8.

Frankl, V. E. (1984). *Man's search for meaning.* New York: Pocket Books.

Fraser, M. (1997). *Risk and resilience in childhood: An ecological perspective.* Washington, DC: NASW Press.

Frazier, P., Conlon, A., & Glaser, T. (2001). Positive and negative life changes following sexual assault. *Journal of Consulting and Clinical Psychology, 69,* 1048–1055.

Freedman, S. R., & Enright, R. D. (1996). Forgiveness as an intervention goal with incest survivors. *Journal of Consulting and Clinical Psychology, 64*(5), 983–992.

Freudenberger, H. J. (1975). The staff burnout syndrome in alternative institutions. *Psychotherapy: Theory, Research and Practice, 12*(1), 73–82.

Fry, P. S. (2001). The unique contribution of key existential factors to the prediction of psychological well-being of older adults following spousal loss. *The Gerontologist, 49,* 69–81.

Furman, L. E. (1994). Religion and spirituality in social work education: Preparing the culturally-sensitive practitioner for the future. *Social Work and Christianity: An International Journal, 21,* 103–117.

Ganje-Fling, M. A., & McCarthy, P. (1996). Impact of childhood sexual abuse on client spiritual development: Counseling implications. *Journal of Counseling & Development, 74,* 253–258.

Garmezy, N. (1987). Stress, competence, and development: Continuities in the study of schizophrenic adults, children vulnerable to psychopathology, and the search for stress resistant children. *American Journal of Orthopsychiatry, 57*(2), 159–173.

Garmezy, N., & Masten, A. (1986). Stress, competence, and resilience: Common frontiers for therapist and psychopathologist. *Behavior Therapy, 17,* 500–521.

Gasker, J. (1999). Freud's therapeutic mistake with Jung's disclosure of childhood sexual abuse: Narrative lessons in the do's and don'ts of validation. *Journal of Poetry Therapy, 13*(2), 81–96.

Gasker, J. (2001). 'I didn't understand the damage it did': Narrative factors influencing the selection of sexual abuse as epiphany. *Journal of Poetry Therapy, 14*(3), 119–133.

Geiger, B. (2002). From deviance to creation: Women's answer to subjugation. *Humanity and Society, 26*(3), 214–227.

Giesbrecht, N., & Sevcik, I. (2000). The process of recovery and rebuilding among abused women in the conservative evangelical subculture. *Journal of Family Violence, 15*(3), 229–248.

Gilfus, M. E. (1999). The price of the ticket: A survivor-centered appraisal of trauma theory. *Violence Against Women, 5*(11), 1238–1257.

Gillum, T. L., Sullivan, C. M., & Bybee, D. I. (2006). The importance of spirituality in the lives of domestic violence survivors. *Violence Against Women, 12*(3), 240–250.

Glaser, B. G. (2001). *The grounded theory perspective: Conceptualization contrasted with description.* Mill Valley, CA: Sociology Press.

Glicken, M. D. (2006). *Learning from resilient people: Lessons we can apply to counseling and psychotherapy.* Thousand Oaks, CA: SAGE Publications.

Goldstein, H. (1990). Strength or pathology: Ethical and rhetorical contrasts in approaches to practice. *Families in Society, 71,* 267–275.

Goodman, L., Dutton, M. A., Weinfurt, K., & Cook, S. (2003). The intimate partner violence strategies index. *Violence Against Women, 9*(2), 163–186.

Gotterer, R. (2001). The spiritual dimension in clinical social work practice: A client perspective. *Families in Society, 82*(2), 187–193.

Graybeal, C. 2001). Strengths-based social work assessment: Transforming the dominant paradigm. *Families in Society, 82*(3), 233–242.

Graham-Bermann, S., & Edleson, J. (2001). *Domestic violence in the lives of children: The future of research, intervention, and social policy.* Washington, DC: American Psychological Association.

Gutierrez, L. (1994). Beyond coping: An empowerment perspective on stressful life events. *Journal of Sociology & Social Welfare, 21*(3), 201–219.

Guzzino, M., & Taxis, C. (1995). Leading experiential vicarious trauma groups for professionals. *Treating Abuse Today, 4,* 27–31.

Hall, T. A. (1995). Spiritual effects of childhood sexual abuse in adult Christian women. *Journal of Psychology and Theology, 23*(2), 129–134.

Harvey, M. R., Mishler, E. G., Koenen, K., & Harney, P. (2001). In the aftermath of sexual abuse: Making and remaking meaning in narratives of trauma and recovery. *Narrative Inquiry, 10*(2), 291–311.

Helgeson, V. S., Reynolds, K. A., & Tomich, P. L. (2006). A meta-analytic review of benefit. Turnings and adaptations in resilient daughters of battered women. *Journal of Nursing Scholarship, 33*(3), 245–251.

Henry, D. L. (1999). Resilience in maltreated children: Implications for special needs adoptions. *Child Welfare, 78*(5), 519–540.

Hepworth, D. H., Rooney, R. H., Rooney, G. D., Strom-Gottfried, K., & Larsen, J. A. (2006). *Direct social work practice: Theory and skills.* Belmont, CA: Thomson Brooks/Cole.

Herman, J. (1997). *Trauma and recovery.* New York: BasicBooks.

Himle, D. P., Jayaratne, S., & Thyness, P. (1991). Buffering effects of four social support types on burnout among social workers. *Social Work Research Abstracts, 27*(1), 22–27.

Hochschild, A. R. (1983). *The managed heart: Commercialization of human feeling.* Berkeley, CA: University of California Press.

Hodge, D. R. (2001). Spiritual assessment: A review of major qualitative methods and a new framework for assessing spirituality. *Social Work, 45*(3), 203–214.

Hollander, J. (2002). Resisting vulnerability: The social reconstruction of gender in interaction. *Social Problems, 49*(4), 474–496.

Horton, A. L., & Johnson, B. L. (1993). Profile and strategies of women who have ended abuse. *Families in Society, 74,* 481–492.

Horwitz, M. (1998). Social worker trauma: Building resilience in child protection social workers. *Smith College Studies in Social Work, 68*(3), 363–377.

Howard, S., Dryden, J., & Johnson, B. (1999). Childhood resilience: Review and critique of the literature. *Oxford Review of Education, 25*(3), 307–323.

Ickovics, J. R., & Park, C. L. (1998). Paradigm shift: Why a focus on health is important. *Journal of Social Issues, 54*(2), 237–244.

Jaffe, P. G., Sudermann, M., & Geffner, R. (2000). Emerging issues for children exposed to domestic violence. *Journal of Aggression, Maltreatment, & Trauma, 3*(1), 1–7.

Jaffe, P. G., Wolfe, D. A., & Wilson, S. K. (1990). *Children of battered women.* Newbury Park, CA: SAGE Publications.

Janoff-Bulman, B. (1992). *Shattered assumptions: Towards a new psychology of trauma.* New York: Free Press.

Jansen, G. G., & Davis, D. R. (1998). Honoring voice and visibility: Sensitive-topic research and feminist interpretive inquiry. *Affilia, 13*(3), 289–311.

Jones, L., Hughes, M., & Unterstaller, U. (2001). Post-traumatic stress disorder (PTSD) in victims of domestic violence: A review of the literature. *Trauma, Violence, & Abuse, 2*(2), 99–119.

Jordan, C., & Franklin, C. (2003). *Clinical assessment for social workers: Quantitative and qualitative methods.* Chicago: Lyceum Books, Inc.

Kelly, L. (1988). *Surviving sexual violence.* Cambridge, UK: Polity.

Kilpatrick, D., Saunders, B., & Smith, D. (2003). *Youth victimization: Prevalence and implications.* U.S. Department of Justice, National Institute of Justice report.

Kilpatrick, K., Litt, M., & Williams, L. (1997). Posttraumatic stress disorder in child witnesses to domestic violence. *American Journal of Orthopsychiatry, 67*(4), 639–644.

Kisthardt, W. (1997). The strengths model of case management: Principles and helping functions. In D. Saleebey, *The strengths perspective in social work practice* (2nd ed., pp. 97–113). New York: Longman.

Kisthardt, W. (1992). A strengths model of case management: The principles and functions of a helping partnership with persons with persistent mental illness. In D. Saleebey, *The strengths perspective in social work practice* (pp. 59–83). New York: Longman.

Knight, C. (2009). *Introduction to working with adult survivors of childhood trauma: Techniques and strategies*. Belmont, CA: Thomson Brooks/Cole.

Kocot, T., & Goodman, L. (2003). The roles of coping and social support in battered women's mental health. *Violence Against Women, 9*(3), 323–346.

Koeske, G. F., & Koeske, R. D. (1989). Work load and burnout: Can social support and perceived accomplishment help? *Social Work, 34*(30), 29–36.

Koeske, G. F., & Koeske, R. D. (1993). A preliminary test of a stress-strain-outcome model for reconceptualization of the burnout phenomenon. *Journal of Social Service Research, 17*(3/4), 107–135.

Kolbo, J. R., Blakely, E. H., & Engelman, D. (1996). Children who witness domestic violence: A review of empirical literature. *Journal of Interpersonal Violence, 11*(2), 281–293.

Koss, M. P., & Harvey, M. R., (1991). *The rape victim: Clinical and community interventions*. Thousand Oaks, CA: SAGE Publications.

Kottler, J. A. (1992). *Compassionate therapy: Working with difficult clients*. San Francisco: Jossey-Bass.

Kushner, H. S. (1981). *When bad things happen to good people*. New York: HarperCollins.

LaFountain, R., Garner, N., & Boldosser, S. (1995). Solution-focused counseling groups for children and adolescents. *Journal of System Therapies, 14*(4), 39–51.

Lahad, M. (2000). Darkness over the abyss: Supervising crisis intervention teams following disaster. *Traumatology, 6*(4), 273–293.

Lambert, J. (2002). *Digital storytelling*. Berkeley, CA: Digital Diner Press.

Laws, K. (1995). *Child abuse: Pathways to successful adjustment*. Manuscript for the Portland Public Schools Project Chrysalis. Portland, OR: RMS Research Corporation.

Lazarus, R., & Folkman, S. (1984). *Stress, appraisal, and coping*. New York: Springer Publishing.

Leffert, N., Benson, P. L., Scales, P. C., Sharma, A. R., Drake, D. R., & Blyth, D. A. (1998). Developmental assets: Measurement and prediction of risk behaviors among adolescents. *Applied Developmental Science, 2*, 209–230.

Lempert, L. B. (1996). Women's strategies for survival: Developing agency in abusive relationships. *Journal of Family Violence, 11*(3), 269–289.

Lev-Wiesel, R., & Amir, M. (2003). Posttraumatic growth among holocaust child survivors. *Journal of Loss and Trauma, 8*, 229–237.

Lewis, C. S., Griffing, S., Chu, M., Jospitre, T., Sage, R. E., Madry, L., & Primm, B. (2006). Coping and violence exposure as predictors of psychological functioning in domestic violence survivors. *Violence Against Women, 12*(4), 340–354.

Lieblich, A., Tuval-Mashiach, R., & Zilber, T. (1998). *Narrative research: Reading, analysis, and interpretation.* Thousand Oaks, CA: SAGE Publications.

Linley, P. A., & Joseph, S. (2004). Positive change following trauma and adversity: A review. *Journal of Traumatic Stress, 17*(1), 11–21.

Lobel, C. M. (1992). Relationship between childhood sexual abuse and borderline personality disorder in women psychiatric inpatients. *Journal of Child Sexual Abuse, 1*(1), 63–80.

Luthar, S. S. (1993). Annotation: Methodological and conceptual issues in research on childhood resilience. *Journal of Child Psychiatry, 34*(4), 441–443.

Luthar, S. S., Cicchetti, D., & Becker, B. (2000). The construct of resilience: A critical evaluation and guidelines for future work. *Child Development, 71*(3), 543–562.

Luthar, S. S., & Zigler, E. (1991). Vulnerability and competence: A review of research on resilience in childhood. *American Journal of Orthopsychiatry, 61*(1), 6–22.

Lynch, S. M., & Graham-Bermann, S. A. (2000). Women abuse and self-affirmation: Influences on women's self-esteem. *Violence Against Women, 6*(2), 178–197.

Mandleco, B., & Perry, C. (2000). An organization framework for conceptualizing resilience in children. *Journal of Child and Adolescent Psychiatric Nursing, 13*(3), 99–111.

Maslach, C. (1982). *Burnout: The cost of caring.* Englewood Cliffs, NJ: Prentice-Hall.

Maslach, C. (1996). *The Maslach burnout inventory* (3rd ed.). Palo Alto, CA: Consulting Psychologists Press.

Maslach, C., & Leiter, M. P. (1997). *The truth about burnout.* San Francisco: Jossey-Bass.

Maslach, C., Schaufeli, W. B., & Leiter, M. P. (2001). Job burnout. *Annual Review of Psychology, 52,* 397–422.

Massey, S., Cameron, A., Ouellette, S., & Fine, M. (1998). Qualitative approaches to the study of thriving: What can be learned? *Journal of Social Issues, 54*(2), 337–355.

Masten, A. S. (2001). Ordinary magic: Resilience processes in development. *American Psychologist, 56*(3), 227–38.

Matsakis, A. (1991). *When the bough breaks.* Oakland, CA: New Harbinger Publications.

McCann, I. L., & Pearlman, L. A. (1990). *Psychological trauma and the adult survivor: Theory, therapy, and transformation.* New York: Brunner/Mazel.

McCann, I. L., & Pearlman, L. A. (1990). Vicarious traumatization: A framework for understanding the psychological effects of working with victims. *Journal of Traumatic Stress, 3*(1), 131–149.

McGee, C. (1997). Children's experiences of domestic violence. *Child and Family Social Work, 2,* 13–23.

McMillen, C., Morris, L. A., & Sherraden, M. (2004). Ending social work's grudge match: Problems versus strengths. *Family in Society, 85*(3), 317–325.

McMillen, C., Zuravin, S., & Rideout, G. (1995). Perceive benefit from child sexual abuse. *Journal of Consulting and Clinical Psychology, 63*(6), 1037–1043.

McNew, J. A., & Abell, N. (1995). Posttraumatic stress symptomatology: Similarities and differences between Vietnam veterans and adult survivors of childhood sexual abuse. *Social Work, 40*(1), 115–126.

McQuade, S., & Ehrenreich, J. H. (1997). Assessing client strengths. *Families in Society, 78*(2), 201–212.

Merrick, E. L., Horgan, C. M., Garnick, D. W., & Hodgkin, D. (2005). Managed care organizations' use of treatment management strategies for outpatient mental health care. *Administration and Policy in Mental Healthy and Mental Health Services Research, 33*(1), 104–114.

Miller, A. (1996). *Prisoners of childhood.* New York: BasicBooks.

Miller, E. D. (2003). Reconceptualizing the role of resiliency in coping and therapy. *Journal of Loss and Trauma, 8,* 239–246.

Miller, J. B. (1976). *Toward a new psychology of women.* Boston: Beacon Press.

Mitchell, K. J., & Finkelhor, D. (2001). Risk of crime victimization among youth exposed to domestic violence. *Journal of Interpersonal Violence, 16*(9), 944–964.

Morrow, S. L., & Smith, M. L. (1995). Constructions of survival and coping by women who have survived childhood sexual abuse. *Journal of Counseling Psychology, 42*(1), 24–33.

Mossige, S., Jensen, T. K., Gulbrandsen, W., Reichelt, S., & Tjersland, O. (2005). Children's narratives of sexual abuse: What characterizes them and how do they contribute to meaning-making? *Narrative Inquiry, 15*(2), 377–404.

Muller, W. (1993). *Legacy of the heart: The spiritual advantages of a painful childhood.* New York: Simon & Schuster.

Naples, N. (2003). Deconstructing and locating survivor discourse: Dynamics of narrative, empowerment, and resistance for survivors of childhood sexual abuse. *Signs: Journal of Women in Culture and Society, 28*(4), 1151–1185.

Norman, J. (2000). Constructive narrative in arresting the impact of posttraumatic stress disorder. *Clinical Social Work Journal, 28*(3), 303–319.

O'Connell-Higgins, G. (1994). *Resilient adults overcoming a cruel past.* San Francisco: Jossey-Bass Publishers.

O'Hanlon, B. (1999). *Do one thing different: Ten simple ways to change your life.* New York: HarperCollins Publishers, Inc.

O'Hanlon, B., & Bertolino, B. (1998). *Even from a broken web: Brief, respectful solution-oriented therapy for sexual abuse and trauma.* New York: W. W. Norton & Company.

O'Hyde, M. (1984). *Sexual abuse: Let's talk about it.* Philadelphia, PA: Westminster Press.

Oko, J. (2006). Evaluating alternative approaches to social work: A critical review of the strengths perspective. *Families in Society, 87*(4), 601–611.

Oktay, J. S. (2004). Grounded theory. In D. Padgett (Ed.), *The qualitative research experience* (pp. 23–46). Belmont, CA: Wadsworth/Thomson Learning.

O'Leary, V. E. (1998). Strength in face of adversity: Individual and social thriving. *Journal of Social Issues, 54*(2), 425–446.

Orava, T. A., McLeod, P. J., & Sharpe, D. (1996). Perceptions of control, depressive symptomatology, and self-esteem of women in transition from abusive relationships. *Journal of Family Violence, 11*(2), 167–186.

Palmer, N. (1991). Feminist practice with survivors of sexual trauma and incest. In B. Bricker-Jenkins, N. R. Hooyman, & N. Gottlieb (Eds.), *Feminist social work practice in clinical settings* (pp. 63–89). Newbury Park, California: SAGE Publications.

Parker, S., & Parker, S. (1991). Female victims of child sexual abuse: Adult adjustment. *Journal of Family Violence, 6*(2), 183–197.

Patten, S., Gatz, Y., Jones, B., & Thomas, D. (1989). Posttraumatic stress disorder and the treatment of sexual abuse. *Social Work, 34*(3), 197–202.

Patterson, J. M. (2002). Integrating family resilience and family stress theory. *Journal of Marriage and Family, 64,* 349–360.

Pearlman, L. A. (1995). Self-care for trauma therapists: Ameliorating vicarious traumatization. In B. H. Stamm (Ed.), *Secondary traumatic stress: Self-care issues for clinicians, researchers, and educators* (pp. 51–64). Lutherville, MD: Sidran Press.

Pearlman, L. A. (1996). Psychometric review of the TSI Belief Scale, Revision L. In B. H. Stamm (Ed.), *Measurement of stress, trauma, and adaptation* (pp. 415–417). Lutherville, MD: Sidran Press.

Pearlman, L. A., & Mac Ian, P. S. (1995). Vicarious traumatization: An empirical study of the effects of trauma work on trauma therapists. *Professional Psychology: Research and Practice, 26*(6), 558–565.

Pearlmann, L. A., & Saakvitne, K. W. (1995). *Trauma and the therapist: Countertransference and vicarious traumatization in psychotherapy with incest survivors*. New York: W. W. Norton & Company.

Peled, E., & Edleson, J. L. (1999). Barriers to children's domestic violence counseling: A qualitative study. *Families in Society, 80*(6), 578–586.

Pellebon, D. A., & Anderson, S. C. (1999). Understanding the life issues of spiritually-based clients. *Families in Society, 80*(3), 229–238.

Polkinghorne, D. E. (1991). Narrative and self-concept. *Journal of Narrative and Life History, 2* & 3, 135–153.

Poulin, J. (2000). *Collaborative social work. Strengths-based generalist practice*. Itasca, IL: F. E. Peacock.

Radey, M., & Figley, C. R. (2007). The social psychology of compassion. *Clinical Social Work Journal, 35*, 207–214.

Rapp, C. A. (1992). The strengths perspective of case management with persons suffering from severe mental illness. In D. Saleebey, *The strengths perspective in social work practice* (pp. 45–58). New York: Pearson Education, Inc.

Rapp, C. A., & Goscha, R. J. (2006). *The strengths model: Case management with people with psychiatric disabilities*. New York: Oxford University Press.

Rappaport, J. (1995). Empowerment meets narrative: Listening to stories and creating settings. *American Journal of Community Psychology, 23*(5), 795–807.

Reamer, F. G. (1997). Managing ethics under managed care. *Families in Society, 78*(1), 96–101.

Riessman, C. (1993). *Narrative analysis*. Newbury Park, CA: SAGE Publications.

Ridgway, P. (2001). Restorying psychiatric disability: Learning from first person recovery narratives. *Psychiatric Rehabilitiation Journal, 24*(4), 335–343.

Riffe, H. A., & Kondrat, M. E. (1997). Social worker alienation and disempowerment in a managed care setting. *Journal of Progressive Human Services, 8*(1), 41–57.

Roche, S. E., & Wood, G. G. (2005). A narrative principle for feminist social work with survivors of male violence. *Affilia, 20*(4). 465–475.

Roth, S., & Cohen, L. J. (1986). Approach, avoidance, and coping with stress. *American Psychologist, 4*(7), 813–819.

Rubin, L. (1996). *The transcendent child*. New York: HarperCollins.

Rutter, M. (1987). Psychosocial resilience and protective mechanisms. *American Journal of Orthopsychiatry, 57*(3), 216–224.

Saakvitne, K. W., Gamble, S., Pearlman, L. A., & Lev, B. T. (2000). *Risking connection: A training curriculum for working with survivors of childhood abuse*. Baltimore: Sidran Press.

Saakvitne, K. W., Tennen, H., & Affleck, G. (1998). Exploring thriving in the context of clinical trauma theory: Constructivist self development theory. *Journal of Social Issues, 54*(2), 279–299.

Safyer, A. W., Griffin, M. L., Colan, N. B., Alexander-Brydie, E., & Rome, J. Z. (1998). Methodological issues when developing prevention programs for low-income, urban adolescents. *Journal of Social Service Research, 23*(3/4), 23–46.

Sahlein, J. (2002). When religion enters the dialogue: A guide for practitioners. *Clinical Social Work Journal, 30*(4), 381–401.

Saleebey, D. (1992). *The strengths perspective in social work practice*. White Plains, NY: Longman.

Saleebey, D. (1996). The strengths perspective in social work practice: Extensions and cautions. *Social Work, 41*(3), 296–305.

Saleebey, D. (1997). The strengths approach to practice. In D. Saleebey (Ed.), *The strengths perspective in social work practice* (2nd ed., pp. 3–19). White Plains, NY: Longman.

Saleebey, D. (2006). *The strengths perspective in social work practice* (4th ed.). New York: Pearson Educational, Inc.

Saleebey, D. (2009). *The strengths perspective in social work practice* (5th ed.). New York: Pearson Educational, Inc.

Salston, M., & Figley, C. R. (2003). Secondary traumatic stress effects of working with survivors of criminal victimization. *Journal of Traumatic Stress, 16*(2), 167–174.

Schwartz, R. H., Tiamiyu, M. F., & Dwyer, D. J. (2007). Social worker hope and perceived burnout: The effects of age, years in practice, and setting. *Administration in Social Work, 31*(4), 103–199.

Senter, K. E., & Caldwell, K. (2002). Spirituality and the maintenance of change: A phenomenological study of women who leave abusive relationships. *Contemporary Family Therapy, 24*(4), 543–564.

Shantall, T. (1999). The experience of meaning in suffering among holocaust survivors. *Journal of Humanistic Psychology, 39*(3), 96–124.

Silver, R. L., Boon, C., & Stones, M. H. (1983). Searching for meaning in misfortune: Making sense of incest. *Journal of Social Issues, 39*(2), 81–102.

Skovholt, T. M. (2001). *The resilient practitioner: Burnout prevention and self-care strategies for counselors, therapists, teachers, and health professionals*. Needham Heights, MA: Allyn and Bacon.

Skovholt, T. M., & Jennings, L. (2004). *Master therapists: Exploring expertise in therapy and counseling*. Boston: Allyn and Bacon.

Smith, J., & Prior, M. (1995). Temperament and stress resilience in school-age children: A within families study. *Journal of American Academy of Child and Adolescent Psychiatry, 34*, 168–179.

Snyder, H. N. (2000). *Sexual assault of young children as reported to law enforcement: Victim, incident, and offender characteristics*. National Center for Juvenile Justice, U.S. Department of Justice.

Spaccarelli, S., & Kim, S. (1995). Resilience criteria and factors associated with resilience in sexually abused girls. *Child Abuse & Neglect, 19*(9), 1171–1182.

Stalker, C. A., Mandell, D., Frensch, K., Harvey, C., & Wright, M. (2007). Child welfare workers who are exhausted yet satisfied with their jobs: How to do they do it? *Child and Family Social Work, 12*(2), 182–191.

Stamm, B. H. (2005). *The ProQOL Manual: The professional quality of life scale: Compassion satisfaction, burnout, and compassion fatigue/secondary trauma scales.* Lutherville, MD: Sidran Press.

Stamm, B. H. (2002). Measuring compassion satisfaction as well as fatigue: Developmental history of the compassion fatigue and satisfaction test. In C. R. Figley (Ed.), *Treating compassion fatigue* (pp. 107–119). New York: Brunner Mazel.

Steed, L. G., & Bicknell, J. (2001). Trauma and the therapist: The experience of therapists working with the perpetrators of sexual abuse. *The Australasian Journal of Disaster and Trauma Studies,* 1, 1–9.

Strauss, A., & Corbin, J. (1990). *Basics of qualitative research.* Newbury Park, CA: SAGE Publications.

Sullivan, W. P., & Rapp, C. A. (1994). Breaking away: The potential and promise of a strengths- based approach to social work practice. In R. G., Meinert, J. T., Pardeck, & W. P. Sullivan (Eds.), *Issues in social work: A critical analysis* (pp. 83–104). Westport, CT: Auburn House.

Tedeschi, R. G., & Calhoun, L. G. (1995). *Trauma & transformation: Growing in the aftermath of suffering.* Newbury Park, CA: SAGE Publications.

Tedeschi, R. G., & Calhoun, L. G. (1996). The posttraumatic growth inventory: Measuring the positive legacy of trauma. *Journal of Traumatic Stress,* 9, 455–471.

Tedeschi, R. G., Park, C. L., & Calhoun L. G. (1998). Posttraumatic growth; Conceptual issues. In R. G. Tedeschi, C. L. Park, & L. G. Calhoun (Eds.), *Posttraumatic growth: Positive changes in the aftermath of crisis* (pp. 1–22). Mahwah, NJ: Lawrence Erlbaum Associates, Publishers.

Tiet, Q. Q., Bird, H., & Davies, M. R. (1998). Adverse life events and resilience. *Journal of the American Academy of Child and Adolescent Psychiatry,* 37(11), 1191–1200.

Tjaden, P., & Thoennes, N. (2000). *Extent, nature, and consequences of intimate partner violence: Findings from the National Violence Against Women Survey.* Washington, DC: Department of Justice (US); Publication NO. NCJ 181867.

Ungar, M. (2003). Qualitative contributions to resilience research. *Qualitative Social Work,* 2(1), 85–102.

Valentine, L., & Feinauer, L. (1993). Resiliency factors associated with female survivors of childhood sexual abuse. *The American Journal of Family Therapy,* 21(3), 216–224.

Wade, A. (1997). Small acts of living: Everyday resistance to violence and other forms of oppression. *Contemporary Family Therapy: An International Journal,* 19(1), 23–39.

Walsh, F. (2003). Clinical views of family normality, health, and dysfunction: From deficit to strength perspective. In F. Walsh (Ed.), *Normal family processes: Growing diversity and complexity* (pp. 27–57). New York: Guilford Press.

Walter, J. L., & Peller, J. E. (1992). *Becoming solution-focused in brief therapy.* New York: Brunner/Mazel.

Washington, O. G. M., & Moxley, D. P. (2001). The use of prayer in group work with African-American women recovering from chemical dependency. *Families in Society,* 82(1), 49–59.

Weick, A., Rapp, C., Sullivan, W. P., & Kisthardt, W. (1989). A strengths perspective for social work practice. *Social Work,* 34, 350–354.

Weingarten, K. (1998). The small and the ordinary: The daily practice of a postmodern narrative therapy. *Family Process*, 37, 3–15.

Wells, K. (1995). The strategy of grounded theory: Possibilities and problems. *Social Work Research, 19*(1), 33–37.

Werner, E., & Smith, R. (1992). *Overcoming the odds: High risk children from birth to adulthood*. Ithaca, NY: Cornell University Press.

Wheeler, B., & Walton, E. (1987). Personality disturbances of adult incest victims. *Social Casework, 68*(10), 597–602.

Whiffen, V., & MacIntosh, H. (2005). Mediators of the link between childhood sexual abuse and emotional distress. *Trauma, Violence, & Abuse, 6*(1), 24–39.

White, M., & Epston, D. (1990). *Narrative means to therapeutic ends*. New York: W.W. Norton & Company.

Wineman, S. (2003). *Power-under: Trauma and nonviolent social change*. Cambridge, MA: Author.

Wolin, S. J., & Wolin, S. (1993). *The resilient self*. New York: Villard Books.

Wrenn, L. J. (2003). Trauma: Unconscious and unconscious meaning. *Clinical Social Work Journal, 31*(2), 123–137.

Yama, M. F., Fogas, B. S., Teegarden, L. A., & Hastings, B. (1993). Childhood sexual abuse and parental alcoholism: Interactive effects in adult women. *American Journal of Orthopsychiatry, 63*, 300–305.

Appendix

A | Solution-Focused Question Types

Lead-in questions: To connect with the client and begin the collaborative process.

- What was it like for you to come here and meet with me?
- If it was your idea to seek help, how did you decide to do it?
- If it was not your idea, how did you decide to show up for this appointment?
- If you have had services in the past—what worked? What do I need to know about what would most help you in our work together?
- What would you like me to help you with in resolving the problem?
- What would you like me to help you with so that our work together is productive?

Goal questions: To clarify what the client wants help with or is motivated to change.

- Specific: How will you know when you have achieved your goal?
- Relevant: How would that make a difference in your life?
- Presence rather than the absence: What will be different for you when the problem is less of a problem or not a problem at all?
- Start rather than end something: What would you like instead?

- In the client's control and achievable: What is a small step you can make toward your goal?
- Challenging but not impossible: What will you need to take this small step?

System/Relationship questions: To highlight important people in clients' lives.

- Who do you think well of and why?
- How has that person helped you?
- What would that person say about the changes you want to make or are making?

Difference questions: To highlight useful differences by comparing and contrasting.

- What's different about you when you are achieving what you want to have happen?
- What difference does it make in your life when the problem is not a problem?

Exception questions: To find times when the typical problem sequence did not happen.

- When is the problem not a problem or less of a problem?
- When in your life have you stood up to the problem?
- Has anyone else noticed when it is not a problem?
- Imagine a future where the problem is less or solved? What changes will others see in you? What will you be doing differently?
- If a miracle was to happen and the problem you are seeking help with was solved, what would be different for you? What part of this miracle would you like to consider trying?

Coping/Agency questions: To amplify client coping skills, strengths, and competencies.

- How did you get that to happen?
- What was it like for you to come here today?
- What did you have to do to get yourself to come here today?
- How did you manage your anxiety and fears about coming here today?

- How have you managed to hold on with everything going on with you?
- How have you managed to keep things from getting worse?
- At its worse, how did you manage? How did you not give up?
- How are things different from when they were at their worse?

Ending questions: To identify what was helpful in the client-worker meeting.

- With everything we've talked about, is there anything in particular that you found helpful?
- Is there anything that I missed that you wish I would have asked you about?

Subsequent session questions: To maintain client change.

- What have you being doing differently this week?
- How have you managed to keep the change going?
- If you got off track, then how will you know when you are back on track?

B

Person Centered Strengths Assessment

The strengths assessment is a tool that was developed for case managers. It is designed to gather information regarding consumers' circumstances in six domains of community living. The goal is to gather information regarding current social circumstances, what people want in each domain, and what resources or successes they have realized in the past in each life domain.

PARTICIPANT_____**DATE**_____

PRIMARY TEAM MEMBER_____

A. HOUSING, A Sense of Home

1. Describe your current housing arrangement:

2. How satisfied are you with current housing circumstances? Do you want to remain there for the next six months or do you want to move?

3. Describe the housing arrangements you have had in the past that have been most satisfying for you.

B. TRANSPORTATION

1. Currently, how do you get around?

2. Do you have any desires regarding expanding your transportation options?

3. What are different ways you used to get around?

C. FINANCIAL/INSURANCE

1. What are your current sources of income? List amount. What in-kind benefits do you receive (food stamps, Medicaid, etc.)?

2. What do you desire regarding your financial situation?

3. What was the most satisfying time in your life regarding your financial situation?

D. VOCATIONAL/EDUCATIONAL

1. Identify as many reasons as you can regarding why you have chosen to pursue getting a job at this time:

2. If you design the job you get, what would it be? Try to be as specific as you can. Where are you working? Indoors or outdoors? Do you work with a group of people or are you alone? Do you go to work in the daytime or at night?

3. Talk about your past job experience. What was the best job you ever held? How long were you there? Identify the particulars of this job that made it so good for you.

4. Why have you left jobs in the past? Try to identify if there is a certain pattern that has been evident in your employment history.

5. What supports do you think you need to be successful in getting and keeping a job?

6. Talk about your use of alcohol and drugs. This includes drugs that are prescribed and those that are not.

7. Most people who are looking for a new job have mixed feelings about this process. How are you feeling about it? What kinds of things concern you or make you feel nervous or anxious about seeking employment?

8. What are the things you are good at? What things do you enjoy doing and believe you do well? Where is your favorite place to hang out? Why do you like it there?

E. SOCIAL SUPPORTS, RELATIONSHIPS, INTIMACY, SPIRITUALITY

1. Talk about the people who are most important in your life. How will getting and keeping a job affect these relationships?

2. What do you want in the nature of a close relationship? Can I help you achieve that?

3. How important is religion, church, or spirituality in your life? Would you like to strengthen your spiritual life? How can I help?

4. When you need support, understanding, or just someone to talk to, where do you go? Can we do more in this area?

5. What do you want and need in the area of social relationships?

F. HEALTH

1. How is your health? What do you do to take care of your health? Do you smoke? What limitations do you experience because of health-related factors? What medications are you currently taking? How is your diet?

2. What do you want and need in the area of health?

G. LEISURE TIME

1. Talk about what you really enjoy doing to kick back and relax. When are you most joyful? When are you most peaceful?

2. Are there things you used to enjoy that you haven't done in awhile?

3. What do you want and need in the area of leisure time?

H. PRIORITIZING

1. With all we have talked about, let's decide on the area of your life with the most immediate and meaningful wants and needs.

Source: www.iidc.indiana.edu/styles/iidc/defiles/CCLC/THE%20 STRENGTHS%20ASSESSMENT.pcp.doc

C

Resiliency Assessment of Childhood Protective Factors

Children do many different things to survive childhood adversity. Please indicate whether during childhood you tried the following strategies. Answer each item as carefully as you can by circling a number next to each statement according to the following scale:

1 = Never
2 = Rarely
3 = Occasionally
4 = Frequently
5 = Very frequently
NA = Not applicable

PSYCHOLOGICAL PROTECTIVE FACTORS: FANTASIZING						
1. I fantasized about having a different family or a different life.	1	2	3	4	5	NA
2. I sought out imaginary friends and/or fantasy worlds.	1	2	3	4	5	NA
PSYCHOLOGICAL PROTECTIVE FACTORS: MENTAL AND PHYSICAL ESCAPES						
3. I stayed away from home as much as possible.	1	2	3	4	5	NA

(Continued)

211

4. I read.	1	2	3	4	5	NA
5. I found place(s) to escape.	1	2	3	4	5	NA
6. I watched TV.	1	2	3	4	5	NA
7. I moved out or ran away from home.	1	2	3	4	5	NA
8. I escaped into nature or the outdoors.	1	2	3	4	5	NA
9. I hid or isolated myself from others.	1	2	3	4	5	NA
10. I escaped into school.	1	2	3	4	5	NA
PSYCHOLOGICAL PROTECTIVE FACTORS: ARTISTIC PURSUITS						
11. I expressed my emotions through music, acting, writing, drawing, painting, or photography.	1	2	3	4	5	NA
12. I used my sense of humor to escape emotional pain or to connect with others.	1	2	3	4	5	NA
SOCIAL PROTECTIVE FACTORS: ADULT CARETAKERS AND MENTORS						
13. I had an adult in my life that cared about me.	1	2	3	4	5	NA
14. I had teachers, coaches, or other adults as role models or mentors.	1	2	3	4	5	NA
SOCIAL PROTECTIVE FACTORS: FRIENDS AND EXTRACURRICULAR ACTIVITIES						
15. I was involved in activities such as sports, art, music, or drama.	1	2	3	4	5	NA
16. I had friends.	1	2	3	4	5	NA
17. I had a job or did volunteer work.	1	2	3	4	5	NA
18. I participated in a community club or organization.	1	2	3	4	5	NA

(Continued)

SPIRITUAL PROTECTIVE FACTORS: BELIEF IN GOD OR A HIGHER POWER, NATURE, RELIGIOUS COMMUNITY, PRAYER/MEDITATION						
19. I felt there was something outside of myself (e.g., God) that loved me.	1	2	3	4	5	NA
20. I believed things happened for a reason.	1	2	3	4	5	NA
21. I connected with nature.	1	2	3	4	5	NA
22. I participated in a religious organization.	1	2	3	4	5	NA
23. I participated in a religious youth group.	1	2	3	4	5	NA
24. I prayed/asked God for help.	1	2	3	4	5	NA

Additional ways you protected yourself:

_____

_____

_____

_____

_____

_____

_____

D

Assessment of Resistance Strategies to Childhood Incest

Children do many different things to survive childhood sexual abuse. Please indicate whether during childhood you tried the following strategies. Answer each item as carefully as you can by circling a number next to each statement according to the following scale:

1 = Never
2 = Rarely
3 = Occasionally
4 = Frequently
5 = Very Frequently
NA = Not Applicable

RESISTANCE TO BEING POWERLESS						
1. I purposely did not do everything the abuser demanded of me.	1	2	3	4	5	NA
2. I physically or verbally challenged the abuser.	1	2	3	4	5	NA
3. I fantasized or dreamed about having more power than the abuser.	1	2	3	4	5	NA

(Continued)

4. I said, "No" to the abuser.	1	2	3	4	5	NA
5. I tried to divert the abuse from happening. (e.g., faking sickness, wearing extra clothes to bed, etc.)	1	2	3	4	5	NA
6. I moved out or ran away from home to stop the abuse.	1	2	3	4	5	NA
RESISTANCE TO BEING SILENCED						
7. I told a family member about the abuse.	1	2	3	4	5	NA
8. I told my stuffed animals, dolls, or other toys about the abuse.	1	2	3	4	5	NA
9. I told my pets about the abuse.	1	2	3	4	5	NA
10. I told my siblings about the abuse.	1	2	3	4	5	NA
11. I told my friends about the abuse.	1	2	3	4	5	NA
12. I told neighbors or community persons about the abuse.	1	2	3	4	5	NA
13. I told God such as through prayer.	1	2	3	4	5	NA
RESISTANCE TO BEING ISOLATED						
14. I sought out activities such as sports, art, music, or drama.	1	2	3	4	5	NA
15. I sensed that there was a God or someone watching over me.	1	2	3	4	5	NA
16. I had friends.	1	2	3	4	5	NA
17. I had teachers, coaches, or other adults as role models or mentors.	1	2	3	4	5	NA
18. I had a job or did volunteer work.	1	2	3	4	5	NA

(Continued)

19. I connected with people because they felt safe and supportive.	1	2	3	4	5	NA
20. I connected with animals/pets.	1	2	3	4	5	NA
21. I sought out a religious community.	1	2	3	4	5	NA
22. I sought connections with family members.	1	2	3	4	5	NA
23. I was connected to nature.	1	2	3	4	5	NA
24. I had imaginary friends and/or fantasy worlds.	1	2	3	4	5	NA

Additional ways you protected yourself:

_____

_____

_____

_____

_____

_____

_____

_____

_____

E Assessment of Intimate Partner Violence Childhood Survival Strategies

Children do many different things to survive exposure to adult interpersonal violence. Please indicate whether during childhood you tried the following strategies. Answer each item as carefully as you can by circling a number next to each statement according to the following scale:

1 = Never
2 = Rarely
3 = Occasionally
4 = Frequently
5 = Very frequently
NA = Not applicable

CREATING PHYSICAL AND MENTAL ESCAPES						
1. I stayed away from home as much as possible.	1	2	3	4	5	NA
2. I was involved in extracurricular activities.	1	2	3	4	5	NA
3. I kept busy.	1	2	3	4	5	NA
4. I would stay with a relative or a friend to escape.	1	2	3	4	5	NA

(Continued)

5. I escaped through the use of art, music, and/or humor.	1	2	3	4	5	NA
6. I watched TV to get away from the violence.	1	2	3	4	5	NA
7. I read a lot as a child.	1	2	3	4	5	NA
8. I would think about other things during the violence.	1	2	3	4	5	NA
9. I ran away from home.	1	2	3	4	5	NA
10. I escaped into nature or the outdoors.	1	2	3	4	5	NA
11. I learned to not show emotion, particularly fear.	1	2	3	4	5	NA
12. I acted like nothing (i.e., violence) was happening.	1	2	3	4	5	NA
13. I used writing as an escape.	1	2	3	4	5	NA
14. I sought out quiet, structured places (e.g., church, library).	1	2	3	4	5	NA
15. I tried to not think about the violence.	1	2	3	4	5	NA
16. I would act like everything was okay in the family.	1	2	3	4	5	NA
ATTEMPTING TO UNDERSTAND FAMILY DYNAMICS						
17. I thought the violence was normal.	1	2	3	4	5	NA
18. I believed my father/stepfather was the cause of the violence.	1	2	3	4	5	NA
19. I knew I was in a situation beyond my control.	1	2	3	4	5	NA
20. I knew the violence wasn't my fault.	1	2	3	4	5	NA
21. I believed that I was worthwhile.	1	2	3	4	5	NA

(Continued)

22. I decided when I grew up to not have violence in my life.	1	2	3	4	5	NA
23. I promised myself that when I grew up and had children that they would not be exposed to violence.	1	2	3	4	5	NA
24. I questioned why no one would intervene.	1	2	3	4	5	NA
25. I saw friends' families where violence didn't occur.	1	2	3	4	5	NA
26. I believed it wasn't my mom's fault.	1	2	3	4	5	NA
27. I wanted to grow up to be different from my parents.	1	2	3	4	5	NA
28. I believed it was my mom's fault.	1	2	3	4	5	NA
BUILDING SUPPORT NETWORKS						
29. I reached out to others for help.	1	2	3	4	5	NA
30. I had someone in my life that cared about me.	1	2	3	4	5	NA
31. I sought out friends.	1	2	3	4	5	NA
32. I sought out teachers, coaches, or other adults as role models or mentors.	1	2	3	4	5	NA
33. I did well in school.	1	2	3	4	5	NA
34. I prayed/asked God for help.	1	2	3	4	5	NA
35. I felt there was something outside of myself (e.g., God) that loved me.	1	2	3	4	5	NA
36. I was sociable.	1	2	3	4	5	NA
37. I connected with nature and/or pets.	1	2	3	4	5	NA

(Continued)

CREATING ORDER WITHIN FAMILIAL CHAOS						
38. I would clean up the house after the violence.	1	2	3	4	5	NA
39. I was an organizer.	1	2	3	4	5	NA
40. I talked to someone about the violence.	1	2	3	4	5	NA
41. I searched out answers for life's problems.	1	2	3	4	5	NA
42. I liked structure where you knew the rules.	1	2	3	4	5	NA
43. I liked things calm and quiet.	1	2	3	4	5	NA
44. I believed things happened for a reason.	1	2	3	4	5	NA
45. I believed I could make things happen.	1	2	3	4	5	NA
46. I wondered why my parents stayed together.	1	2	3	4	5	NA
47. I wondered why the violence continued.	1	2	3	4	5	NA
48. I made plans for my future.	1	2	3	4	5	NA
DEVELOPING AND EXECUTING SAFETY PLANS						
49. I found place(s) to hide from the violence.	1	2	3	4	5	NA
50. I made a plan to escape.	1	2	3	4	5	NA
51. I kept important phone numbers I could use for help.	1	2	3	4	5	NA
52. I recognized cues in the batterer (e.g., drinking alcohol) that alerted me to danger.	1	2	3	4	5	NA
53. I called the police or 911.	1	2	3	4	5	NA
54. I would stay at someone's house to get away from the violence.	1	2	3	4	5	NA

(Continued)

55. I just wanted the violence to end.	1	2	3	4	5	NA
56. I was hypervigilant to signs of violence.	1	2	3	4	5	NA

INTERVENING WITH THE BATTERER						
57. I argued with the batterer to divert the violence.	1	2	3	4	5	NA
58. I physically intervened between my mother and father.	1	2	3	4	5	NA
59. I did not show fear.	1	2	3	4	5	NA
60. I asked my father to stop the violence.	1	2	3	4	5	NA
61. I verbally intervened between my parents.	1	2	3	4	5	NA
62. I rebelled.	1	2	3	4	5	NA
63. I would lock my father out of the house.	1	2	3	4	5	NA
64. I was the mediator, the go-between my parents.	1	2	3	4	5	NA
65. I stood up to my father.	1	2	3	4	5	NA

PROTECTING AND COMFORTING MOTHERS AND SIBLINGS						
66. I learned to be self-reliant.	1	2	3	4	5	NA
67. I told my mother the violence isn't right.	1	2	3	4	5	NA
68. I gathered my siblings to hide them.	1	2	3	4	5	NA
69. I told my mom to leave my dad.	1	2	3	4	5	NA
70. I helped my mom to physically leave my dad.	1	2	3	4	5	NA
71. I wanted my mom to leave my dad.	1	2	3	4	5	NA

(Continued)

72. I was protective of my siblings.	1	2	3	4	5	NA
73. I had a lot of family responsibility.	1	2	3	4	5	NA
74. I was protected by my older siblings.	1	2	3	4	5	NA
75. I raised myself and my siblings.	1	2	3	4	5	NA

Additional ways you protected yourself:

_____

_____

_____

_____

_____

F

Assessment of Adult Recovery Strategies from Intimate Partner Violence

Women do many different things to recover from intimate partner violence. Please indicate whether you tried the following strategies. Answer each item as carefully as you can by circling a number next to each statement according to the following scale:

1 = Never
2 = Rarely
3 = Occasionally
4 = Frequently
5 = Very frequently
NA = Not applicable

EXERCISING ONE'S TENACITY TO SURVIVE AND PERSEVERE						
1. I try to not let what happened to me (e.g., domestic violence) "break" me.	1	2	3	4	5	NA
2. I am able to make plans for my future.	1	2	3	4	5	NA
3. I believe I can make things happen.	1	2	3	4	5	NA

(Continued)

4. I believe I can heal.	1	2	3	4	5	NA
5. I am able to make decisions about my life.	1	2	3	4	5	NA
6. I resist feeling powerless or helpless.	1	2	3	4	5	NA
7. I choose who and when to disclose about the domestic violence.	1	2	3	4	5	NA
8. I try to not let the abuser control my life.	1	2	3	4	5	NA
9. I confront family members, friends, etc. who deny or minimize what happened to me.	1	2	3	4	5	NA
10. I seek out self-help books to gain understanding and better myself.	1	2	3	4	5	NA
11. I believe my struggles make me stronger.	1	2	3	4	5	NA
12. I do not give up or quit.	1	2	3	4	5	NA
13. I believe I can achieve my dreams and aspirations.	1	2	3	4	5	NA
14. I am resourceful.	1	2	3	4	5	NA
ACCESSING SOCIAL SUPPORTS						
15. I reach out to family and friends.	1	2	3	4	5	NA
16. I have someone in my life that cares about me.	1	2	3	4	5	NA
17. I am involved in a religious community.	1	2	3	4	5	NA
18. I have a job or do volunteer work.	1	2	3	4	5	NA
19. I feel there is something outside of myself (e.g., God) that loves me.	1	2	3	4	5	NA

(Continued)

20. I pray/ask God or a Higher Power for help.	1	2	3	4	5	NA
21. I tend to connect with nature and/or pets.	1	2	3	4	5	NA
22. My children are a source of strength for me.	1	2	3	4	5	NA
23. When needed, I use medical and mental health services.	1	2	3	4	5	NA
24. I am able to be in a nonviolent intimate relationship.	1	2	3	4	5	NA
25. I am furthering my education.	1	2	3	4	5	NA
26. I have coworkers who are supportive of me.	1	2	3	4	5	NA
27. I use domestic violence services.	1	2	3	4	5	NA
28. I have a minister/priest/ spiritual leader I talk to.	1	2	3.	4	5	NA
TRANSFORMING SUFFERING THROUGH GIVING BACK TO OTHERS						
29. I want to make a difference in the lives of others.	1	2	3	4	5	NA
30. I believe there is a reason for the struggles I've endured.	1	2	3	4	5	NA
31. I am an advocate for others who are mistreated.	1	2	3	4	5	NA
32. I hope that something good can come out of the harm I experienced.	1	2	3	4	5	NA
33. I search out answers for life's problems.	1	2	3	4	5	NA
34. I choose to be a good friend.	1	2	3	4	5	NA
35. I choose to be a good parent, partner, and/or spouse.	1	2	3	4	5	NA

(Continued)

36. I choose to forgive the batterer.	1	2	3	4	5	NA
37. I choose to not harm others.	1	2	3	4	5	NA
38. I choose to give back to others/community.	1	2	3	4	5	NA

Additional recovery strategies:

_____

_____

_____

_____

_____

_____

_____

_____

Professional Quality of Life Scale

COMPASSION SATISFACTION AND FATIGUE SUBSCALES—REVISION IV

[Helping] people puts you in direct contact with their lives. As you probably have experienced, your compassion for those you *[help]* has both positive and negative aspects. We would like to ask you questions about your experiences, both positive and negative, as a *[helper]*. Consider each of the following questions about you and your current situation. Select the number that honestly reflects how frequently you experienced these characteristics in the last 30 days.

0=Never	1=Rarely	2=A Few Times	3=Somewhat Often	4=Often	5=Very Often

	1.	I am happy.
____	1.	I am happy.
____	2.	I am preoccupied with more than one person I *[help]*.
____	3.	I get satisfaction from being able to *[help]* people.
____	4.	I feel connected to others.
____	5.	I jump or am startled by unexpected sounds.
____	6.	I feel invigorated after working with those I *[help]*.
____	7.	I find it difficult to separate my personal life from my life as a *[helper]*.

_____ 8.   I am losing sleep over traumatic experiences of a person I [help].
_____ 9.   I think that I might have been "infected" by the traumatic stress of those I [help].
_____ 10. I feel trapped by my work as a [helper].
_____ 11. Because of my [helping], I have felt "on edge" about various things.
_____ 12. I like my work as a [helper].
_____ 13. I feel depressed as a result of my work as a [helper].
_____ 14. I feel as though I am experiencing the trauma of someone I have [helped].
_____ 15. I have beliefs that sustain me.
_____ 16. I am pleased with how I am able to keep up with [helping] techniques and protocols.
_____ 17. I am the person I always wanted to be.
_____ 18. My work makes me feel satisfied.
_____ 19. Because of my work as a [helper], I feel exhausted.
_____ 20. I have happy thoughts and feelings about those I [help] and how I could help them.
_____ 21. I feel overwhelmed by the amount of work or the size of my case [work] load I have to deal with.
_____ 22. I believe I can make a difference through my work.
_____ 23. I avoid certain activities or situations because they remind me of frightening experiences of the people I [help].
_____ 24. I am proud of what I can do to [help].
_____ 25. As a result of my [helping], I have intrusive, frightening thoughts.
_____ 26. I feel "bogged down" by the system.
_____ 27. I have thoughts that I am a "success" as a [helper].
_____ 28. I can't recall important parts of my work with trauma victims.
_____ 29. I am a very sensitive person.
_____ 30. I am happy that I chose to do this work.

Self-scoring directions, if used as self-test:

1. Be certain you respond to all items.
2. On some items the scores need to be reversed. Next to your response write the reverse of that score (i.e. 0=0, 1=5, 2=4, 3=3).

Reverse the scores on these 5 items: 1, 4, 15, 17 and 29. Please note that the value 0 is not reversed, as its value is always null.

3. Mark the items for scoring:
   a. Put an *X* by the 10 items that form the *Compassion Satisfaction Scale*: 3, 6, 12, 16, 18, 20, 22, 24, 27, 30.
   b. Put a *check* by the 10 items on the *Burnout Scale*: 1, 4, 8, 10, 15, 17, 19, 21, 26, 29.
   c. *Circle* the 10 items on the *Trauma/Compassion Fatigue Scale*: 2, 5, 7, 9, 11, 13, 14, 23, 25, 28.
4. Add the numbers you wrote next to the items for each set of items and compare with the theoretical scores.

Your Scores on the ProQOL: Professional Quality of Life Screening

Based on your responses, your personal scores are below. If you have any concerns, you should discuss them with a physical or mental health care professional.

Compassion Satisfaction_____

Compassion satisfaction is about the pleasure you derive from being able to do your work well. For example, you may feel like it is a pleasure to help others through your work. You may feel positively about your colleagues or your ability to contribute to the work setting or even the greater good of society. Higher scores on this scale represent a greater satisfaction related to your ability to be an effective caregiver in your job.

The average score is 37 (SD 7; alpha scale reliability .87). About 25% of people score higher than 42 and about 25% of people score below 33. If you are in the higher range, you probably derive a good deal of professional satisfaction from your position. If your scores are below 33, you may either find problems with your job, or there may be some other reason—for example, you might derive your satisfaction from activities other than your job.

Burnout_____

Most people have an intuitive idea of what burnout is. From the research perspective, burnout is associated with feelings of hopelessness and difficulties in dealing with work or in doing your job effectively. These negative feelings usually have a gradual onset. They can reflect the feeling that your efforts make no difference, or they can be associated with a very high workload or a nonsupportive work environment. Higher scores on this scale mean that you are at higher risk for burnout.

The average score on the burnout scale is 22 (SD 6.0; alpha scale reliability .72). About 25% of people score above 27 and about 25% of people score below 18. If your score is below 18, this probably reflects positive feelings about your ability to be effective in your work. If you score above 27 you may wish to think about what at work makes you feel like you are not effective in your position. Your score may reflect your mood; perhaps you were having a "bad day" or are in need of some time off. If the high score persists or if it is reflective of other worries, it may be a cause for concern.

Compassion Fatigue/Secondary Trauma_____

Compassion fatigue (CF), also called secondary trauma (STS) and related to vicarious trauma (VT), is about your work-related, secondary exposure to extremely stressful events. For example, you may repeatedly hear stories about the traumatic things that happen to other people, commonly called VT. If your work puts you directly in the path of danger, such as being a soldier or humanitarian aide worker, this is not secondary exposure; your exposure is primary. However, if you are exposed to others' traumatic events as a result of your work, such as in an emergency room or working with child protective services, this is secondary exposure. The symptoms of CF/STS are usually rapid in onset and associated with a particular event. They may include being afraid, having difficulty sleeping, having images of the upsetting event pop into your mind, or avoiding things that remind you of the event.

The average score on this scale is 13 (SD 6; alpha scale reliability .80). About 25% of people score below 8 and about 25% of people score above 17. If your score is above 17, you may want to take some time to think about what at work may be frightening to you or if there is some other reason for the elevated score. While higher scores do not mean that you do have a problem, they are an indication that you may want to examine how you feel about your work and your work environment. You may wish to discuss this with your supervisor, a colleague, or a health care professional.

Source: © B. Hudnall Stamm, 1997–2005. *Professional Quality of Life: Compassion Satisfaction and Fatigue Subscales, R-IV (ProQOL).* http://www. isu.edu/~bhstamm. This test may be freely copied as long as (a) author is credited, (b) no changes are made other than those authorized below, and (c) it is not sold. You may substitute the appropriate target group for *[helper]* if that is not the best term. For example, if you are working with teachers, replace *[helper]* with teacher. Word changes may be made to any word in italicized square brackets to make the measure read more smoothly for a particular target group.

Disclaimer

This information is presented for educational purposes only. It is not a substitute for informed medical advice or training. Do not use this information to diagnose or treat a health problem without consulting a qualified health or mental health care provider. If you have concerns, contact your health care provider, mental health professional, or your community health center.

Index